AF811870

Palgrave Studies in Economic History

Series Editor
Kent Deng, London School of Economics, London, UK

Palgrave Studies in Economic History is designed to illuminate and enrich our understanding of economies and economic phenomena of the past. The series covers a vast range of topics including financial history, labour history, development economics, commercialisation, urbanisation, industrialisation, modernisation, globalisation, and changes in world economic orders.

More information about this series at
http://www.palgrave.com/gp/series/14632

Sara Torregrosa Hetland

The Spanish Fiscal Transition

Tax Reform and Inequality in the Late Twentieth Century

palgrave
macmillan

Sara Torregrosa Hetland
Lund University
Lund, Skåne Län, Sweden

ISSN 2662-6497 ISSN 2662-6500 (electronic)
Palgrave Studies in Economic History
ISBN 978-3-030-79540-5 ISBN 978-3-030-79541-2 (eBook)
https://doi.org/10.1007/978-3-030-79541-2

© The Editor(s) (if applicable) and the Author(s), under exclusive licence to Springer Nature Switzerland AG 2021
This work is subject to copyright. All rights are solely and exclusively licensed by the Publisher, whether the whole or part of the material is concerned, specifically the rights of translation, reprinting, reuse of illustrations, recitation, broadcasting, reproduction on microfilms or in any other physical way, and transmission or information storage and retrieval, electronic adaptation, computer software, or by similar or dissimilar methodology now known or hereafter developed.
The use of general descriptive names, registered names, trademarks, service marks, etc. in this publication does not imply, even in the absence of a specific statement, that such names are exempt from the relevant protective laws and regulations and therefore free for general use.
The publisher, the authors and the editors are safe to assume that the advice and information in this book are believed to be true and accurate at the date of publication. Neither the publisher nor the authors or the editors give a warranty, expressed or implied, with respect to the material contained herein or for any errors or omissions that may have been made. The publisher remains neutral with regard to jurisdictional claims in published maps and institutional affiliations.

Cover credit: cinoby/GettyImages

This Palgrave Macmillan imprint is published by the registered company Springer Nature Switzerland AG
The registered company address is: Gewerbestrasse 11, 6330 Cham, Switzerland

To my parents, who were part of those at the bottom.

Acknowledgements

This book is based on my Ph.D. dissertation, which was defended at the University of Barcelona in January 2016. Five years have passed since then—but no, I have not spent these five years writing the book: I had two children in the mean time, which delayed the whole process of making the thesis into a monograph. During this time, the Spanish tax system has undergone some changes, but I still think that it rests on the foundations that were built during the Transition.

I want to start the book by saying thank you to those who helped me the most. In Barcelona, I had the support of my two supervisors, Alfonso Herranz and Alejandro Esteller, who were all I could have expected. Their patience, perspectives, and encouragement contributed greatly to my work in the thesis and beyond. A big "thank you both" goes here again.

The inspiration for this study draws strongly from the studies of Francisco Comín on the history of the Spanish tax system, and he has always been generous when I have approached him. I also remember a particular conversation with Carles Sudrià, one of my master's teachers at the

University of Barcelona, which led me into the study of this particular period of Spanish tax history. Others who provided me with useful comments and discussions were (in alphabetical order) Miguel Artola, Nadja Dwenger, Sergio Espuelas, Miguel Martorell, Alessia Matano, Jorge Onrubia, Fernando Rodrigo, and Emmanuel Saez.

Our work as scholars is always built on the efforts of others. In this sense, I benefited from the earlier work of a team at the University Carlos III de Madrid, led by Javier Ruiz-Castillo, on the Spanish Household Budget Surveys. I am also very grateful for the help received at several archives and libraries, particularly the *Archivo Central del Ministerio de Hacienda* and the library of the *Instituto de Estudios Fiscales.*

I found a great place to work at the University of Barcelona, with a constructive scholarly community, and where my troubles as a Ph.D. student were shared with dear friends—Roser, Marisol, Rodrigo, Èric, Oriol, and Elena. I also spent some months visiting the Center for Equitable Growth in the University of California—Berkeley, and the Department of Economic History and Human Geography at Umeå University, where I benefited from the insights of other groups. The north turned out to be a great place to finish writing about the south. This has also been the case for the last months, when I went back to this "old" work from my current workplace at Lund.

I should say that I am in debt with all Spanish taxpayers, who funded this research with a scholarship under the programme *"Formación del Profesorado Universitario"*.

Always grateful for the love and encouragement of friends and family. You know who you are, and how important you are. And of course: thank you, Cristián, my teammate at so many levels.

Contents

1 Introduction 1
- 1.1 A Belated Transition 3
- 1.2 Taxation, Inequality, and Democratisation 9
- 1.3 A Brief History of Modern Tax Systems in the West 13
- References 19

2 The Fiscal System of Late Francoism 27
- 2.1 The Long Life of Liberal Taxation 29
- 2.2 Stabilisation, Growth, and a "Missed Opportunity" 36
- 2.3 The Early Seventies: Attempts at Reform 42
- References 52

3 Why the Reform Was Necessary 57
- 3.1 The Level of Taxation and Spending 59
- 3.2 The Distribution of the Tax Burden 67
- 3.3 Demands for Decentralisation 76
- References 81

4 The Political Economy of the Fiscal Transition 83
4.1 Political Transition, Political Parties, and the Electoral System 85
4.2 A Changing Economic Context 90
4.3 The Reform Process: Party Stances in Parliament 95
4.4 Pressure Groups 104
References 112

5 Winners and Losers 117
5.1 How to Measure Progressivity 119
5.2 Who Paid the Taxes? 127
5.3 Who Received the Benefits? 137
References 146

6 Bypassing the Progressive Income Tax 153
6.1 The Pillars of Compliance: Coercion, Consent… and Information 155
6.2 The Struggle for Generality in Spanish Income Taxation 159
6.3 Evasion and Inequality After the Tax Reform 165
References 178

7 An Assessment of the Tax Reform 185
7.1 Modernisation and Convergence 186
7.2 Fiscal Federalism and Its Discontents 191
7.3 Public Opinion and Legitimacy 195
7.4 Inequality: Unresolved Business? 199
References 209

8 Conclusions: The Spanish Fiscal Transition and Beyond 215
8.1 Looking Forward 218
8.2 Fiscal Transitions in the Late twentieth Century 222
References 230

Index 235

List of Figures

Fig. 1.1 Tax revenue as a percentage of GDP in Spain and the EU-14, 1940–2020 (*Source* Tax revenue of the Spanish state from Comín & Díaz [2005], total tax revenue of Spain [all public administrations] until 1990 from Torregrosa-Hetland [2015], Spanish GDP from Prados de la Escosura [2017]. The rest from *OECD Statistics*) 8

Fig. 2.1 Tax revenue as a percentage of GDP in Spain, 1900–1976 (*Source* Comín & Díaz [2005], with GDP from Prados de la Escosura [2017]. *Notes* The graph shows the sum of direct and indirect taxes in the source, so social contributions and other public revenues are excluded) 30

Fig. 2.2 Revenue of the income tax as a percentage of GDP, Spain 1933–1977 (*Source* Comín & Díaz [2005] until 1957, Torregrosa-Hetland [2015] from 1958, with GDP from Prados de la Escosura [2017]) 34

Fig. 2.3 Returns and actual payers of income tax, Spain 1933–1977 (*Source* Number of returns, and returns with positive tax due taken from Gota Losada [1970] and Valdés [1982]; data for 1967 obtained from the General Archive of the Ministry of Public Finance [ACMH-9039]. Number of households from census of 1970, 1981 and 1991, as well as household surveys of 1964 and 1973. Note: the number of households was extended backwards using an estimate of the average number of individuals therein [the expected bias would be a slight overestimation of the series shown in the initial period]) 39
Fig. 2.4 Social contributions as a percentage of GDP in Spain, 1940–1970 (*Source* Vergés [1974] and the Spanish National Accounts, Contabilidad Nacional de España, base 1970 [1979], with GDP from Prados de la Escosura [2017]. *Notes* The discontinuity in 1967, related to the entry into effect of the 1963 law, is probably due to the inclusion of some of the contributions previously administered by private entities ["*entidades colaboradoras*"]. The increase was probably smoother than it appears in the data) 43
Fig. 2.5 The structure of taxation in Spain, 1960–1990 (*Source* Torregrosa-Hetland [2015], with GDP from Prados de la Escosura [2017]) 48
Fig. 3.1 Percentage of survey respondents who stated that "taxes are high/very high", 1970–2000 (*Source* Alvira et al., 2000; Alvira & García, 1976, 1981; Strümpel & Alvira, 1975) 61
Fig. 3.2 Perception of the balance between taxes paid and services received, 1975–1998 (*Source* Alvira et al., 2000; Alvira & García, 1976, 1977, 1981, 1987) 63
Fig. 3.3 Survey respondents who considered the tax system unfair, 1965–2000 (*Source* Alvira & García, 1976; Strümpel, 1967; Strümpel & Alvira, 1975; and *Centro de Investigaciones Sociológicas* for 1985–2000) 70

Fig. 3.4 Desired, perceived, and actual distribution of the tax burden (1971) (*Source* Instituto de Estudios Fiscales [1972] and author's calculations. *Notes* The figure does not reflect the whole population, but only certain categories (see text). The survey data was given in income ranges; each group is represented here at the average percentile of observations in their range (for the corresponding social categories). These rates are defined with the denominator including not only market income but also transfers. See Chapter 5 for more details) 73

Fig. 3.5 Desired reduction of tax burden (1971) (*Source* Instituto de Estudios Fiscales [1972] and author's calculations. *Notes* Same as Fig. 3.4) 74

Fig. 4.1 Annual growth in real GDP per capita, 1960–2000 (*Source* Prados de la Escosura, 2017) 91

Fig. 4.2 Annual rates of inflation, 1960–2000 (*Source* Calculated using the consumer price index from the *Instituto Nacional de Estadística*) 92

Fig. 4.3 International openness of the Spanish economy, 1960–2000 (*Source* Trade openness from Tena (2005), financial de jure openness from Chinn and Ito [2006]) 94

Fig. 5.1 Taxes and phases of income (*Source* Compiled by author) 122

Fig. 5.2 Alternative approach to taxes and phases of income (*Source* Compiled by author) 123

Fig. 5.3 Effective tax rates over income distribution in 1970 (*Source* Author's calculations) 128

Fig. 5.4 Effective tax rates over income distribution in 1982 (*Source* Author's calculations) 129

Fig. 5.5 Effective tax rates over income distribution in 1990 (*Source* Author's calculations) 129

Fig. 5.6 Direct taxes and social contributions in five countries (*Source* For Spain, author's calculations. France, United Kingdom, and United States from Piketty and Saez [2007]. Sweden, from Bengtsson et al. [2016]. *Notes* [1] In the data for France, P40–60 is P0–90. [2] In the data for France, the US, and the UK, the last two values represented are, respectively, those for P99–99.5 and the mean of rates for P99.5–99.9, P99.9–99.99, and P99.99–100. Similarly, for Sweden, the first value is P0–40 and the last two values, P99–99.9 and P99.9–100. This means that the top rates in Spain refer to relatively [slightly] lower percentiles) 131

Fig. 5.7 Effective tax rates with benefits as part of pre-tax income, 1970–1990 (*Source* author's calculations. *Note* The vertical axis is also here capped at 60%, which only affects percentile 1 in 1990) 133

Fig. 5.8 Effective tax-and-transfer rates across the income distribution, 1970–1990 (*Source* Author's calculations. *Notes* Average effective tax-and-transfer rates by deciles. Rates are capped at −20%: for the deciles not shown, transfers make up practically all income. In 1990, a calculation with only public benefits and excluding the rest of transfers is possible, and proves very similar to the total shown. See Torregrosa-Hetland [2015a]. It is possible, however, that private transfers were of more relative importance in earlier years) 139

Fig. 5.9 Tax-and-transfer redistribution in several countries (*Sources* For Spain, author's calculations. For Argentina, Cornia et al. [2011]; for Brazil, Lustig [2011]; for Chile, Jorratt [2010]; for Colombia, Barreix et al. [2006]; for Mexico, Goñi et al. [2011], Uruguay, Roca [2010]; United States, Congressional Budget Office [2012]; and United Kingdom, Barnard et al. [2011]. *Notes* SP [Spain], AR [Argentina], BR [Brazil], CH [Chile], CO [Colombia], ME [Mexico], UR [Uruguay], UK [United Kingdom], US [United States of America]) 141

Fig. 6.1 Results of inspection of personal income tax (1942–1990) (*Source* Torregrosa-Hetland [2015a]. *Notes* "Discovered tax due" is that obtained by inspection, and is shown as percentage of each year's total tax due. "Discovered non-filers" are individuals who did not present a return and were caught; they are displayed as a percentage of each year's number of filers. "Inquiries" represents the total number of formal investigations [which refer both to filers and non-filers], while "Inquiries with tax due" is the number of those which resulted in a positive amount to pay for the taxpayer. Inquiries are also shown as a percentage of each year's filers) 161

Fig. 6.2 Tax due detected by inspection of personal income tax (1942–1990), as a percentage of GDP (*Sources* Same as Fig. 6.1, with GDP from Prados de la Escosura [2017]) 164

Fig. 6.3 Aggregate discrepancy between tax returns and National Accounts (1971–1990) (*Source* Torregrosa-Hetland [2015a], based on tax statistics, household budget surveys, and the National Accounts. See the source for methodological details) 167

Fig. 6.4 Tax compliance in personal income tax, Spain and other countries (*Sources* For Spain, author's calculations and Esteller-Moré [2011]. Remaining countries from Albarea et al. [2020], Alm et al. [1991], Benedek & Lelkes [2011], Bernardi [1996], Bernardi & Bernasconi [1997], Black et al. [2012], Engel et al. [1999], Gómez-Sabaini & Morán [2020], Internal Revenue Service [1996], Jiménez et al. [2010], Johns & Slemrod [2010], Kleven et al. [2011], Leventi et al. [2013], Marino & Zizza [2012], and Swedish National Tax Agency [2008]) 173

Fig. 7.1 Perceptions of fraud after the tax reform (*Source* Alvira et al., 2000) 198

Fig. 7.2 Public social spending in Spain (1940–2000). (a) Old age, disability and unemployment, (b) Family, health and education (*Source* Espuelas, 2013a. *Notes* Functional classification, following the OECD classification. Disability therefore includes temporary payments in case of sickness or work accident. The categories do not coincide with the differentiation between spending in monetary transfers and in kind) 205

List of Tables

Table 2.1	Tax bases for social security contributions by categories of workers	41
Table 2.2	Selected taxes as a percentage of GDP in Spain and other Western European countries, 1970	44
Table 3.1	Opinions about fairness of direct and indirect taxation, 1971 (percentage)	72
Table 4.1	District malapportionment in Spain and other countries (percentage)	88
Table 4.2	Loosemore–Hanby index of disproportionality in Spain and other countries (percentage)	89
Table 4.3	Parties benefiting from electoral rules, 1977–1986	90
Table 4.4	The process of tax reform: main laws	96
Table 4.5	Tax caps for social security contributions by categories of workers, 1979–1990	105
Table 5.1	Tax incidence assumptions	122
Table 5.2	Progressivity and redistribution indices, 1970–1990	134
Table 5.3	Taxation and income inequality (Gini index), 1970–1990	136
Table 6.1	Generality of personal income taxation in Spain (1933–2000)	160

Table 6.2 Compliance with Spanish income tax according to the Commission (1979–1986) 164
Table 6.3 Compliance rates by income source, 1982 and 2001 (percentages) 169
Table 6.4 Impact of fraud on tax progressivity and inequality 171
Table 7.1 Selected taxes as a percentage of GDP in Spain and other Western European countries, 1990 and 2018 187
Table 7.2 Inequality in disposable income, 1973–1990 (Gini index) 202
Table 7.3 Levels and growth of disposable equivalent income, 1973–1990 203

1
Introduction

In many senses, the Spain of the early seventies is hardly recognisable today. An underdeveloped country ruled by a right-wing dictatorship, in which the population had very low education levels and women were legally subjugated to their fathers or husbands, gave way to a modern society comparable to others in Western Europe. Political, economic, and social change, even with all its deficiencies, was undoubtedly profound. The process included change in the tax system, which underwent a thorough reform to follow new principles: this is referred to here as the *fiscal transition.* It was a fundamental part of the political transition.

The following pages look at the changes in the Spanish tax system between 1960 and 1990, with some incursions into earlier and later years, and a focus on the relationships between taxation, inequality, and democratisation. The aim is to see whether taxes contributed to reducing inequality, and indeed whether they *managed* to reduce inequality, given that the country underwent a transition to democracy. Indeed, democratisation has often been understood as a result of distributive tensions between the elite and the masses, and therefore as a process that would promote redistribution.

© The Author(s), under exclusive license to Springer Nature Switzerland AG 2021

S. Torregrosa Hetland, *The Spanish Fiscal Transition*, Palgrave Studies in Economic History,
https://doi.org/10.1007/978-3-030-79541-2_1

Spain in the late twentieth century is not just an academic case study; it should interest a wider audience. It was one of several transitions to democracy during the same period, along with Portugal and Greece in Europe but also many other countries in Latin America (with which there are many similarities, including, albeit more recently, comparable levels of economic development). In each of these transitions, right-wing dictatorships reluctantly gave way to democratic regimes, where options for tax reform were heightened. The results were not always as expected. The Spanish case is not unique, but it is an example of a rather peaceful transition.

We will see how Spain attempted to follow the Western European taxation model, both for the sake of imitation and to make integration easier; but convergence with this model, as well as economic convergence, remained unfinished. The interpretation offered here is that this attempt at convergence in the late seventies proved rather more difficult than it might have been in earlier decades. The golden age of economic growth gave way to a period of economic, financial, and industrial crisis, and to the rapid second globalisation. This new context put a spokes in the wheel of progressive tax reform. Ultimately, Spain never fully attained the classic model of Western European postwar taxation. When income tax was introduced in the country in 1978, it was already under attack elsewhere, from various fronts. An international wave of reforms in the eighties would soon change the characteristics of tax systems, the expectations of them, and the emphasis placed on progressivity and redistribution. Very high top income tax rates were never really effective in Spain, and were soon reduced in line with international trends. Evasion was long overlooked. The same constraints may have been found in other places as well, or will be found in the future, which is why this book might offer some lessons that will be summarised in the final chapter.

The book asks the following questions: How did democracy affect the taxes that Spaniards paid? Did an increase in political equality lead to a (similar) increase in economic equality? What were the social demands with regard to taxes? How were tax reform decisions made? And, how compliant were citizens with the new system?

In this first chapter, the basics of the tax reform are introduced, placed in historical context, and situated in the relevant literature, while some central concepts will be defined. Chapters 2 and 3 deal with the situation before the fiscal transition; they ask how the tax system worked before, especially during Francoism, why it needed to change, and what were the nature of the demands from the public, the intellectual community, and politicians. Chapter 4 describes the process of reform, and how it was conditioned by several factors. Chapters 5 and 6 place the focus on the effects of the tax reform on inequality: how progressive did the system become, and what impacts did fraud have on the income tax? Chapter 7 offers a broader assessment of the tax reform from additional points of view, while Chapter 8 concludes.

1.1 A Belated Transition

Spain was late in applying modern forms of taxation, because it was afflicted with a backward-looking dictatorship for almost 40 years. The victory of the rebels in the Civil War (1936–1939) put the dictator Francisco Franco in power, where he remained until his death in 1975. During this time, the country first went through an autarkic period (marked by very difficult postwar years, which have been called "the years of hunger"; Arco Blanco, 2020; Barciela López, 2003), and later, from the sixties, experienced economic opening and rapid growth (Prados De La Escosura et al., 2012). Throughout, the structures of the state remained old-fashioned. This was an interventionist state, which regulated economic and social life profoundly, but a poor state. Tax revenues were low because the dictatorship did not want to tax where economic capacity was present.

After Franco's death in November 1975 (which was a "death foretold" for some time), things changed rather quickly. In what was a tumultuous period of Spanish history, the short government of Carlos Arias Navarro attempted continuity, but this proved to be impossible. Adolfo Suárez was then appointed prime minister in July 1976,[1] and in the following months crafted an agreement with politicians who emerged from both the dictatorship (like Manuel Fraga, who had been minister of information and tourism in the sixties and minister of the interior during the Arias government) and the democratic opposition (such as the Communist Santiago Carrillo). The agreement was embodied in the *Ley de Reforma Política*, approved by way of a referendum in December 1976. This allowed free elections to be held in June 1977, and also marked the start of constitutional talks, culminating with the approval of the Constitution through another referendum in December 1978. The construction of the new regime was accompanied by intense social mobilisation, terrorist activity, and political violence, and was even threatened by a military *coup d'état* in February 1981. But it nevertheless endured.

The process of political transition has been somewhat idealised in the historiography: in contrast to what happened after 1931, this time violence was limited and a modern and functioning democracy was ultimately established. The same applied to the *fiscal* transition: it set down the roots of a modern tax system that worked towards the reduction of inequalities. More recently, however, the political transition has faced increased criticism, with questions aimed, for example, at its peaceful character and its long-term effects on welfare (Baby, 2018; Navarro, 2002). The economic transition has also been analysed, in a recent contribution (De la Torre & Rubio-Varas, 2021). From the perspective of several decades on from these episodes, they can be revisited in order to improve our understanding of them. This book is part of that trend.

In 1975, Spain was clearly heading towards a multi-dimensional crisis. Opposition movements had developed during the previous decades, having grown in strength from the sixties (Molinero & Ysàs, 2008; Saz, 2010). In the ruling bloc, some discrepancies became visible, with certain factions recognising the difficulties in maintaining the regime after Franco's death, and talks emerging about limited political liberalisation (while others were in favour of continuity). At the same time, the economic context was very worrisome: the effects of the first oil crisis would soon put an abrupt end to the growth cycle of the previous decade, even if the increase in international prices was initially absorbed by the public sector (Rubio-Varas & Muñoz, 2021). A recent book has considered the years of transition to democracy as one of the "turning points" in Spanish history (Betrán & Pons, 2020).

In the usual interpretation, the transition to democracy was the product of the inability of both sides to take full control of the situation.

Colomer (1998) mentioned, in this regard, Przeworski's considerations about uncertainty during political transitions, which brought stances towards moderation (Przeworski, 1986). Martínez-Alier and Roca Jusmet (1988) have also pointed to fear of a military coup as the cause for moderation within labour unions and leftist parties, which led them to a more cooperative attitude towards the political and economic pacts. A coalescence of interests gave rise to an "agreed reform" or "transition through transation" (Powell, 2015), in which an intermediate path was taken between full continuity and democratic breakout. Francoist institutions were progressively dismantled, without violating the existing legal framework, in a process orchestrated by the Prime Minister Adolfo Suárez. Opposition parties were successful in their demands for constitutional talks and full legalisation—although in the case of the Communist Party of Spain (*Partido Comunista de España*), this came quite late and probably impacted negatively on their electoral results. The supporters of the dictatorship, on the other hand, were indulged with the creation of an upper chamber in parliament (the Senate) and the establishment of an electoral system skewed in their favour (Lago & Montero, 2005).

The 1977 elections were won by Suárez's coalition, the Union of the Democratic Centre (*Unión de Centro Democrático*, UCD). This was a heterogeneous group, formed only some months previously by liberals, Christian democrats, and social democrats. For the latter camp, who occupied the left wing of this coalition, tax reform was a priority—and was also recognised as necessary by many in other parties and in broader society. Thus, the transition to democracy brought about a comprehensive transformation of the tax system, which is widely regarded as a fundamental aspect of Spain's regime change. This transformed system would follow new principles and support different spending. In this sense, the tax reform of 1977 has some parallels with that of 1845, which established the liberal tax system that remained essentially in place until the late seventies. At that time of the earlier reform—the mid-nineteenth century—liberal politics had only just stabilised in the country, replacing absolutist rule after several decades of violent conflict. The reform, led by the Moderate Party (*Partido Moderado*) also involved a comprehensive overhaul of the tax system, to make it consistent with the new politics.

The characteristics and evolution of this liberal tax system are discussed in Chapter 2.

The historiography has generally pointed out that, in the late seventies, the coincidence of political and economic crises made decision-making difficult, delaying the response to severe economic problems (De la Torre & Rubio-Varas, 2021; García Delgado, 1990). When decisions were finally taken, they were taken through consensus, following the lead of the vice president for economic affairs, Enrique Fuentes Quintana: the Moncloa Pacts of October 1977 represented an agreement between the government and the new political parties to introduce a programme of economic stabilisation and institutional reform (Comín, 2007; Cuevas & Pons, 2020). The Moncloa Pacts combined measures for the short term (crisis resolution) and the long term (institutional changes, including liberalisation and fiscal reform). In addition, an increase in expenditure on transfers and social services was agreed upon, in exchange for wage moderation to fight rampant inflation (Trullén, 1993). This would be financed through the tax reform.

The tax reform programme of 1977 was indeed a comprehensive one. It proposed the adoption in Spain of a Western European taxation model in which personal income taxation would be at the centre, together with wealth, inheritance, and value added taxes. This system was to be fairer, more efficient, and also more flexible than the existing one. It would provide the state with higher revenue, which it needed to spend on modern infrastructure, education, and welfare state development. It also meant convergence with the countries of the European Economic Comission, and would thus facilitate the long-desired integration. With respect to fairness, the Moncloa Pacts explicitly established the need for direct and indirect taxation to make equal contributions to the public budget.

Francisco Fernández Ordóñez, the minister who fathered the reform, was an advocate of progressivity (or, at least, of a decrease in the regressive nature of the existing system) and of the expansion of public services. He also placed huge importance on fighting tax evasion, primarily by fostering voluntary compliance: he meant to take relations between Spain's (nascent) citizens and its (newly democratic) state into a new era, based on responsibility and fair exchange. In his view, reducing inequality through the tax system was less conflictive than attempting to do so in the wage bargaining process, and this equity objective was crucial for the legitimation of a market economy, particularly in the context of the prevailing crisis: "*The fragile Spanish economy is going through difficult times, and we think that adequate restructuring will only be possible if there is fairness in the distribution of sacrifices and the part of the effort that we all must share. As much as we respect the market economy as the main instrument for obtaining resources, we firmly demand the public sector's correcting action through the tax system and redistributive expenditure*" (Fernández Ordóñez, 1980, p. 60; author's translation). By "we", Fernández Ordóñez meant the members of his Social Democratic Party (*Partido Social Demócrata*), one of the constituent groups of the UCD in 1977.

The main milestones of the tax reform were the introduction of personal income tax (1978) and value added tax (1986). Both became central to the funding of public expenditure in the following years. In 1977, a wealth tax had been introduced, together with some impactful measures for fighting tax fraud.[2] Wealth tax, as well as inheritance tax (reformed in 1987), always represented only small shares of the budget; they were seen more as control instruments for personal taxation. Corporate income tax was also reformed in 1978. Social contributions, which then represented half of public revenues, experienced only minor changes.[3]

It should be noted at this point that the spirit of consensus that characterised the start of the tax reform did not last long. Indeed, the politics of consensus were replaced by the politics of competition once the constitution was passed and new elections were on their way (in 1979). This explains the delay in the reform of indirect taxation and in the development of the tax administration, which were only undertaken by socialist governments that enjoyed large majorities in the second half of the eighties. Value added tax was a condition for the accession to the EEC in 1986, as were reforms of excises, public monopolies, and tariffs.[4] During the first years the application of the tax reforms were defective because of a lack of administrative capacity and obstruction by financial institutions, and tax evasion prospered as a result. This practice was fought more decidedly after 1985.

The reforms brought about a substantial modernisation of public finances, and allowed an increase in revenues as well as the funding of a nascent welfare state—even if they initially came with considerable budget deficits (Albi, 1990; Espuelas, 2013; Fuentes Quintana, 1990). The process of convergence with more advanced countries in Europe remained nevertheless incomplete: as shown in Fig. 1.1, total tax revenue in terms of GDP approached that of the EU core (represented here with the average of the EU-14), but a significant differential remained. The distance, furthermore, was increased by the crises of the early nineties and of 2008, illustrating the system's vulnerability.[5]

Since 1990, no comprehensive tax redesign has been undertaken, although partial modifications have been abundant, including to the central components of the system (personal income tax, value added tax, and corporation tax). Increases in value added tax rates have been implemented several times in conjunction with reductions in social security contributions. The democratic period also entailed decentralisation

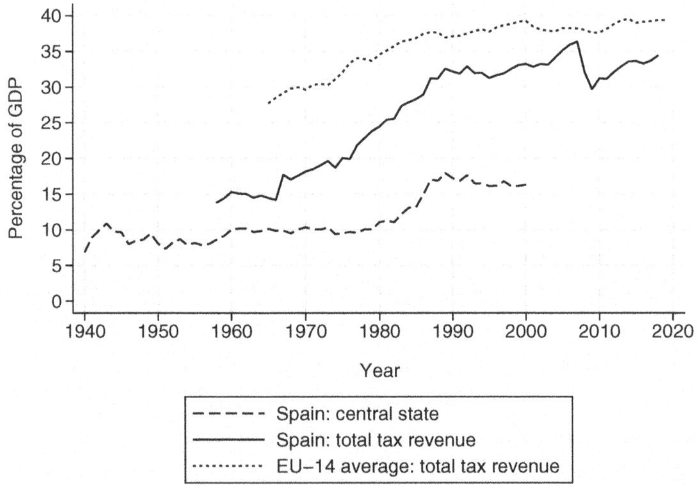

Fig. 1.1 Tax revenue as a percentage of GDP in Spain and the EU-14, 1940–2020 (*Source* Tax revenue of the Spanish state from Comín & Díaz [2005], total tax revenue of Spain [all public administrations] until 1990 from Torregrosa-Hetland [2015], Spanish GDP from Prados de la Escosura [2017]. The rest from *OECD Statistics*)

towards the regional governments of expenditure and revenue, including, since 1996, some regulatory capacities.[6]

The story of the tax reform has been analysed from several perspectives, in addition to the accounts of some of the lead actors of the day (Fernández Ordóñez, 1980; Fuentes Quintana, 1990, 2004; Lagares, 1999). Valiño (1989) provided a review of the legislative innovations from the point of view of a public finance scholar, something that Martínez-Vázquez and Sanz-Sanz (2007) took through to the early 2000s. Gandarias (1999) added the insights of a political scientist. Pan-Montojo (1996) and Comín (2007) applied the approach of the historian. The past work of this book's author has been aimed at a quantitative analysis of the effects of the reform on the income distribution and the funding of welfare state efforts. Whether all these changes resulted in a transition towards progressivity is the main focus of the rest of the book.

1.2 Taxation, Inequality, and Democratisation

Taxation can affect inequality through several channels, including by redistributing income and by impacting how income is generated and shared in the market. On the other hand, inequality may also affect taxation, for example, by conditioning the types of social agreements possible (Lupu & Pontusson, 2011) or the revenue potential of different tax alternatives. Democracy is often an implicit third leg, but in this particular account it is explicit, and central. Popular demands will affect taxation to the extent that the system is democratic. Therefore, the expansion or nature of democracy will also be very important for the design and operation of the tax system, and thus for inequality.

This book focuses on the impact of taxation on inequality through redistribution, although we make reference to the other relations as well. Redistribution is defined as a reduction in inequality caused by a given tax (or spending) instrument. Tax redistribution is usually measured as the difference in the value of an inequality index before and after taxes (in other words, between inequality of gross income and inequality of net income). Often used to this end is the Reynolds-Smolensky index, which corresponds to the difference in the Gini index; it is also sometimes expressed as a percentage reduction in pre-tax inequality.

A tax will be redistributive if it takes more money (in relative terms) from the rich than from the poor, i.e. because it is progressive. Progressivity equates to the increase in the tax rate as income grows. This tax rate is the *effective* tax rate, not the nominal one: it is affected both by legal rates and by how the tax base is defined and adjusted. But a tax also needs to raise substantial revenue to have an impact on inequality reduction; otherwise it might be very progressive but only mildly redistributive. Formulae for these concepts are given in Chapter 5.

Let us discuss briefly why we might care about progressivity. This is a big word, and not one that has enjoyed the best press in recent years—but it has been central in tax policy discussions for a long time. The idea that taxes should be progressive originated in the intellectual circles of political economy in the late nineteenth century; notable exponents were Francis Edgeworth and Edwin Seligman (Mehrotra, 2013). Progressivity was the culmination of the "ability to pay" idea, used as an argument for the creation of income taxes: the tax burden should fall more on wealthier people—because it was easier for them to pay. It should not be apportioned based on who benefited from public expenditure, neither levied, for convenience, on consumption (Steinmo, 2003). As we will see in the next subsection, in practical terms the advent of progressivity was also the result of political mobilisation to tax the rich, amid increasing democratisation and the revenue needs of the world wars. Progressive income taxes were at the heart of modern tax systems in the mid-twentieth century, but were later criticised, especially after 1970, for their excessive complexity and for negatively affecting economic activity.

Today, although support for progressivity seems to have weakened, inequality still ranks high in the worries of many. The rise in inequality since the eighties, particularly in Anglo-Saxon economies, has motivated a return of inequality to the centre of the economic and political debate (Atkinson, 2018; Atkinson & Piketty, 2007). But if we care about inequality, we might as well care about progressive taxation. Progressive (or regressive) taxation impacts the distribution of disposable income, i.e.

the revenues that we bring home and decide how to spend after having paid our taxes. This might be because of the payments we make, but also through the effects of taxes on the distribution of market income itself. That taxation affects incentives is no secret. It might affect incentives to work and to save, but also to bargain for higher wages (Piketty et al., 2011). In this way, many scholars have related progressive taxation with lower levels of market income inequality; that is, of income before tax (Roine et al., 2009; Rubolino & Waldenström, 2020). Some also care about the fairness of tax payments themselves, so that tax progressivity is a social demand in itself (Mehrotra, 2013; Singhal, 2013; Smith, 1989, p. 65).[7]

In recent decades, inequality has not increased as steeply in Spain as in some of the other Western countries with which it is usually compared. Prados de la Escosura (2008) showed that Spanish inequality, as measured by the Gini index, reached its maximum levels during World War I *and* the early fifties, decreasing thereafter until around 1980. The share in total income of the top 0.01% of the population fell between 1933 and 1970 (Alvaredo & Saez, 2009). Both the Gini and the top income shares point to some increase in inequality after 1980 (albeit much smaller than, for example, in the United States). Since then, the distribution of income has oscillated with the occurrence of economic crises. Notably, this latest increase in inequality took place in the democratic period, contradicting what might have been expected from the regime change.[8]

The relationship between democracy and redistribution has been the focus of much writing in the last few decades. Classic models predicted that democratisation would bring about increases in redistribution, following the intuition of Meltzer and Richard (1981), which is based on the median voter theorem. This theorem states that the voter situated in the middle position is the decisive one, such that policies will tend to match their preferences. The basics of the argument have been applied to the theory of political transitions: democratic countries are expected to be more redistributive than their non-democratic counterparts (Acemoglu & Robinson, 2001; Boix, 2003). If democratisation is an extension of decision power from the elites down towards the masses (as in a progressive downwards expansion of suffrage), this will change the median voter to one situated further down the distribution. This poorer median voter is likely to favour more redistribution than their richer counterpart. We would therefore expect the impact of taxes *and benefits* to change as a result of a regime transition—if this entails an effective modification of power and decision-making institutions. *Ceteris paribus*, the increase in redistribution would lead to a decrease in inequality.

The logic of these arguments has not been consistently backed by empirical studies. Aidt and Jensen (2009) pointed to the significant impact of franchise expansion on the *adoption* of progressive income taxes before 1939, but Scheve and Stasavage (2012) were unable to confirm that this applied to the *intensification* of inheritance taxation (1816–2000). Lindert (1994) found that democratisation had a positive impact on social spending in various countries between 1880 and 1930, but a recent study on fiscal redistribution in the United Kingdom between 1820 and 1913 did not yield similar evidence (Aidt et al., 2020). Mulligan et al. (2004) did not detect significant differences between the socioeconomic policies of democracies and non-democracies in the period 1960–1990. In a survey of empirical works, Gradstein and Milanovic (2004) noted some evidence of increases in redistribution after democratisation, but not always with the corollary of reductions in inequality (which is consistent with the observations of Timmons, 2010a). Indeed, democratic transitions might also have triggered other economic changes pushing in the opposite direction (notably in the ex-communist countries).

Recent studies have advanced more nuanced theories on the distributive impacts of democratisation, to which this book connects. For instance, Acemoglu and Robinson (2001, 2008) underlined the possibility that the elite may de facto block the implementation of aggressive redistributive policies, with the threat of economic or even political reversal. Boix (2003) likewise considered high redistribution as a potentially destabilising factor for democracy; thus, democratic transitions would be more likely under low levels of inequality, and where domestic capital has a higher capacity to escape taxation. Albertus and Menaldo (2014) suggested that redistribution will only make significant progress after a transition if the power of the elite was effectively challenged in the process, which is of course not always the case. This book provides an additional case study: one within the group of late democratic transitions (the "third wave") touched upon above. These transitions took place after 1970, starting with Greece, Portugal, and Spain and followed by countries in Latin America, Asia, and Africa. The countries that underwent third-wave transitions differ in many respects but, as noted, they have some common features, among which the fact that they were peripheral during the period of the third industrial revolution and the second globalisation. Redistribution and democratisation cannot be considered in isolation from this fact.

Globalisation has swept the world in two waves, the first gaining momentum in the second half of the nineteenth century and the second since 1970. Precisely, in the period studied here the movement of goods, inputs, and investments was made easier, cheaper, and faster—at an increasing rate, even if there have been setbacks. Economic openness undoubtedly affects the prospects of redistribution, since it gives the owners of internationally mobile assets (i.e. capital more than labour) greater leverage with which to escape taxation (Bates & Lien, 1985; Freeman & Quinn, 2012). On the other hand, others have argued that globalisation can be compatible with redistribution through offsetting by way of other mechanisms, primarily social spending, and labour regulation (Huberman & Lewchuk, 2003; Rodrik, 1998). The net effect thus remains to be seen, and may depend on several factors.

1.3 A Brief History of Modern Tax Systems in the West

The tax history of Western countries is a history of expanding state capacities, although it is far from a linear one: if they wanted more revenue, modern European states had to *invest* in their taxation power (Besley & Persson, 2009). But it is also, relatedly, a history of changing fiscal contracts. A fiscal contract is an implicit agreement whereby citizens pay taxes in exchange for public goods and services: since tax enforcement is never perfect, the payment of taxes is to some extent voluntary, and the state needs to give something in return (Levi, 1988).

During the early modern period, investments in fiscal capacity were often the result of inter-state warfare (Dincecco & Prado, 2012; Tilly, 1990). The *ancien régime* taxation systems struggled to become centralised, and states that were more successful in expanding revenues did so by taxing international trade, and by combining taxation with the raising of debt in emerging financial markets (Cardoso & Lains, 2010; Yun-Casalilla et al., 2012). The establishment of liberal political systems, normally as a result of revolutions, gave way to parallel reforms in the tax systems—one might say, in the fiscal contracts. Tax reforms entailed an attempt at homogenisation: between territories and between citizens, through abolition of the previous feudal privileges, even if there were limitations to this (Dincecco, 2009; Neal, 2010). At the same time, the liberal states protected new rights and developed new functions. The expression of this tax system was established in Spain in 1845 (Comín, 2010)—and so it cannot be said to have been a backward country at that point.

Western tax systems evolved in response to economic, social, and political change. The late nineteenth and early twentieth centuries saw the introduction of modern income taxes in several advanced European countries, their colonies, and the Americas. These followed the aforementioned notion of "ability to pay", which also inspired the emergence of progressive inheritance-tax schedules. The appearance of modern income taxes has been presented as an attempt to shift some of the tax burden from agriculture (i.e. landholders) onto new segments of society—the dynamic, industrial, mobile part of the economy (Mares & Queralt, 2015). In addition, the extension of the franchise favoured the adoption of income tax, but only after a threshold, since potential voters at the top would probably not favour the introduction of a new tax they themselves would be paying (Aidt & Jensen, 2009).

It was only later that income taxes started to become steeply progressive and used as instruments for redistribution. The political and economic crises of the first half of the twentieth century, the World Wars, and the Great Depression, fuelled pressures for a fairer distribution of the tax burden (Piketty, 2003; Scheve & Stasavage, 2016; Thorndike, 2012). Income taxes, initially falling only on the economic elite, became general taxes, paid by broad segments of the population, as the combined effect of regulatory changes *and* the cumulative impacts of inflation (Torregrosa-Hetland & Sabaté, 2021). This process took place in many Western countries—but not in Spain (Comín, 1988). The fiscal cleavage was thus generated.

After a turbulent half century, in the fifties Western countries entered a golden age of economic growth and social stability (Eichengreen, 2007). The increased levels of tax collection during the wars did not go back to normal immediately after—in what was called a "ratchet effect" (Peacock & Wiseman, 1961). Instead, new tax capacity was used to fund other social needs, leading to the development of welfare states. The postwar fiscal contract was based on a new institutional arrangement. In Steinmo's words, "*The compromise between Left and Right entailed a* de facto *consensus that both progressive taxation and welfare state programs were to be permanent features in democratic capitalist states*" (Steinmo, 1993, p. 26).

New tax capacity was linked to improved tax administration, including the use of pay-as-you-earn schemes, which are facilitated by the cooperation of big business (Kleven et al., 2015). This was the heyday of progressive taxation, represented by strong income taxes with high top tax rates. But it was also the period of a new tax innovation in Europe—value added tax—and of expansions in social security contributions, both of which underpinned increases in revenue (Peters, 1991). At the same time, the European integration process motivated talks about tax harmonisation, reflected in the Neumark Report of 1962.

It was only in the seventies that Spain attempted to close the gap with Western Europe and adopt the postwar tax model. Democratisation made this possible; but a new economic context and new economic thinking would make it difficult. The seventies and eighties witnessed the emergence of a different paradigm that opposed markedly progressive taxes (on the grounds that they hindered economic growth) and proposed reductions to tax rates (particularly for the rich) along with expansions of the tax base, by limiting deductions (Buggeln et al., 2017; Steinmo, 1993). Most famously, this paradigm was represented by the tax reforms of Ronald Reagan, but the movement also brought significant changes in many other countries throughout the world.

The tax reforms of the eighties were a reaction against progressivity and redistribution. The argument was that very high tax rates discouraged people from working and saving and turned them into tax evaders, while easy access to welfare benefits made them lazy. Moreover, complex tax structures, intended to enhance progressivity but also to promote other societal goals, made systems incomprehensible for the public. In other words, the state had overstepped its boundaries.

But how progressive were tax systems in reality? To what extent did they redistribute income? This is not easy to measure, especially in historical terms, in part because it is very data intensive. Thus, scholars have used approximations such as top marginal tax rates in income taxes, shares of different taxes out of total revenue, or similar measures (Peters, 1991; Scheve & Stasavage, 2016; Steinmo, 1989, 1993). These approximations clearly show the retreat of progressivity that came with the changes in the composition of taxation and in the income tax schedules during the seventies and eighties.

However, more recent analyses using microdata show that redistribution generally increased in the same period in many developed countries: it did so despite legal reforms that reduced progressivity, and *as a response to rising market inequality.*[9] Increased redistribution did not manage to counteract the growth in the inequality of market incomes, meaning that disposable income became more unequal as well (Caminada et al., 2017; Jesuit & Mahler, 2017). These studies use data from the Luxembourg Income Study, measuring redistribution by personal income taxes, workers' social contributions, and household transfers; they do not include the effects of indirect taxes, which is arguably a major shortcoming.[10] How the picture would be affected over time if indirect taxes and spending in kind were included is still, mostly, an open question.[11] A very recent contribution (Bozio et al., 2020) offers a possible answer by comparing the cases of the United States and France. In both countries, inequality was reduced in the period before 1983, mostly because of falling pre-tax inequality. But afterwards the opposite was true: pre-tax inequality increased, and so did post-tax inequality, even though total redistribution expanded (in this case, it includes estimations of the effect of both indirect taxes and in kind and collective expenditure).

The picture of the post 1980-era, with these wider definitions, is thus consistent with the aforementioned studies.

As for comparison across countries, Steinmo (1989) and Lindert (2004) suggested that more progressive systems tended to be smaller and therefore less redistributive as a whole, while the "big welfare spenders" (such as Sweden) were based on heavy taxation of the lower classes (via consumption and labour taxes). This would occur because of political resistance to more salient direct taxes (Wilensky, 2002) or economic considerations (Lindert, 2004), and is in parallel to the famous "paradox of redistribution" in spending (Korpi & Palme, 1998). The idea was confirmed by Prasad and Deng (2009) for the period 1979–2004; according to their findings, taxes in the United States were more progressive than those of several European countries, which had bigger welfare states.[12] Indeed, using the theory of the fiscal contract, some have argued that spending on the poor is generally funded by taxes on the poor (Kato, 2003; Timmons, 2005, 2010b). This would leave little space for redistribution by taking from the rich. It is therefore interesting to ask what place Spain, and other late transitioners, occupied in this setting. We will see that they resorted to regressive taxation. But did this allow them to develop highly redistributive systems?

Notes

1. These appointments were made by the King Juan Carlos I, who Franco himself designated his successor as head of state in 1969.
2. Lifting of banking secrecy, introduction of tax offence, and related issues—together with the granting of a tax amnesty. More on this in Chapter 4.
3. In this book, it is not only taxes *stricto* sensu that are considered. A tax is defined as a compulsory contribution without a clear equivalent "compensation". In this sense, social contributions are included in all the analyses, in as much as they do not represent an "actuarially fair" system.
4. Tariffs were of considerable importance in the sixties (a common feature of underdeveloped countries), but this was subsequently lost due amid commercial liberalization. State monopolies, banned by EU legislation, were replaced by excises.

5. As this book is being written, the coronavirus crisis is ongoing in Western Europe as well as the rest of the world, putting a strain on public finances everywhere. Its full effects are yet to be seen. At the end of the second quarter of 2020, Spain had one of the highest ratios of government debt to GDP in the EU, having increased by almost 12 points in just one year (data from Eurostat, Quarterly government debt).
6. This refers to autonomous communities under the common regime; regions with charter regimes have more powers and acquired them early on in the transition. See Chapter 7.
7. Smith (1989) reports the results of an international survey from 1987 saying that "*there seems to be something approaching a consensus when we asked specifically about* progressive *taxation. About two-thirds to three-quarters of respondents in all nations agreed that high income earners should be taxed more heavily than those on low incomes*". The survey was conducted within the International Social Survey Programme, in the following seven countries: Britain, United States of America, Australia, West Germany, Netherlands, Italy, and Hungary.
8. Both cited studies deal with inequality of gross income (i.e. pre-tax), even though Prados de la Escosura (2008) uses some data on net income as well (for the end of the period). In another work, this author has found that inequality in terms of disposable income stayed rather constant after democratisation (Torregrosa-Hetland, 2016), contradicting the widely held view of sharp decrease (Alcaide, 2000). This discussion will be revisited in Chapter 8.
9. Indeed, redistribution depends not only on the legal rules but also on the level of inequality actually in existence. A given income tax structure will result in more redistribution if it is applied to more unequally distributed income. The issue is further considered in Chapter 5.
10. By this measure, inequality was reduced by an average of 15 Gini points in fifteen developed countries around 1985, and by 18 Gini points around 2013 (Caminada et al., 2017). Jesuit and Mahler (2017)'s analysis of twenty developed countries between 1967 and 2010 showed redistribution to have increased in 1970–1995 (from 10 to 20 Gini points on average), remaining quite stable thereafter. Disposable income inequality started to increase, slowly, in 1985.
11. Garfinkel et al. (2006) looked at this for 2001 and found that differences between countries representing diverse welfare state models were substantially reduced, but they do not offer a temporal perspective.

12. There is room for more research on this topic in historical terms; another of this author's current projects is dedicated to it.

References

Acemoglu, D., & Robinson, J. A. (2001). A theory of political transitions. *American Economic Review, 91*(4), 938–963.

Acemoglu, D., & Robinson, J. A. (2008). Persistence of power, elites, and institutions. *American Economic Review, 98*(1), 267–293.

Aidt, T. S., & Jensen, P. S. (2009). The taxman tools up: An event history study of the introduction of the personal income tax. *Journal of Public Economics, 93*(1–2), 160–175.

Aidt, T., Winer, S., & Zhang, P. (2020). Franchise extension and fiscal structure in the United Kingdom 1820–1913: A new test of the Redistribution Hypothesis. In *Cambridge working papers in economics* (No. 2008). Faculty of Economics, University of Cambridge.

Albertus, M., & Menaldo, V. (2014). Gaming democracy: Elite dominance during transition and the prospects for redistribution. *British Journal of Political Science, 44*(03), 575–603.

Albi, E. (Ed.). (1990). *La Hacienda Pública en la Democracia. Estudios en homenaje al profesor Enrique Fuentes Quintana.* Ariel.

Alcaide, J. (2000). La renta nacional de España y su distribución. Serie años 1898 a 1998. In J. V. Fuertes (Ed.), *1900–2000. Historia de un esfuerzo colectivo: cómo España superó el pesimismo y la pobreza* (pp. 741, 810). Fundación BSCH.

Alvaredo, F., & Saez, E. (2009). Income and wealth concentration in Spain from a historical and fiscal perspective. *Journal of the European Economic Association, 7*, 1140–1167.

Arco Blanco, M. Á. del (Ed.). (2020). *Los "años del hambre". Historia y memoria de la posguerra franquista.* Marcial Pons.

Atkinson, A. (2018). *Inequality: What can be done?* Harvard University Press.

Atkinson, A., & Piketty, T. (2007). *Top incomes over the 20th century: A contrast between Continental European and English-speaking countries.* Oxford University Press.

Baby, S. (2018). *El mito de la transición pacífica. Violencia y política en España (1975–1982).* Akal.

Barciela López, C. (Ed.). (2003). *Autarquía y mercado negro : el fracaso económico del primer franquismo, 1939–1959.* Crítica.

Bates, R. H., & Lien, D.-H.D. (1985). A note on taxation, development, and representative democracy. *Politics and Society, 14*, 53–70.

Besley, T., & Persson, T. (2009). The origins of state capacity: Property rights, taxation, and politics. *American Economic Review, 99*(4), 1218–1244.

Betrán, C., & Pons, M. A. (Eds.). (2020). *Historical turning points in Spanish economic growth and development, 1808–2008.* Springer International Publishing.

Boix, C. (2003). *Democracy and redistribution.* Cambridge University Press.

Bozio, A., Garbinti, B., Goupille-Lebret, J., Guillot, M., & Piketty, T. (2020). *Predistribution vs. Redistribution: Evidence from France and the U.S* (2020/22; World Inequality Lab—Working Paper).

Buggeln, M., Daunton, M., & Nützenadel, A. (2017). The political economy of public finance: Taxation, state spending and debt since the 1970s. In *The political economy of public finance: Taxation, state spending and debt since the 1970s.* Cambridge University Press.

Caminada, K., Wang, J., Goudswaard, K., & Wang, C. (2017). *Income inequality and fiscal redistribution in 47 LIS-countries, 1967–2014* (No. 724; Working Paper Series).

Cardoso, J. L., & Lains, P. (2010). Paying for the liberal state: The rise of public finance in nineteenth-century Europe. In *Paying for the liberal state: The rise of public finance in nineteenth-century Europe.* Cambridge University Press.

Colomer, J. M. (1998). *La transición a la democracia: el modelo español.* Anagrama.

Comín, F. (1988). *Hacienda y economía en la España contemporánea (1800–1936).* Instituto de Estudios Fiscales.

Comín, F. (2007). Reaching a political consensus for tax reform in Spain: The Moncloa Pacts, Joining the European Union and the rest of the journey. In J. Martínez Vázquez & J. F. Sanz Sanz (Eds.), *Fiscal reform in Spain. Accomplishments and challenges* (pp. 8–57). Edward Elgar.

Comín, F. (2010). Public finance and the rise of the liberal state in Spain, 1808–1914. In J. L. Cardoso & P. Lains (Eds.), *Paying for the liberal state. The rise of the public finance in nineteenth-century Europe* (pp. 214–250). Cambridge University Press.

Comín, F., & Díaz, D. (2005). Sector público administrativo y estado del bienestar. In A. Carreras & X. Tafunell (Eds.), *Estadísticas Históricas de España. Siglos XIX-XX: Vol. II* (pp. 873–964). Fundación BBVA.

Cuevas, J., & Pons, M. A. (2020). *1977: Hopes fulfilled—Building democracy in turbulent economic times* (pp. 159–194). Palgrave Macmillan.

De la Torre, J., & Rubio-Varas, M. (Eds.). (2021). *Economía en transición. Del tardofranquismo a la democracia*. Marcial Pons.

Dincecco, M. (2009). Fiscal centralization, limited government, and public revenues in Europe, 1650–1913. *Journal of Economic History, 69*(1), 48–103.

Dincecco, M., & Prado, M. (2012). Warfare, fiscal capacity, and performance. *Journal of Economic Growth, 17*(3), 171–203.

Eichengreen, B. (2007). *The European economy since 1945: Coordinated capitalism and beyond*. Princeton University Press.

Espuelas, S. (2013). *La evolución del gasto social público en España, 1850–2005* (Vol. 63). Banco de España.

Fernández Ordóñez, F. (1980). *La España necesaria*. Taurus.

Freeman, J., & Quinn, D. (2012). The economic origins of democracy reconsidered. *American Political Science Review, 106*, 58–80.

Fuentes Quintana, E. (1990). *Las reformas tributarias en España. Teoría, historia y propuestas*. Crítica.

Fuentes Quintana, E. (2004). Los Pactos de la Moncloa y la Constitución de 1978. In E. Fuentes Quintana (Ed.), *Economía y economistas españoles* (Vol. 8, pp. 163–238). Círculo de Lectores.

Gandarias, E. (1999). *La política de la reforma fiscal: de la dictadura a la democracia*. Centro de Estudios Avanzados en Ciencias Sociales, Instituto Juan March.

García Delgado, J. L. (1990). *Economía Española de la Transición y la Democracia, 1973–1986*. Centro de Investigaciones Sociológicas.

Garfinkel, I., Rainwater, L., & Smeeding, T. M. (2006). A re-examination of welfare states and inequality in rich nations: How in-kind transfers and indirect taxes change the story. *Journal of Policy Analysis and Management, 25*(4), 897–919.

Gradstein, M., & Milanovic, B. (2004). Does Libertè = Egalité? A survey of the empirical links between democracy and inequality with some evidence on the transition economies. *Journal of Economic Surveys, 18*(4), 515–537.

Huberman, M., & Lewchuk, W. (2003). European economic integration and the labour compact, 1850–1913. *European Review of Economic History, 7*(1), 3–41.

Jesuit, D. K., & Mahler, V. A. (2017). Fiscal redistribution in comparative perspective: Recent evidence from the Luxembourg income study (LIS) data centre. In *The political economy of public finance: Taxation, state spending and debt since the 1970s* (pp. 177–198). Cambridge University Press.

Kato, J. (2003). *regressive taxation and the welfare state: Path dependence and policy diffusion*. Cambridge University Press.

Kleven, H. J., Kreiner, C. T., & Saez, E. (2015). *Why can modern governments tax so much? An agency model of firms as fiscal intermediaries.*

Korpi, W., & Palme, J. (1998). The paradox of redistribution and strategies of equality: Welfare state institutions, inequality, and poverty in the Western countries. *American Sociological Review, 63*(5), 661–687.

Lagares, M. J. (1999). La Hacienda Pública en las Facultades de Ciencias Económicas y en la sociedad española durante la segunda mitad del siglo XX. In E. Fuentes Quintana (Ed.), *Economía y economistas españoles* (Vol. 7, pp. 571–617). Galaxia Gutenberg.

Lago, I., & Montero, J. R. (2005). "Todavía no sé quiénes, pero ganaremos": Manipulación política del sistema electoral español. *Zona Abierta, 110*(111), 279–348.

Levi, M. (1988). *Of rule and revenue*. University of California Press.

Lindert, P. (1994). The rise of social spending, 1880–1930. *Explorations in Economic History, 31*(1), 1–37.

Lindert, P. H. (2004). *Growing public*. Cambridge University Press.

Lupu, N., & Pontusson, J. (2011). The structure of inequality and the politics of redistribution. *American Political Science Review, 105*(02), 316–336.

Mares, I., & Queralt, D. (2015). The non-democratic origins of income taxation. *Comparative Political Studies, 48*(14), 1974–2009.

Martínez-Alier, J., & Roca Jusmet, J. (1988). Economía política del corporativismo en el Estado Español: Del franquismo al posfranquismo. *REIS, 41*, 25–62.

Martínez-Vázquez, J., & Sanz-Sanz, J. F. (Eds.). (2007). *Fiscal reform in Spain.* Edward Elgar.

Mehrotra, A. K. (2013). *Making the modern American fiscal state: Law, politics, and the rise of progressive taxation, 1877–1929*. Cambridge University Press.

Meltzer, A. H., & Richard, S. F. (1981). A rational theory of the size of government. *Journal of Political Economy, 89*, 914–927.

Molinero, C., & Ysàs, P. (2008). *La anatomía del franquismo: de la supervivencia a la agonía: 1945–1977*. Crítica.

Mulligan, C. B., Gil, R., & Sala-i-Martin, X. (2004). Do democracies have different public policies than nondemocracies? *Journal of Economic Perspectives, 18*(1), 51–74.

Navarro, V. (2002). *Bienestar insuficiente, democracia incompleta.* Anagrama.

Neal, L. (2010). Conclusion: The monetary, fiscal, and political architecture of europe, 1815–1914. In *Paying for the liberal state: The rise of public finance in nineteenth-century Europe* (pp. 279–302). Cambridge University Press.

Pan-Montojo, J. L. (1996). Una larga e inconclusa transición: la reforma tributaria, 1977–1986. In J. Tusell & A. Soto (Eds.), *Historia de la transición. 1975–1986* (pp. 264–304). Alianza.

Peacock, A. T., & Wiseman, J. (1961). *The growth of public expenditure in the United Kingdom.* Princeton University Press.

Peters, G. B. (1991). *The politics of taxation: A comparative perspective.* Wiley-Blackwell.

Piketty, T. (2003). Income inequality in France, 1901–1998. *Journal of Political Economy, 111*(5), 1004–1042.

Piketty, T., Saez, E., & Stantcheva, S. (2011). *Optimal taxation of top labor incomes: A tale of three elasticities* (Issue 8675).

Powell, C. (2015). Spain: Transition by transaction. In S. Bitar & A. F. Lowenthal (Eds.), *Democratic transitions: Conversations with world leaders* (pp. 345–352). Johns Hopkins University Press.

Prados de la Escosura, L. (2008). Inequality, poverty and the Kuznets curve in Spain, 1850–2000. *European Review of Economic History, 12*, 287–324.

Prados de la Escosura, L. (2017). *Spanish economic growth, 1850–2015.* Springer International Publishing.

Prados De La Escosura, L., Rosés, J. R., & Sanz-Villarroya, I. (2012). Economic reforms and growth in Franco's Spain. In *Revista de Historia Economica —Journal of Iberian and Latin American Economic History* (Vol. 30, Issue 1, pp. 45–89). Cambridge University Press.

Prasad, M., & Deng, Y. (2009). Taxation and the worlds of welfare. *Socio-Economic Review, 7*, 431–457.

Przeworski, A. (1986). Some problems in the study of the transition to democracy. In G. O'Donnell, P. C. Schmitter, & L. Whitehead (Eds.), *Transitions from authoritarian rule* (pp. 44–63). Johns Hopkins University Press.

Rodrik, D. (1998). Why do more open economies have bigger governments? *Journal of Political Economy, 106*(5), 997–1032.

Roine, J., Vlachos, J., & Waldenström, D. (2009). The long-run determinants of inequality: What can we learn from top income data? *Journal of Public Economics, 93*(7–8), 974–988.

Rubio-Varas, M., & Muñoz, B. (2021). Energía en transición. In J. De la Torre & M. Rubio-Varas (Eds.), *Economía en Transición. Del tardofranquismo a la democracia* (pp. 33–60). Marcial Pons.
Rubolino, E., & Waldenström, D. (2020). Tax progressivity and top incomes evidence from tax reforms. *Journal of Economic Inequality, 18*(3), 261–289.
Saz, I. (2010). La lucha por la libertad en España desde una perspectiva comparada (1962–1977). In C. Navajas & D. Iturriaga (Eds.), *Novísima: II Congreso Internacional de Historia de Nuestro Tiempo* (pp. 71–80).
Scheve, K., & Stasavage, D. (2012). Democracy, war, and wealth: Lessons from two centuries of inheritance taxation. *American Political Science Review, 106*(1), 81–102.
Scheve, K., & Stasavage, D. (2016). *Taxing the rich: A History of fiscal fairness in the United States and Europe*. Princeton University Press.
Singhal, M. (2013). *Quantifying preferences for redistribution.*
Smith, T. W. (1989). Inequality and welfare. In R. Jowell, S. Witherspoon, & L. Brook (Eds.), *British social attitudes: Special international report*. Gower.
Steinmo, S. (1989). Political institutions and tax policy in the United States, Sweden, and Britain. *World Politics, 41*(4), 500–535.
Steinmo, S. (1993). *Taxation and democracy. Swedish, British, and American approaches to financing the modern state*. Yale University Press.
Steinmo, S. (2003). The evolution of policy ideas: Tax policy in the 20th century. *The British Journal of Politics & International Relations, 5*(2), 206–236.
Thorndike, J. J. (2012). *Their fair share: Taxing the rich in the age of FDR*. Urban Institute Press.
Tilly, C. (1990). *Coercion, capital, and European states, AD 990–1990*. B. Blackwell.
Timmons, J. (2005). The fiscal contract: States, taxes, and public services. *World Politics, 57*, 530–576.
Timmons, J. F. (2010a). Does democracy reduce economic inequality? *British Journal of Political Science, 40*(4), 741–757.
Timmons, J. F. (2010b). Taxation and representation in recent history. *Southern Political Science Association, 72*(1), 191–208.
Torregrosa-Hetland, S. (2015). *Tax system and redistribution: The Spanish fiscal transition (1960–1990)*. University of Barcelona.
Torregrosa-Hetland, S. (2016). Sticky income inequality in the Spanish transition (1973–1990). *Revista de Historia Economica - Journal of Iberian and Latin American Economic History, 34*(1).

Torregrosa-Hetland, S., & Sabaté, O. (2021). Income tax progressivity and inflation during the World Wars. *European Review of Economic History* (forthcoming).
Trullén, J. (1993). *Fundamentos económicos de la Transición política española. La política económica de los acuerdos de la Moncloa.* Ministerio de Trabajo y Seguridad Social.
Valiño, A. (1989). *La reforma tributaria de 1977*. Universidad Complutense de Madrid.
Wilensky, H. L. (2002). *Rich democracies: Political economy, public policy, and performance*. University of California Press.
Yun-Casalilla, B., O'Brien, P. K., & Comín, F. (2012). (eds.) *The rise of fiscal states: A global history 1500–1914*. Cambridge University Press.

2

The Fiscal System of Late Francoism

In the early seventies, it was widely recognised that the Spanish tax system was in need of reform. Mistrusted by the public, criticised by the academic community, and disregarded by many, it barely fulfilled the objectives of any tax system. Spanish taxes generated very low revenue by international standards, and did so with numerous inefficiencies and administrative complications. Finally, they were as a whole regressive, thereby contributing to increase income inequality.

The tax system was mainly based on indirect taxes, which are in principle borne by consumers when paying for goods and services. This form represented an average of 36% of total tax revenue in the years 1970–1975. The general consumption tax of the time, the *impuesto general sobre el tráfico de empresas* (IGTE), barely raised 6% of total tax revenue during this period—a similar magnitude as a whole range of other indirect levies, such as taxes on luxury items; excises; and transaction, stamp, and customs duties. The IGTE was a turnover tax, which has been shown to be technically inferior to a value added tax.[1] In addition, there was no

© The Author(s), under exclusive license to Springer Nature Switzerland AG 2021
S. Torregrosa Hetland, *The Spanish Fiscal Transition*, Palgrave Studies in Economic History, https://doi.org/10.1007/978-3-030-79541-2_2

real income tax in Spain in 1975. Direct taxation was very underdeveloped and still anchored to the old nineteenth-century taxes imposed on different sources of income (especially, by now, the tax on wages and salaries, the *impuesto sobre las rentas del trabajo personal*, which likewise raised 6% of tax revenue in 1970–1975). Social contributions, on the other hand, had been growing strongly since the sixties, and accounted for 42% of tax revenue by the early seventies. These were also regressive taxes that fell on wages and salaries.

All in all, Spanish tax revenue stood at 19% of GDP during the final years of Franco's rule. This was a meagre budget.

In all these respects, the Spanish tax system was very different from those of neighbouring countries usually taken as benchmarks—for example, France, the United Kingdom, and Germany (Comín, 1993; Martínez-Vázquez & Sanz-Sanz, 2007). In each of these countries, a modern personal income tax was paid yearly by a majority of the population, and therefore constituted a central revenue instrument. Value added taxes had been introduced in thirteen European countries before 1975 (Ebrill et al., 2001; Seelkopf et al., 2019), following the lead of France, where it raised nearly 8% of GDP by the early seventies. The total tax revenue in these respective countries was higher than in Spain—typically over 30% of GDP—which also meant that social contributions represented a smaller share. Given harmonisation initiatives within the European Economic Community (EEC), Spain's tax backwardness was an additional obstacle for the country's aspiration of eventually joining in European integration.

However, even if several prominent aspects of nineteenth-century taxation were still in place by 1977, fiscal reform was not completely absent during the Francoist period. It's more about the *kind* of reform that took place. For example, taxes on consumption were expanded in the aftermath of the Civil War, and presumptive taxation of company profits was reinforced during the fifties and sixties. The rest of the chapter presents an overview of the history of the Spanish tax system before and during Francoism, discussing the main changes as well as the proposals that were *not* implemented despite some high-level initiatives.

2.1 The Long Life of Liberal Taxation

As far as Spanish taxation is concerned, the *Ancien Régime* came to an end in 1845 after previous advances and retreats. That year, the government from the Moderate party enacted a comprehensive tax reform that repealed the principles, if perhaps not all the practices, of absolutist taxation.

The minister of public finance at the time, Alejandro Mon, introduced a tax system inspired by the French example. Mon's system was directed towards the proportional taxation of different sources of income (from land, real estate, industry, and trade). Revenue collection was supposed to be conducted with as little intromission as possible in taxpayers' business, and was therefore often based on indirect modes of assessment and apportionment that had a long history in Spain. This type of taxes are called "schedular" or "real" taxes, as opposed to personal taxation, which takes into account the total income of the taxpayer.

Even though land tax became very important, the bulk of taxation was indirect: through fiscal monopolies, excises, and customs duties. The latter two accounted for an increasing proportion of revenue during the second half of the nineteenth century. The growth in tariffs was related to reduced protectionism and expansion of foreign trade, as in other countries at the time. These principles of liberal taxation governed Spanish public finances for a long time (Comín, 1988, 2010; Fuentes Quintana, 1990).[2]

The system of 1845 was completed with Minister Raimundo Fernández Villaverde's reforms around 1900. He created a new tax to be levied on salaries, capital returns, and corporate profits—income streams that had been made more important by economic development. This was thus an adaptation of the tax system to gradual economic change, and did not entail breaking with the model. Villaverde's attempt that same year to introduce progressive rates to the inheritance tax was unsuccessful (San Julián-Arrupe, 2012).

In contrast, the late nineteenth to the early twentieth century was a period of tax innovation in many Western European countries. Personal income taxes were introduced in places such as Italy (1864), Sweden (1902), and France (1911), following, with some delay, the lead of the

United Kingdom (1842) (Aidt & Jensen, 2009). The progressive character of these taxes, as well as of inheritance taxes, was often reinforced before or during the First World War.[3] In Spain, several income tax proposals were formulated during 1910–1932, but none was successful. This is perhaps unsurprising given that the political system remained very oligarchic, despite the establishment of universal male suffrage in 1890. Progressivity made a very limited entrance to the Spanish fiscal system in 1907, applying only to inheritances between unrelated individuals (Comín et al., 1995).

Spain also remained exempt from the trend of expansion in tax revenues. Indeed, these essentially stagnated at 8% of GDP during the whole 1900–1958 period (see Fig. 2.1). The tax burden even *decreased* during the First World War, when Spanish neutrality favoured an expansion of the economy—precisely an illustration of how rigid and unresponsive to growth taxes were. This deepened the divide between Spain (and other peripheral countries) and the classic experience of Western

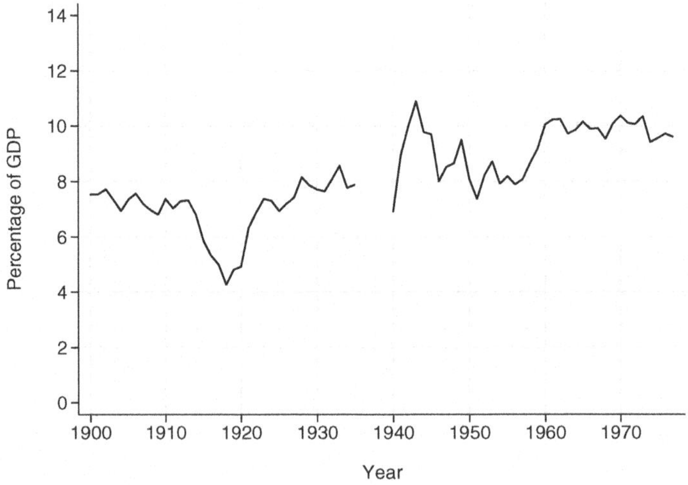

Fig. 2.1 Tax revenue as a percentage of GDP in Spain, 1900–1976 (*Source* Comín & Díaz [2005], with GDP from Prados de la Escosura [2017]. *Notes* The graph shows the sum of direct and indirect taxes in the source, so social contributions and other public revenues are excluded)

Europe, where the two world wars and their aftermaths brought about significant increases in tax revenue.

The Second Spanish Republic (1931–1936), with Jaume Carner occupying the Ministry of Public Finance, introduced an income tax in 1932. It was called *contribución general sobre la renta*, and broke with the principles of schedular taxation in its attempt to take into account the total income of the taxpayer as its base. Rates went from 1% for the lowest bracket to a maximum of 11%. It was, however, only a complementary tax, since schedular taxes were kept as the basis of the tax system. The new income tax was to be paid by those with income over 100,000 pesetas, which meant well below 1% of the adult population, severely limiting the tax's revenue potential as well as its impact on income distribution. In 1933, there were only 1446 payers of income tax in Spain (Alvaredo & Saez, 2009; Gota Losada, 1970).

After the fascist victory in the Civil War, fiscal reform took a different direction. The first minister of public finance under Franco was José Larraz, who took office in August of 1939 and left it in May of 1941. A very extensive account of his trajectory and initiatives is provided by Comín and Martorell (2013), upon which this summary is based.[4] A man of Catholic orientation, with an orthodox economic education and previous experience at the Bank of Spain, Larraz was often left exasperated by the lack of basic economic knowledge of Franco and his team. After the Civil War he aimed at economic and monetary stabilisation, and at enacting a tax reform to increase government revenues (in order to cover expenditure with ordinary revenue—a challenging undertaking in a country that had been impoverished by three years of warfare). The tax system that Larraz inherited in 1939 was not only short of revenue-generating potential, but also very complex, with very many different taxes that contributed only small quantities to the public treasury—or even bypassed it altogether, going directly to other institutions.

Larraz's reform increased indirect taxation, mainly through the consolidation of several pre-existing taxes on specific products into the new tax on *usos y consumos*, which was also extended to additional items. The tax was levied on producers (for administrative simplicity), but was supposed to apply to final consumers through expenditure. This was the main product of Larraz's tax reform, and accounted for between 18 and 28%

of state revenue during 1941–1960 (Comín & Martorell, 2013, p. 248). It also further disincentivised consumption during the postwar period of shortage. But despite being called a single tax, in truth it retained the same regulations as its predecessors, with a multiplicity of rates.

Comín and Martorell (2013) referred to Larraz as a very academic person who based his proposals on previous study of the tax history of Spain and other Western European countries. He was aware that tax innovation after the First World War I had meant the introduction of general taxes on income and consumption in many places. But Larraz, although favourable to tax modernisation (within the parameters of orthodoxy), felt that consumption tax was the only one of the two options that could generate considerable revenue in the Spain of the forties. The development of income tax would be less viable, given that it required extensive administrative resources and improvements to tax morale.[5] Larraz's reform did slightly reinforce income taxation, by reducing its threshold (to 70,000 pesetas) and increasing the tax rates, but it was still very marginal in terms of revenue.[6]

Larraz also adjusted the rates and bases of the schedular taxes (on land, industrial activity, etc.).[7] These adjustments contributed to increases in tax revenue in the immediate years (see Fig. 2.1), but the system was not fit to produce sustained revenue under the high levels of inflation experienced during the postwar period (inflation during the forties was an average of 13% per year, with extreme fluctuations; data from Carreras & Tafunell, 2018). Schedular taxes were, in the words of the Spanish economist Manuel de Torres, "petrified" (Torres, 1956). The level of tax revenues went back to its previous level of around 8% of GDP during the remainder of the forties and the fifties.

All in all, the tax system of 1940 went unchanged until the reforms of Mariano Navarro Rubio in 1957 and 1964, which are explored in the next section. During the fifties, however, the (so-called) income tax was reformed. And the direction of this reform was hotly debated—albeit within small circles of influential businessmen, economists, and politicians—between those who wanted the income tax to incentivise savings and private investment, and those who envisioned it as an instrument of redistribution. The latter group was led by the prominent economist

Manuel de Torres, and had links with the *Falange* party and its newspaper *Arriba*. This group ultimately succeeded in imposing its vision on the law, after provoking the withdrawal of a pre-existing proposal. According to Comín and Martorell (2013), the clash between these two blocs resulted in the resignation of Francisco Gómez de Llano, the minister of public finance from 1951 to 1957.

In fact, both proposals had some similarities, such as an increase in the income tax threshold. Indeed, the limit on the obligation to file a return had been brought down to 60,000 pesetas in 1943, and was set at 100,000 with the reform enacted in December 1954. The rationale was that the continuous increase in the number of tax returns had made their administration very difficult or almost impossible. Tax evasion, therefore, was deemed to be very high, and this was reflected in the fact that a very high percentage of tax payments, over 60% in the early sixties, derived from inspections (see Chapter 6). Increasing the threshold would reduce the number of taxpayers, and facilitate relations between them and the tax administration. This would ultimately reduce fraud—even if it would not increase the "generality" of the tax throughout the population. It was thus a different path to that initially foreseen by Carner in 1932, who thought that the tax should be progressively extended to finally substitute the schedular taxes, as had occurred in other Western European countries.

The increase in the threshold was combined with the reestablishment of certain criteria associated with the obligation to file a return—based on certain expenditures and external indications of wealth—which was expected to improve compliance within the target segment. Moreover, tax rates were reduced, and now went from a minimum of 2.5% to a maximum of 33% (for income over a million pesetas).

By 1957 the number of actual taxpayers had increased somewhat (from 16,545 in 1954 to 30,944), but the number of total returns had almost quadrupled (from 27,653 to 109,026) (Gota Losada, 1970). This increase, however, seems to have been well below the initial expectations: according to the economist Juan Velarde in *Arriba*, more than 125,000 returns were already expected by 1955 (Comín & Martorell, 2013, p. 338). The ultimate effects on revenue can be seen in Fig. 2.2, which shows the whole period 1933–1977 (from the introduction of the

Fig. 2.2 Revenue of the income tax as a percentage of GDP, Spain 1933–1977 (*Source* Comín & Díaz [2005] until 1957, Torregrosa-Hetland [2015] from 1958, with GDP from Prados de la Escosura [2017])

contribución general sobre la renta until the last year before the tax reforms of the fiscal transition). This tax never constituted an important source of public revenue, fluctuating around 0.15% of GDP during the dictatorship, but it decreased in 1955 to a near all-time low of 0.10% (it even decreased in nominal terms!), from which it progressively recovered its previous levels.[8]

The meagre revenue collected through the income tax illustrates, as noted, that the principles of liberal taxation governed Spanish public finances for a long time. Income from different sources was taxed under different schedules (in theory proportionally, but with regressive effects because of the modes of assessment). Indirect taxation represented the bulk of revenue, with maximum levels around 70% in the mid-sixties (data from Comín & Díaz, 2005). Francisco Comín, one of the preeminent scholars of the Spanish tax system, singled out this, along with the inability to enact a modern income tax before 1978, as "*the visible expression of resistance to changing the patterns of distribution of the tax burden established in the mid-nineteenth century*" (Comín et al., 1995, p. 343; author's translation).

With regard to social security, during the early part of this period the system was contributory. Insurance for different risks (accidents, retirement, and maternity) had been introduced during the first half of the twentieth century, a process that is reviewed in Barrada (1999) and Pons and Silvestre (2010).[9] These risks were covered across different accounts administered by a myriad of institutions, but mostly the *Instituto Nacional de Previsión*. They were generally funded through contributions by both firms and workers, with a given percentage out of wages. Importantly, not all of the population was covered (it was primarily targeted at formal urban workers), nor were all taxpayers subject to the same conditions.

The dictatorship promoted the development of this model, providing some protection for old age, sickness, family, and, eventually, in 1961, unemployment. This has been interpreted as an instrument for securing some legitimacy among the working class—but the other side of the coin was low wages and no freedom of association (Guillén, 1997). Importantly, social insurance schemes that were formerly based mostly on "defined contributions" were transformed into "defined benefit" schemes, and became financially unsound over time (González Catalá & Vicente Merino, 1987).[10] Fixed benefits could be increased for political reasons, without ensuring their funding within the system. Moreover, up to the early sixties these insurance schemes were geared towards workers up to a certain wage level, which was fixed in nominal terms: the cap lost real value over time, especially with the high inflation of the fifties, decreasing the total number of contributors. Pensions paid out by the system were very low and clearly insufficient to cover the basic needs of the beneficiaries (Comín & Martorell, 2013; González Murillo, 2008).

In 1941, a complementary regime called *mutualismo laboral* was introduced. This provided additional protection to workers, normally at the firm level, and was under the umbrella of the Ministry of Labour. During the forties and fifties there was some institutional unification of schemes, with the creation of the *seguros sociales unificados* in 1948 (joining the schemes for pensions, family, and sickness administered by the *Instituto Nacional de Previsión*), and the coordination of payments between these and the *Mutualismo*. But the overlap between these two institutions, covering the same risks with different contributions and different account books, was only put to an end in 1967. Diversity continued to exist, though, given that very different conditions were established for specific groups of workers. These social insurance systems (in the plural) were therefore very distant from the type of general, national social security that was being developed in Western European countries in the postwar period.

Under Francoism there was no longer an actuarial relation between payments and benefits, and so social insurance contributions essentially became a tax. Thus, it is important to keep in mind that workers paid more in taxes, as compulsory payments generally speaking, than might appear to be the case if we only look at "taxes" strictly defined.

2.2 Stabilisation, Growth, and a "Missed Opportunity"

By the late fifties, the Spanish economy was on the way to an external payments crisis, with growing inflation and external deficit, and scarce foreign reserves (Prados de la Escosura et al., 2012). To confront this situation, the Stabilization and Liberalization Plan was devised and implemented in 1959—even though some related and preparatory measures had already been taken in 1957. The plan combined a classic stabilisation operation with internal and external liberalisation of the Spanish economy, and was reinforced with the incorporation of Spain into several international institutions. It has therefore been considered a watershed in the economic policy of the Francoist dictatorship—the final abandonment of autarkic orientation (Martínez-Ruiz & Pons, 2020).

The Stabilization and Liberalization Plan was a success in many respects, and gave way to a period of rapid and unparalleled growth in the Spanish economy during the following decade (Prados de la Escosura, 2017). In some accounts, the sixties have therefore been considered a "missed opportunity" to enact a modernising tax reform (Fuentes Quintana, 1990).[11] The rationale for this is that an expansion of public revenues could be easier under a context of growth, which might allow to combine an increasing tax burden with the growth of net income in the hands of the taxpayers. Indeed, when tax reform finally took place, it came alongside, and was conditioned by, a deep economic crisis (Torregrosa-Hetland, 2021).

A tax reform was enacted prior to the Stabilization plan, but in relation to it, in 1957. In introducing this reform, the minister of public finance Mariano Navarro Rubio sought an increase in tax revenues that would, in turn, reduce public deficits—one of the causes of high inflation in the preceding years. In 1964, during the high-growth period, the same minister launched a new reform that now had a purported redistributive objective. We will now discuss the basic changes introduced with both.

With regard to the tax reform of 1957, one of its main novelties was the creation of the corporation tax per se—that is, with that name and aimed exclusively at the taxation of businesses. The echoes of those who argued in 1954 for a tax system that supported savings and private investment could be heard in the reform of 1957, which created a "fund for investments" whereby part of the business profits could be saved, exempt from taxation, for later investments. This reform, among others, has been analysed by Comín and Vallejo (2012), who documented the influence of interest groups in the final result.

But companies, like other types of taxpayers, were not even expected to pay according to their actual profits. Navarro Rubio's way of confronting fraud was to institutionalise negotiation of tax bases with groups of taxpayers. These collective tax bases were then distributed within the group, according to certain "objective" indicators. In essence, this procedure resembled the forms of apportioning taxes of the nineteenth century—forms that stood to benefit the powerful taxpayers within each group. This type of collective assessment applied to indirect as well as direct taxes, and was known as "*régimen de convenios*" and "*evaluación global*", respectively. As well as reducing fraud, Navarro Rubio presented it as a mechanism to encourage cooperation and to have taxpayers check up on each other.

The complexity of the Spanish tax system was maintained and even reinforced. Companies not only paid the corporate tax, but also a fixed quota within the industrial tax (*licencia fiscal*). Part of the reform of 1957 was indeed (and again) a reorganisation of existing taxes under new names, without affecting their character. The labour tax (*impuesto sobre los rendimientos del trabajo personal*) and the capital tax (*impuesto *sobre las rentas del capital*) were created in this way. These were mostly, as before, proportional taxes. The industrial tax, for example, taxed estimated "profits" at a 20% rate. The labour tax also had a single rate (15%), but a scheme for reductions in the tax base would have made it somewhat progressive. The capital tax, on the other hand, entailed tax rates between 8 and 30%. In the case of the income tax, rates were increased above the million peseta mark, to a maximum of 44%.[12]

All in all, the reform allowed a budget balance to be attained in 1958, through an increase in revenue that was combined with greater spending control. Tax collection jumped to 10% of GDP within some years (see Fig. 2.1). But short-term success in revenue, and increases in the number of payers of several taxes, was not followed by the sustained expansion in public revenues that one might expect to find in a modern tax system. Not that this was, really, an objective of Navarro Rubio.

The second reform took place in 1964. As mentioned, in the minister's account this second reform intended to redistribute the burden, after having succeeded in increasing public revenues and compliance by way of the first. The introduction to the main law comprising the reform stated that "*the political guidelines of the Spanish State require permanent redistributive action, benefiting the lower income sectors of the population [...] Economic growth policy must implicitly include the provision of adequate mechanisms to channel improvements in income to those who are to be its legitimate beneficiaries*".[13] In the fiscal arena, this was inspired by the principle of progressivity in the distribution of the tax burden. Some parts of this text would definitely raise eyebrows among experts on Francoist politics. They may have smelled like modern taxation, but they were not.

One of the main novelties of the 1964 reform was the introduction of a so-called "general income tax" (*impuesto general sobre la renta de las personas físicas*) to replace the old one. But again this did not mean the elimination of schedular taxes on different sources of income. Rather, the "general tax" was superimposed on them, which meant that the tax base was determined by the rules of the schedular taxes, and that payments within these were deductible against the general tax due (before, they had been deductible as part of the entire tax base). The marginal tax rates were increased, ranging from 16 to 61.4%, but these rates are not comparable to the ones in the old tax since they now included schedular taxation as well.[14]

The threshold for general income tax was increased from 25,000 to 60,000 pesetas. This brought it to the same level as the threshold for labour tax (which was also strongly increased, from 18,000 pesetas in 1954). But in practice, if the tax base was under 200,000 pesetas, only schedular taxes were paid, and this limit went up to 300,000 pesetas if the taxpayer only had an income from labour. Therefore, for the great majority of taxpayers, progressivity was nowhere in sight. The number of actual payers of income tax dropped again in 1967, when these rules were in place (see Fig. 2.3). This, of course, is in direct opposition to establishing a general, modern income tax.

The corporation tax was modified similarly, to be called "general" and include schedular taxes. It kept its 30% rate (lower for partnerships

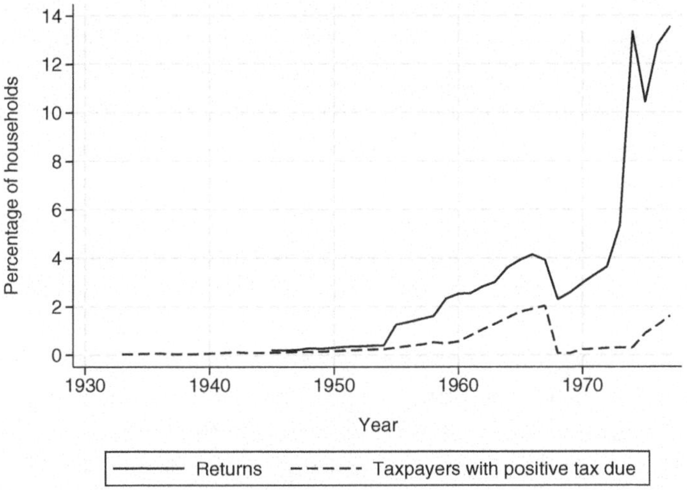

Fig. 2.3 Returns and actual payers of income tax, Spain 1933–1977 (*Source* Number of returns, and returns with positive tax due taken from Gota Losada [1970] and Valdés [1982]; data for 1967 obtained from the General Archive of the Ministry of Public Finance [ACMH-9039]. Number of households from census of 1970, 1981 and 1991, as well as household surveys of 1964 and 1973. Note: the number of households was extended backwards using an estimate of the average number of individuals therein [the expected bias would be a slight overestimation of the series shown in the initial period])

and limited partnerships). The reform also introduced several novelties related to amortisation, avoiding double taxation of dividends, and reserves for investment. But all in all, the changes to income taxation in 1964 were far from revolutionary, as they did not alter the basic principles of distribution of the tax burden.

With respect to indirect taxation, a general consumption tax was created in 1964, in the form of the *impuesto general sobre el tráfico de empresas*. This was a turnover tax, applied to every transaction in the life of the different goods. It came to replace the pre-existing *impuesto general sobre el gasto*, which in reality was an umbrella term for a long series of specific taxes on different products (for example, gasoline, textiles, alcohol, or sugar). This was a step forward in terms of modernisation, even if by this time several Western European countries were introducing a more technically advanced form of general consumption taxation—namely, a value added tax (Ebrill et al., 2001). Alongside the general consumption tax, some excises continued to exist, as well as specific taxation of luxury goods and services (such as vehicles, tobacco, cosmetics, etc.).

The main changes during the sixties were actually to social security contributions.[15] These contributions were not included within the tax system, operating independently and under the authority of a different ministry (Labour). A reform in 1963 (put into effect in 1967), the *Ley de Bases de la Seguridad Social*, reorganised the system and unified the payment of social security contributions. The new contributions were not assessed on full wages, but on certain "bases" established by decree for different categories of workers ("*bases tarifadas*"). In practice, these set a very low cap, exempting a significant proportion of high salaries (they were around 40% of wages/salaries in the mid-sixties, but only 20% in better-paid categories, according to Vergés, 1974). The system of "*bases tarifadas*" was the culmination of a process of exempting wage increases from taxation during previous years—a trend that continued over the following years, with bases growing less than wages (Barrada, 1999; Serrano & Malo, 1979). Social contributions were therefore highly regressive, and increasingly so. Table 2.1 illustrates this by showing the tax bases established between 1963 and 1970, which contrast with the evolution of wages during the same period. Nominal wages in industry

Table 2.1 Tax bases for social security contributions by categories of workers

	1963	1967	1968	1969	1970	Growth 1963–1970 (%)
In pesetas per month						
1: Engineers and Graduates	5600	5670	5970	6330	6630	18
2: Assistants (graduated)	4700	4770	5070	5370	5670	21
3: Administrative and workshop heads	3900	3960	4260	4530	4830	24
4: Assistants (not graduated)	3400	3420	3720	3960	4260	25
5: Administrative officers	2800	3150	3450	3660	3960	41
6: Subordinates	2000	2610	2880	3060	3600	80
7: Administrative assistants	1800	2520	2880	3060	3600	100
In pesetas per day						
8: 1st and 2nd category officers	80	96	105	112	130	63
9: 3rd and 4th category officers	70	90	100	106	124	77
10: Workmen	60	84	96	102	120	100
11: 3rd and 4th year apprentices	48	56	60	64	76	58
12: 1st and 2nd year apprentices	25	35	40	43	48	92
Pro memoria: average monthly wage in selected occupations						
Financial institutions	6605	11,501	12,653	14,285	16,531	150
Graphic arts and publishing	3610	6240	6701	7411	8275	129
Mining (metalic minerals)	3302	6106	6547	7258	8006	142
Textile	2899	5184	5491	5894	6490	124
Trade	2726	4896	5395	6048	6566	141
Construction	2458	4301	4781	5261	6067	147

Source Tax bases from *Boletín Oficial del Estado*. Hourly wages from Maluquer de Motes and Llonch Casanovas (2005, Table 15.24)
Notes The tax base for Category 7 corresponds to the minimum wage. Monthly wages have been estimated by applying a factor of 193 to hourly data. This results from a 45 hours week, which was standard for several occupations in the sixties (Maluquer de Motes & Llonch Casanovas, 2005, Table 15.32)

and services more than doubled, while the increase in the tax bases was below 100%, and less than a third in the highest-paid categories.

The model remained "Bismarckian" in that it was not universal but based on participation via contributions, and the conditions varied for different professional groups. Some of these groups enjoyed more favourable conditions, from an actuarial point of view: for example, protection for agrarian and self-employed workers was partially financed by superavits from the general workers scheme—therefore representing solidarity among workers but not generally in society. Guillén (2000) stressed that some aspects of the law of 1963, such as an increase in state participation in funding, or the involvement of workers in system management, were never put into practice.

In spite of this, the revenue brought in with social contributions increased strongly after 1967—which means, of course, that there was a greater tax burden on labour. These revenues were directed to fund pensions and health care, but also other investment projects, given the generation of considerable surpluses during the sixties. Social contributions were estimated to represent 18% of wages in 1963–1966, then 29% by 1973–1974 (Vergés, 1974). Figure 2.4 represents these contributions as a percentage of GDP, similarly to what we have shown for total taxes and income tax in Figs. 2.1 and 2.2, respectively. They fluctuated between 3 and 4% of GDP during the fifties and increased beyond 6% by the end of the sixties. This meant a considerable expansion of tax revenue during this last decade, which is not shown in Fig. 2.1 because it took place outside the "tax system" per se. In political terms, social contributions were easier to raise than taxes.

2.3 The Early Seventies: Attempts at Reform

All in all, therefore, the sixties can be considered a "missed opportunity" for reform. Throughout this decade of economic growth, social change, and increased openness, the Spanish state continued to be poor in terms of resources. Western European countries were by 1970 raising around 30% of their GDP in taxes—much higher than Spain's 18% (see Table

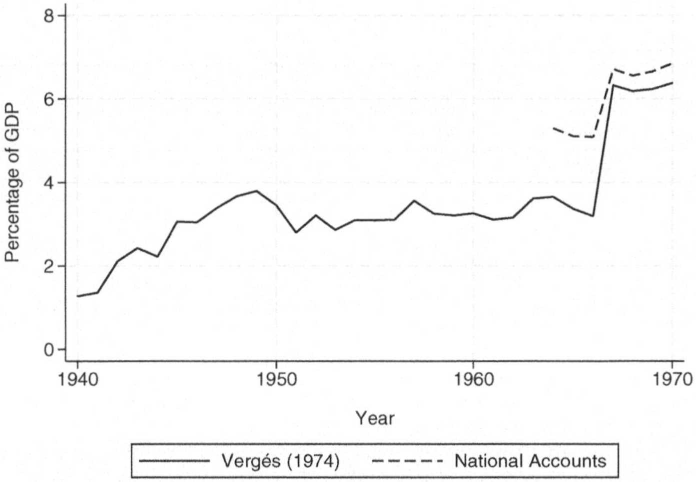

Fig. 2.4 Social contributions as a percentage of GDP in Spain, 1940–1970 (*Source* Vergés [1974] and the Spanish National Accounts, Contabilidad Nacional de España, base 1970 [1979], with GDP from Prados de la Escosura [2017]. *Notes* The discontinuity in 1967, related to the entry into effect of the 1963 law, is probably due to the inclusion of some of the contributions previously administered by private entities ["*entidades colaboradoras*"]. The increase was probably smoother than it appears in the data)

2.2). Even Italy, arguably the country closest economically to Spain, had an advantage of six percentage points.

The structure of taxation was also different. In Northwestern Europe, income tax represented between a third and half of total tax revenues, which indicates higher progressivity and also suggests a broader development of the "fiscal contract". For its part, France raised much more through income tax than did Spain—almost 4% of GDP rather than 0.1. The average in the EU-14 was near 8% of GDP. Three of the countries in Table 2.2 had implemented a value added tax by 1970 (France, Germany, and Sweden), while a sales tax was in place in the United Kingdom. The fact that these single, general taxes accounted for a higher share of GDP (and public income) than in Spain points towards a higher level of tax modernisation and efficiency.

However, with respect to social security contributions, Spanish revenue does not stand out for the wrong reasons: the growth in this

Table 2.2 Selected taxes as a percentage of GDP in Spain and other Western European countries, 1970

	Total tax revenue	Personal income tax	General consumption tax	Social security contributions
Sweden	35.6	17.7	3.7	5.3
United Kingdom	35.0	11.0	2.4	4.9
France	33.7	3.6	8.6	12.2
Germany	31.6	8.4	5.4	9.6
Italy	24.8	–	3.3	9.4
Spain	18.2	0.1	1.3	6.7
EU-14	29.7	7.9	4.4	6.7

Source OECD Statistics except for Spain from Torregrosa-Hetland (2015), with GDP from Prados de la Escosura (2017)
Note Countries are in descending order by total tax revenue. Italy in 1970 also had a schedular income tax, which makes its data incomparable with the rest. EU-14 includes all countries in EU-15 except for Spain

income source during the sixties had put it at standard European levels, and it kept on increasing in subsequent years. In this regard, Spain's backwardness lay in the lack of generality of its system: there were multiple uncoordinated managing entities, several specific regimes, very low state involvement in funding, and no development of social services.

Some observers in Spain were certainly aware of this situation, and during the first half of the seventies a discussion about tax reform was in the air. Of course, this does not mean that the average Spaniard engaged in sophisticated conversations about tax bases and rates, even if they did have some general opinions (see Chapter 3). But in intellectual circles, some ideas were emerging. For several economists and high-ranking public officials, the poverty of the Spanish state was a problem because it meant a scarcity of resources not only for potential redistribution, but also for investment aimed at economic growth, such as in education or infrastructure. Furthermore, a long-held aspiration of becoming "part of Europe" was hampered by the tax differential.

Since 1953, experts in tax law had been holding a yearly conference called *Semana de Estudios de Derecho Financiero* ("Financial Law Studies Week"). Among the regular participants were Ministers of Public Finance, senior officials in the tax administration, and prominent academic economists. In the *Semanas*, the "hottest topics" about taxation in the country were discussed, often with an eye on what was happening elsewhere in Europe. Even if the conference was somewhat technical, the list of topics shows where attention was focused: for example, both in 1966 and 1972 the topic was "international economic relations"; in 1968, "The future of fiscal systems"; and in 1969, "value added tax". During the conference of 1968, Professor José María Naharro Mora (who had played a prominent role in the discussion about the income tax reform in 1954) gave a talk titled "the future structure of the fiscal system", which represents the extent of a general consensus among the intellectual elite around the problems and needed reforms. With regard to the problems, Naharro mentioned the weakness of income taxation, the complexity of indirect taxation, and the insufficient resources of the tax administration. This professor, as well as his audience, was well aware of the "relative tax underdevelopment" of the country, and of the need to converge with its European neighbours. He warned, however, against trying to make this transition too quickly, particularly with respect to extending the income tax, so as to not jeopardise the flow of public funds. It was commonly expected that expenditure needs would grow over the subsequent years, not least because of investment needs in areas such as education. Reinforcing indirect taxation, even if the system was already skewed towards it, seemed a promising avenue since this would provide flexibility in revenues and favour savings. In contrast, the stance taken by the prominent tax inspector Alfonso Gota Losada in the same 1968 conference was more openly favourable to developing income tax following European guidelines; he also mentioned the work of the Neumark commission in proposing harmonisation of direct taxation.

Another forum for debate was the meetings organised by the *Círculo de Economía*. The *Círculo*, established in 1958 by a group of prominent Catalan businessmen, functioned as a think tank in constant dialogue with economists working in the public administration, such as Juan Sardá, Enrique Fuentes Quintana, and Luis Ángel Rojo. In Madrid, the *Club Siglo XXI*, founded in 1969, also organised debates and conferences about Spanish political and economic life. The economic and political elite used these institutions as meeting points, where they disseminated ideas about Europeanisation and modernisation. Tax modernisation, of course, was a necessary part of these processes.

In this context, some very detailed plans for reform were written. Their cradle was the *Instituto de Estudios Fiscales*, a research and training institution attached to the Ministry of Public Finance and created in 1969. Its director at the time was Enrique Fuentes Quintana, with César Albiñana the assistant director. Around them, a group of economists and public finance specialists worked to craft a comprehensive tax reform project. The aim was the adoption of a European-style taxation model in Spain, with personal income taxation at the centre, and complemented by net wealth, inheritance, and value added taxes. Such a system was intended to be fairer, more efficient, and more flexible.[16] It would provide the state with the increased revenues needed, in the minds of its proponents, for a higher level of development. Fuentes Quintana wrote that Spanish democratisation would likely bring about long-supressed demands for higher public spending, and that these demands would be impossible to meet within the current tax system (Instituto de Estudios Fiscales, 1973). The proposed tax system would also mean convergence with Europe, facilitating the long-desired process of integration into the EEC (which required some tax harmonisation, in the spirit of the 1962 Neumark Report).[17]

The institute's concrete proposals can be read in two volumes known as the *Libro Verde* (1973) and the *Libro Blanco* (1976), both of which were re-published in 2002 (Instituto de Estudios Fiscales, 1973, 1976). In the *Libro Verde*, as part of its criticism of the current tax system, the Institute conducted a detailed analysis of the distribution of the tax burden, showing it to be regressive at the top (effective tax rates were decreasing for the richest). Importantly, these proposals did not include social contributions, which are a regressive component; see Chapter 5. The proposed tax system would get around this problem by emphasising the role of personal income tax. Inheritance and net wealth taxes were meant to act as complements, providing information about taxpayers but not much revenue. Turnover tax should be replaced by a value added tax, as in the European Commission countries. Importantly, the books also contained guidelines about the administrative reform that would be necessary to operate the new system.

The first plan was presented by the minister of public finance Alberto Monreal Luque to Franco's government in April 1973, but without success. Indeed, after doing so, Monreal was dismissed and his project hidden from public knowledge (most copies of the *Libro Verde* were destroyed). After this episode, Fuentes Quintana and members of the institute became convinced that a modernising tax reform of this sort could never be passed under Franco's dictatorship. Democratisation was a prerequisite.[18] After the dictator's death, a second project, very similar to the first, was presented by Minister Juan Miguel Villar Mir, only to be also postponed. Manuel Jesús Lagares, another economist involved, provided a detailed account of the process (Lagares, 1999).

During the last years of the dictatorship, there was some expansion in "general" income tax in terms of the number of returns (Fig. 2.3). Between 1973 and 1974 the number of returns jumped from less than 500,000 to 1.3 million, but out of these, the number of taxpayers making actual payments of progressive income tax (and not only of schedular taxes) barely changed, going from 27,733 to 28,720 (data from Valdés [1982]). In 1977 the number of actual taxpayers reached almost 164,000, making up 12% of the total (up from 2.2% in 1974). These increases in the number of returns were certainly a challenge for the tax administration of the time, for which scarcity of personnel and lack of mechanisation made it very difficult to process large volumes of individual information. But these were modest changes in comparison with the jump in returns that would be seen in 1980, after the reform: from 2.8 to 5.4 million returns, and from 274,000 to 3,827,000 positive ones (71% of the total). The expansion in the number of returns in the early seventies, however, did not lead to an expansion in the revenue generated by the tax, as a percentage of GDP, as can be seen in Fig. 2.2.

With regard to social security, a reform in 1972 sought to increase the revenues yielded by the system, gradually bringing the "bases" in line with real wages and salaries. This alignment process was meant to culminate in 1975, but continued up to 1978 (González Catalá & Vicente Merino, 1987). By the end of the seventies, Spain's social security system generated as much revenues as all its other taxes altogether. Pensions had also been raised in 1972, and were now calculated according to contributions over the last two years: ultimately, this meant that expenditure in the system grew more quickly than revenues. Furthermore, the social security system was still highly complex, with considerable differences between worker groups, and possible negative effects on employment. By the mid-seventies, many advocated integrating the social security system within the public budget, in order to fund its expenditure, partly or wholly, through general taxation. Increased state participation in the funding of social security had been established in the 1972 reform, but not put into practice.

Figure 2.5 presents the share of direct taxes, indirect taxes, and social contributions in GDP from 1960 to 1990. This makes it possible to evaluate the nature of the tax system during the late Franco regime and to see the effects of the fiscal transition. By Franco's death in 1975, indirect taxes were still more important than direct taxes, which had been a long-standing characteristic of the Spanish tax system. But indirect taxes were stagnating or slightly decreasing in relation to GDP at that point, which shows the rigidity of some taxes that were fixed in nominal or physical terms (excises), as well as the lack of revenue from the oil monopoly, during 1974 and 1975, in response to the first oil shock (Rubio-Varas & Muñoz, 2021). Direct taxes, on the other hand, had been on the increase

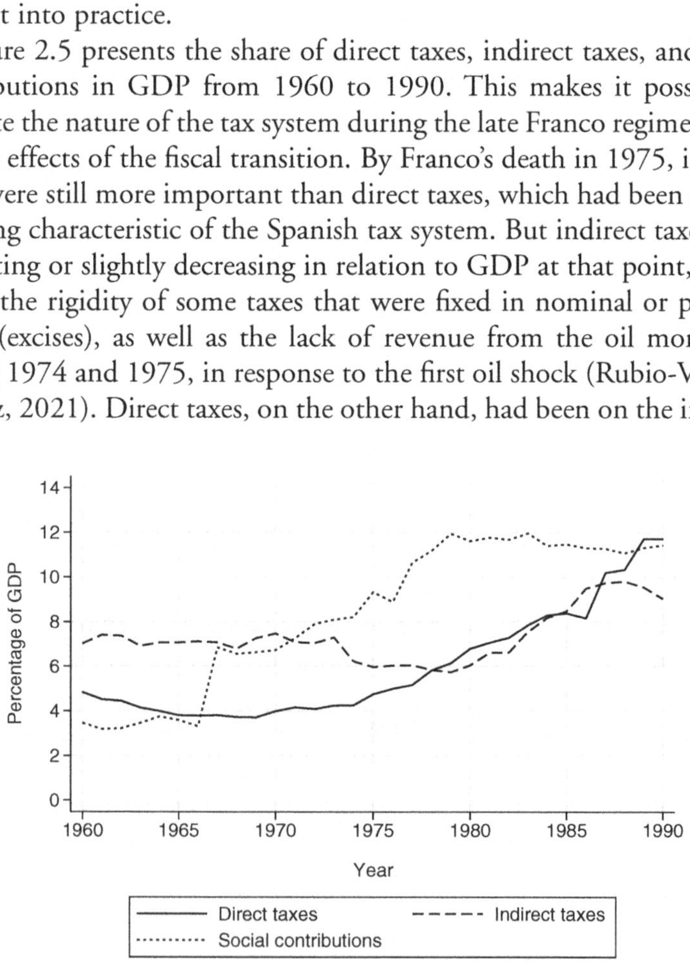

Fig. 2.5 The structure of taxation in Spain, 1960–1990 (*Source* Torregrosa-Hetland [2015], with GDP from Prados de la Escosura [2017])

since around 1970—an increase mostly explained by labour tax, which more than doubled its revenue in real terms between 1970 and 1975 (going from 0.9 to 1.6% of GDP). This is related to an extension in the wage-earner rate and payroll increases, but also to high inflation (above 5% annually) in combination with thresholds and deductions fixed in nominal terms, which sparked criticism (see Chapter 3). However, the fastest-growing component was social contributions, which represented around 9% of GDP in the final years of the dictatorship, up from 6.7% in the late sixties. All in all, tax revenues were increasing at the end of the dictatorship, to a total of 20% of GDP (still far from Western European levels), but they were doing so primarily by putting additional pressure on workers.

The Spanish tax system of 1977 had widely recognised problems. It provided scarce revenue, and was very rigid—meaning that economic growth did not translate into higher public revenues. It was also regressive, since indirect taxes and social contributions comprised the bulk of it, and progressive income taxation was practically non-existent. The types of taxes were many, and they were complicated to file and administer. Furthermore, it was common knowledge that the rich evaded their share of taxation.

All in all, this meant that it was difficult for the state to perform certain functions—such as spending on education and infrastructure—that were essential for economic development, let alone the redistribution of income to reduce inequalities. In any case, Franco's Spain clearly did not include redistribution among its objectives. But democratic Spain might do.

Notes

1. Turnover taxes are imposed at each phase of a product's life, meaning that the tax in the first phase is included in the price at the next one, generating what is known as a cascade effect. As a consequence, the tax is not neutral across all goods, since production takes place with different degrees of vertical integration. A value-added tax is also charged at each phase, but allows firms to deduct the price of acquisition of intermediate goods, thus avoiding the cascade effect.

2. This chapter describes the general Spanish tax system. Some regional particularities existed, especially in the regions with "fueros" (local laws and privileges): the Basque Country and Navarre, while the Canary Islands had special treatment regarding indirect taxation. The systems of Navarre and the Basque province of Álava will be described briefly in Chapter 3 when we approach the issue of decentralisation during the political transition. Analyses of both the Basque and the Navarrese cases during the nineteenth century can be found in De la Torre and García-Zúñiga (1998) and Fernández de Pinedo and Fernández (1998), respectively.
3. For example, in the United Kingdom a "super-tax" on high incomes was introduced with the People's Budget of 1909. One year later, Swedish reformers introduced an imputation for wealth in the income tax base, as well as higher rates (Torregrosa-Hetland & Sabaté, 2021). In several countries, top marginal tax rates increased significantly during the First World War (Scheve & Stasavage, 2016).
4. An overview of Larraz's personality and reforms, as well as of those who followed him in office, can be found in Fuentes Quintana (1997).
5. In the words of Larraz, Spain was a country of "bad tax citizenship", which made it difficult to have an operational income tax (Comín & Martorell, 2013, p. 238). It is also true that Franco had a personal stance against income taxation, which has been well documented; for example, on the same page Comín and Martorell cited Larraz, who stated that the *Generalísimo* "was not sympathetic to global and ordinary taxation of income" (author's translation).
6. This can of course be blamed on lack of taxpayer cooperation and weak enforcement capacities, but Larraz's reform also abolished the payment obligation based on "external signs", which required people to file a return if they, for example, had certain vehicles, obtained personal services, and so on.
7. The rates were 17.5% for the rural tax, 21.5% for the urban tax, 15% on (most) salaries, and 20% on interest. Corporations paid a nominal rate between 11 and 25% according to the relationship between capital and profits. In the case of income tax, on the other hand, marginal rates were between 7.5 and 40%. Source: *Ley de 16 de diciembre de 1940, de Reforma Tributaria* (Boletín Oficial del Estado, 22/12/1940).
8. Note that besides tax rate and threshold adjustments, an income tax is supposed to be elastic and thus to increase the revenue generated along with economic growth. But the growth period of the sixties was

not reflected in increased revenue from the old income tax. Fraud and regulatory changes kept it checked.

9. Unemployment insurance had also been introduced in 1931, but it was eliminated shortly after and thus not in place during the early Francoist period that we review here (Pons & Silvestre, 2010).
10. For a precise definition of the terms "defined contribution" and "defined benefit" see Barr (2004).
11. This idea already appears in the income-tax reform proposals of Manuel de Torres and his acolytes during the fifties. In their view, a vigorous expansion of income tax would have been impossible in the critical economic context of the postwar forties (plagued by scarcity and inflation), but the resumption of economic growth in the next decade made it viable.
12. Source: *Ley de 26 de diciembre de 1957, de Reforma Tributaria* (Boletín Oficial del Estado, 27/12/1957).
13. Author's translation. Source: *Ley 41/1964, de 11 de junio, de Reforma del Sistema Tributario* (Boletín Oficial del Estado, 13/6/1964).
14. The maximum rates were applied to taxpayers with income over 1.6 million pesetas. Source: *Decreto 3358/1967, de 23 de diciembre, texto refundido del Impuesto General sobre la Renta de las Personas Físicas* (Boletín Oficial del Estado, 18/3/1967). Rates for schedular taxes were as follows: 14% for labour tax (but lower rates for particular groups, such as insurance agents or translators), 15% for dividends, 20% for interest (in 1967 this was increased to 24%, except for the case of public debt). Total payment from general income tax and the schedular taxes was set at 50% of the tax base, after deductions.
15. Social security contributions are included in our account of the tax system throughout the book. Even though these are earmarked revenues, intended to finance future pensions, in reality there is no full actuarial connection between payments and future pensions in the system. Social security combines an insurance element with a redistribution element across individuals with different life expectancies, income levels, and working life experiences. Furthermore, pensions are subordinated to political decisions. This makes it justified to consider pensions as social spending and social contributions as taxes.
16. These terms are often used in public finance discussions. What constitutes a *fair* system is of course open to debate. In this period, the dominant conception of fairness was based on the principle of "ability to pay", often conceived as progressivity. An *efficient* system is supposed to create the least possible deadweight loss due to taxation, such as by avoiding excessive

complexity or taxing goods with inelastic demand. Lastly, *flexibility* refers to the ability of the tax system to generate revenue increases when the economy expands. See the discussion by Adolf Wagner (originally written in 1890) published in Musgrave and Peacock (1958).

17. Talks in Spain about tax reform during this period were influenced by the Report of the Fiscal and Financial Committee on tax harmonization, coordinated by Fritz Neumark, whose conclusions were published in 1962. The committee advocated harmonisation as a way to facilitate competition in the European Common Market. In hindsight, harmonisation has taken more steps towards indirect taxation (particularly VAT), but the Neumark Committee also included recommendations for making direct taxation similar across countries. This also included standardised definitions of tax bases, deductions, and rates of corporate and individual income taxes.
18. Fuentes Quintana made this point, for example, in the newspaper ABC, 19th May 1977, p. 65: "La reforma fiscal será inviable sin un sistema democrático". He then returned to it in Fuentes Quintana (1990), quoting Francisco Fernández-Ordóñez, who finally initiated the reform during the first democratic government: "*Laureano López Rodó also intervened* [in the tax debates of 1977 in Parliament] *to say that reforms of this nature had already been made during the previous regime [...], and I replied that yes, I was aware of reform projects, a reform project presented by the Minister of Finance, Monreal Luque. And he presented it to Franco, on a day like today, and was fired the next day*" (author's translation, from Delgado, 2007, p. 129).

References

Aidt, T. S., & Jensen, P. S. (2009). The taxman tools up: An event history study of the introduction of the personal income tax. *Journal of Public Economics, 93*(1–2), 160–175.

Alvaredo, F., & Saez, E. (2009). Income and wealth concentration in Spain from a historical and fiscal perspective. *Journal of the European Economic Association, 7*(5), 1140–1167.

Barr, N. A. (2004). *The economics of the welfare state*. Oxford University Press.

Barrada, A. (1999). *El gasto público de bienestar social en España de 1964 a 1995*. Fundación BBVA.

Carreras, A., & Tafunell, X. (2018). *Entre el Imperio y La Globalización. Historia Económica de la España Contemporánea*. Crítica.

Comín, F. (1988). *Hacienda y economía en la España contemporánea (1800–1936)*. Instituto de Estudios Fiscales.

Comín, F. (1993). Reforma tributaria y política fiscal. In J. L. García Delgado (Ed.), *España. Economía* (6th ed., pp. 1073–1121). Espasa Calpe.

Comín, F. (2010). Los seguros sociales y el Estado del Bienestar en el siglo XX. In J. Pons & J. Silvestre (Eds.), *Los orígenes del Estado del Bienestar en España, 1900–1945: Los seguros de accidentes, vejez, desempleo y enfermedad* (pp. 17–49). Prensas Universitarias de Zaragoza.

Comín, F., & Díaz, D. (2005). Sector público administrativo y estado del bienestar. In A. Carreras & X. Tafunell (Eds.), *Estadísticas Históricas de España. Siglos XIX–XX: Vol. II* (pp. 873–964). Fundación BBVA.

Comín, F., & Martorell, M. (2013). *La Hacienda Pública en el franquismo. La guerra y la autarquía (1936–1959)*. Instituto de Estudios Fiscales.

Comín, F., Pan-Montojo, J., Pro, J., Vallejo, R., & Zafra, J. (1995). *La práctica fiscal en la España contemporánea. Una historia de la Administración tributaria (1800–1990)*. Instituto de Estudios Fiscales.

Comín, F., & Vallejo, R. (2012). La reforma tributaria de 1957 en las Cortes franquistas. *Investigaciones De Historia Económica—Economic History Research, 8*(3), 154–163.

De la Torre, J., & García-Zúñiga, M. (1998). Hacienda foral y crecimiento económico en Navarra durante el siglo XIX. In J. De la Torre & M. García-Zúñiga (Eds.), *Hacienda y crecimiento económico. La reforma de Mon, 150 años después* (pp. 183–210). Marcial Pons.

Delgado, S. (2007). *Francisco Fernández Ordóñez: un político para la España necesaria (1930–1992)*. Biblioteca Nueva.

de Torres, M. (1956). *Juicio sobre la actual política económica española*. Aguilar.

Ebrill, L., Keen, M., Bodin, J.-P., & Summers, V. (2001). *The modern VAT*. http://www.imf.org.

Fernández de Pinedo y Fernández, E. (1998). Haciendas forales y desarrollo económico en el País Vasco (1841–1920). In J. de la Torre & M. García-Zúñiga (Eds.), *Hacienda y crecimiento económico: la reforma de Mon, 150 años después* (pp. 171–182). Marcial Pons.

Fuentes Quintana, E. (1990). *Las reformas tributarias en España. Teoría, historia y propuestas*. Crítica.

Fuentes Quintana, E. (Ed.). (1997). *La Hacienda en sus ministros.* Prensas Universitarias de Zaragoza.
González Catalá, V., & Vicente Merino, A. (1987). *Análisis económico-financiero del Sistema español de Seguridad social (1964–1985).* Ministerio de Trabajo y Seguridad Social.
González Murillo, P. (2008). El franquismo social: Propaganda y seguros a través del Instituto Nacional de Previsión (1939–1962). In S. Castillo (Ed.), *Solidaridad, Seguridad, Bienestar: Cien años de protección social en España* (pp. 89–124). Ministerio de trabajo e inmigración.
Gota Losada, A. (1970). La realidad de la imposición personal sobre la renta. *Hacienda Pública Española, 3*, 17–41.
Guillén, A. (2000). *La construcción política del sistema sanitario español: de la posguerra a la democracia.* Exlibris Ediciones.
Guillén, A. M. (1997). Un siglo de previsión social en España. *Ayer, 25*, 151–178.
Instituto de Estudios Fiscales. (1973). *Informe sobre el sistema tributario español.* IEF.
Instituto de Estudios Fiscales. (1976). *Sistema tributario español: Criterios para su reforma.* IEF.
Instituto Nacional de Estadística. (1979). *Contabilidad Nacional de España. Base 1970. Años 1964–1976, 1977 provisional y avance de 1978.* INE.
Lagares, M. J. (1999). La Hacienda Pública en las Facultades de Ciencias Económicas y en la sociedad española durante la segunda mitad del siglo XX. In E. Fuentes Quintana (Ed.), *Economía y economistas españoles* (Vol. 7, pp. 571–617). Galaxia Gutenberg.
Maluquer de Motes, J., & Llonch Casanovas, M. (2005). Trabajo y Relaciones Laborales. In A. Carreras & X. Tafunell (Eds.), *Estadísticas Históricas de España: Siglo XIX–XX* (pp. 1155–1245). Fundación BBVA.
Martínez-Ruiz, E., & Pons, M. A. (2020). 1959: The stabilization plan and the end of autarky. In C. Betrán & M. A. Pons (Eds.), *Historical turning points in Spanish economic growth and development, 1808–2008* (pp. 123–158). Palgrave.
Martínez-Vázquez, J., & Sanz-Sanz, J. F. (Eds.). (2007). *Fiscal reform in Spain.* Edward Elgar.
Pons, J., & Silvestre, J. (Eds.). (2010). *Los orígenes del Estado del Bienestar en España, 1900–1945.* Prensas Universitarias de Zaragoza.
Prados de la Escosura, L. (2017). *Spanish economic growth, 1850–2015.* Springer International Publishing.

Prados de la Escosura, L., Rosés, J. R., & Sanz-Villarroya, I. (2012). Economic reforms and growth in Franco's Spain. *Revista De Historia Economica—Journal of Iberian and Latin American Economic History, 30*(1), 45–89.
Rubio-Varas, M., & Muñoz, B. (2021). Energía en transición. In J. De la Torre & M. Rubio-Varas (Eds.), *Economía en Transición. Del tardofranquismo a la democracia* (Chapter 2). Marcial Pons.
San Julián-Arrupe, J. (2012). Economic ideas and redistributive policy in the Spanish parliament: The 1900 debate on fiscal progressivity introduction. *Revista de Historia Industrial. Economía y Empresa, 21*(3), 49–71.
Scheve, K., & Stasavage, D. (2016). *Taxing the rich: A history of fiscal fairness in the United States and Europe*. Princeton University Press.
Seelkopf, L., Bubek, M., Eihmanis, E., Ganderson, J., Limberg, J., Mnaili, Y., Zuluaga, P., & Genschel, P. (2019). The rise of modern taxation: A new comprehensive dataset of tax introductions worldwide. *Review of International Organizations, 16*, 239–263.
Serrano, A., & Malo, J. L. (1979). *Salarios y mercado de trabajo en España*. Blume.
Torregrosa-Hetland, S. (2015). *Tax system and redistribution: The Spanish fiscal transition (1960–1990)*. PhD thesis, University of Barcelona.
Torregrosa-Hetland, S. (2021). La reforma fiscal de 1977–86 y su marco económico. In J. De la Torre & M. Rubio-Varas (Eds.), *Economía en Transición. Del tardofranquismo a la democracia* (Chapter 4). Marcial Pons.
Torregrosa-Hetland, S., & Sabaté, O. (2021). *Income taxes and redistribution in the early 20th century*. Lund Papers in Economic History: General Issues; no. 224.
Valdés, T. (1982). *Los métodos de análisis discriminante como herramienta al servicio de la inspección fiscal*. Instituto de Estudios Fiscales.
Vergés, J. (1974). *Seguridad Social Española: análisis económico-financiero y cuentas del periodo 1940–1970*. Universidad Autónoma de Barcelona.
Wagner, A. (1958). Three extracts on public finance. In R. A. Musgrave & A. T. Peacock (Eds.), *Classics in the theory of public finance* (pp. 1–15). Springer.

3

Why the Reform Was Necessary

Between 1977 and 1986, the tax system inherited from Francoism was almost completely overthrown. Most of the change actually happened in the very first years of the transition. A wealth tax was introduced in 1977; tax fraud was declared a crime at the same time, and people started paying income taxes by the millions after 1979.

According to Francisco Fernández Ordóñez, something as unpopular as "*scratching one's pocket*" became "*even popular, which is incredible, because it annoyed us all*" (Delgado, 2007; author's translation). Such was, of course, his self-satisfied view as the minister behind the reform. But the revenue data does show how the balance between direct and indirect taxes changed strongly in a few years: indirect taxes yielded 26% more than direct taxes in 1975, while in 1980 it was direct taxes that were 12% above indirect ones. This had been an explicit objective of the tax reform, and was even stated in the Moncloa Pacts of October 1977. And as discussed in Chapter 2, the preponderance of indirect over direct taxation had been a long-standing feature of the Spanish tax system.

© The Author(s), under exclusive license to Springer Nature Switzerland AG 2021
S. Torregrosa Hetland, *The Spanish Fiscal Transition*, Palgrave Studies in Economic History, https://doi.org/10.1007/978-3-030-79541-2_3

How was this possible? After forty years of tax rigidity, of excessive persistence of the liberal tax system's principles, a young and still unconsolidated democracy turned the tax system upside down. This chapter discusses the needs and reasons for the tax reforms, delving deeper into the criticisms and demands from the tax system that were outlined in the previous chapter. Why was the tax reform necessary? What were its main objectives?

The reason the reform took place so soon after the political transition was that it was "ready" beforehand. There were detailed proposals in the tax administration, in the reports and plans written by the *Instituto de Estudios Fiscales* mentioned in Chapter 2. In addition, and also importantly, there was a rather widespread societal consensus that reform was necessary. Public opinion cannot lead policy under a dictatorship, but it is expected to do so—at least to a certain extent—under a democracy.

A consensus certainly existed among the elites, even if there were, of course, disagreements at the level of the finer details (these will be addressed in Chapter 4). The general public was also favourably predisposed to tax reform, although evidence to this end during the dictatorship is perhaps best taken with a pinch of salt. Contemporary sociological surveys point towards dislike of the existing tax system on several grounds. Of course, different groups of taxpayers disliked various taxes and aspects of the system—generally those that affected them the most. But it can be concluded that taxes were widely considered to be high, complicated, and unfair.

The *Instituto de Estudios Fiscales* began to conduct surveys about Spaniards' tax attitudes in the mid-sixties, in cooperation with scholars from the University of Cologne, Günter Schmölders and Burkhard Strümpel. The *Centro de Investigaciones Sociológicas* conducted similar surveys from 1980, and international initiatives such as the International Social Survey Program or the World Values Surveys took the evidence towards the present day. Early studies were generally focused on opinions about legitimacy and tax evasion—a matter which might seem more aseptic to the dictatorship than more fundamental criticisms. Unfortunately, the survey evidence is scattered and heterogeneous across time, but it still allows several conclusions to be inferred. Also reviewed here are petitions to public administrations, excerpts from the press, political parties' programmes, and other sources.

Not only did the Spanish people generally dislike their tax system, but they also desired important changes in public spending. Investment in infrastructure was regarded as necessary, and so was the expansion of welfare services, including education and health. Increased spending in these areas could not be achieved within the current tax system: it was too inefficient and regressive. Thus, the public increasingly came to see tax reform as a necessary means for many of the changes they desired in Spanish society. There were also voices calling for decentralisation, which included the power to tax (a power that some, but not all, regions had retained during Francoism). This was granted eventually, although it was a gradual process. These demands are discussed in the following sections.

A final note: it was through the series of events between 1977 and 1979 that the reform took place remarkably quickly. But after an initial push, conflict and obstacles became more formidable, and the process slowed down significantly. This will be discussed in Chapter 4.

3.1 The Level of Taxation and Spending

Very few people want to see an increase in their own taxes, but most of us are content to relinquish some of our income in exchange for the greater good of public spending. Insufficient public revenues had led to insufficient public spending in Spain, something that more and more people were becoming aware of, especially in the intellectual elite. Taxes, therefore, would need to be increased.

Opinion favourable to this kind of reform could already be seen in parts of the Spanish media during the fifties, despite the limitations on public discussion in a dictatorship in which a free press did not exist. Comín and Martorell (2013, pp. 303 and ff.), described the formation of a group of critical economists who wrote for the newspaper *Arriba* under the influence of Manuel de Torres. The group was led by Juan Velarde and included Enrique Fuentes Quintana and César Albiñana (Fuentes and Albiñana were both mentioned in Chapter 2 for their later role in the *Instituto de Estudios Fiscales*). For these economists, it was clear that the tax system raised insufficient revenue, which meant that the state could not engage in the expenditure needed for economic development. For example, Alfredo Cerrolaza wrote in 1954 that the level of tax revenue that year was, in real terms, only 75% that of 1935, twenty years earlier.[1] In his view, this meant that deficit was *not* caused by excessive spending, but by paucity of revenue. (Chapter 2 noted that a central objective of Navarro Rubio's tax reform a few years later, in 1957, was to reduce deficit, and that he tackled this both by increasing revenue and restraining spending).

Tax revenue was scarce because taxes were inelastic. This applies especially to the direct, schedular taxes, a point developed by Fuentes Quintana in his writings (Fuentes Quintana, 1978). Torres coined the term "petrification" for this phenomenon, as mentioned in Chapter 2. Schedular taxes became petrified because their indirect forms of assessment were often based on nominal quantities, so they became outdated by inflation.

Manuel de Torres also criticised the system for being too complex. The fact that taxpayers had to file a whole range of tax returns, regardless of the quantities they ended up paying, constituted what he called an "indirect tax burden". This concept exists today in public economics as compliance costs, and was also a complaint of taxpayers in the sixties. Hernández Moyés (2006) analysed the opinions of "taxpayers" during Francoism—a term she used, in common with other public writings in this period, to refer to those who filed tax returns: firm-owners or wealthy household heads, represented by amendments in the Francoist *Cortes*.[2] Taxpayers' complaints show that they considered the system burdensome, overly complex, and plagued by legal insecurity. They also tended to think that inspection bodies had excessive power, and that public spending was of low utility or poorly administered. For example, with regard to the latter, in 1974 Manuel Escudero Rueda said in the *Cortes*: *"I want to emphasise that one of the causes that contribute to tax fraud is the lack of trust of the Spanish taxpayer in the effective execution of public administration"* (cited in Hernández Moyés, 2006, p. 217; author's translation).

That a tax system has high compliance costs is a reflection of poor regulation and administration. Simplicity is recognised as a virtue of tax systems, even if it necessitates some trade-off with other desirable characteristics. But filing taxes in the Spain of the sixties was undoubtedly burdensome, since firms and individuals needed to comply with a range of minor taxes—which were in turn administered and inspected by different bodies. Many direct taxpayers found taxes "difficult" or "very difficult" to understand, and a significant proportion of them hired professionals to "do their taxes", according to a survey conducted in 1971 (García, 1975). Compliance costs were a challenge in the tax system of late Francoism—and one that was not resolved very satisfactorily by subsequent reforms.

In any case, taxes were generally low as a percentage of national income (as seen in Chapter 2). But this does not mean that they were low for everyone, or that everyone wanted them to increase. The surveys undertaken from the mid-sixties generally showed that respondents perceived their taxes as very high.[3] This was also true after the tax reform—in fact increasingly so, in line with the actual evolution of tax revenues (see Fig. 3.1). This perception of a high tax burden started to wane around

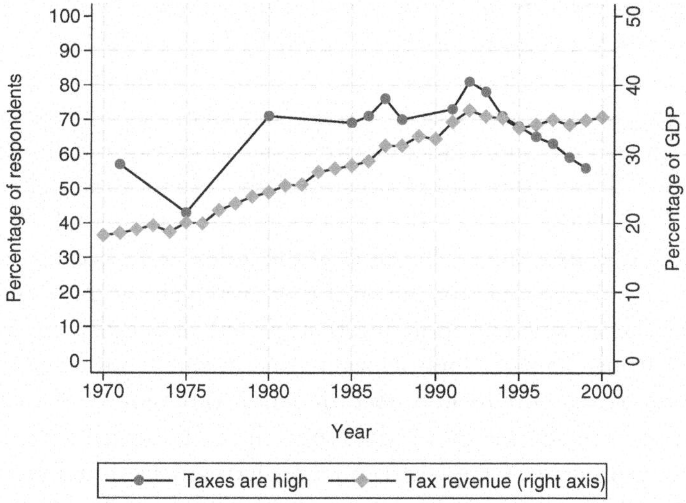

Fig. 3.1 Percentage of survey respondents who stated that "taxes are high/very high", 1970–2000 (*Source* Alvira et al., 2000; Alvira & García, 1976, 1981; Strümpel & Alvira, 1975)

1990 as the ratio of tax revenues to GDP stabilised, following the Treaty of Maastricht and subsequent efforts to control public expenditure.

These respondents, it should be noted, are not completely homogeneous over time: the first survey (1965) was only conducted in cities, the second (1971) only surveyed "direct taxpayers",[4] and subsequent ones opened up the reference population to "household heads". The responses are not, therefore, representative of the general population, but at best of adult males.

That Spaniards thought they paid high taxes, even though we know they were low by international standards, should not come as a surprise. After all, across different countries it is quite common for people to dislike paying taxes, and to consider their own burdens too high, while wanting those of others to increase. Survey respondents were often more sensitive to the need to contribute when questions made the connection with public spending explicit; this was the case for example in the study by Edlund (2000) on Sweden between 1981 and 1997.[5]

Indeed, the perception of the tax burden may well depend not only on its actual level but also on the public services provided—and the Francoist state provided limited and low-quality services. During the years following the tax reform, taxpayers seem to have immediately noticed the increase in their taxes, while the benefits of extended expenditure took longer or were less clearly visible (especially in the case of non-cash benefits). This is indicated by the "index of taxpayer feeling" shown in Fig. 3.2. This index seeks to capture the extent to which citizens perceived a balance between the taxes they paid and the public services they received in exchange. The value of the index never became positive, which means that people did not feel they were getting more than they paid for (this is also common internationally), but satisfaction slowly increased from the early eighties as a consequence of the reforms. Of course, the balance might be very different at different levels of income distribution, which the index does not show. Decreasing regressivity during the period (see Chapter 5) could push dissatisfaction down. At the same time, the economic cycle might also be expected to affect perceptions of the tax burden; this is seen, for example, in the crisis of the early nineties, as shown in Figs. 3.1 and 3.2.

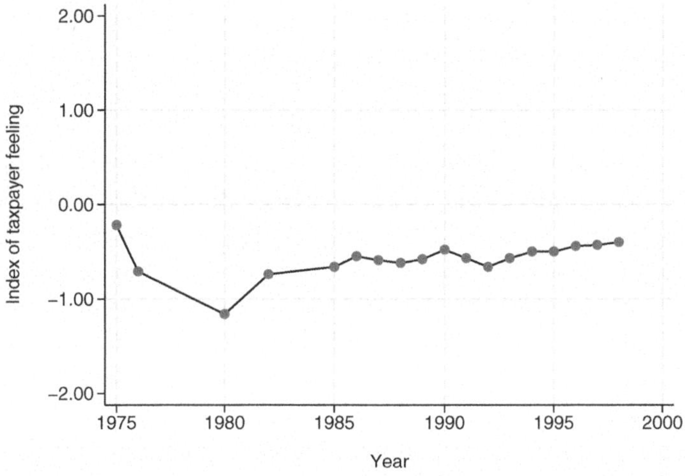

Fig. 3.2 Perception of the balance between taxes paid and services received, 1975–1998 (*Source* Alvira et al., 2000; Alvira & García, 1976, 1977, 1981, 1987)

This section began by noting that taxes were a means towards an end: the end was higher public spending, which was a demand to which many of the sources attest. After years of insufficient public budgets, deficits in public spending were prevalent: for example, in urban planning, education, and health services. These were especially visible in certain urban areas that had received strong immigration flows during Francoism, where a dynamic protest movement developed through neighbourhood associations (Molinero & Ysàs, 1999). Many also knew that the economy needed greater developmental investments to foster and sustain economic growth. Additionally, democratisation would bring freer expression of the long-muted demands for better social protection.

In 1974, 50% of household heads claimed that they would like to see an increase in public spending. This percentage was higher among those with middle or higher education (64–65%), as well as highly qualified white-collar professionals (74%), while it was lowest among those dwelling in very small towns, the oldest, and the poorest and richest segments of the population (13% of the richest group responded that spending should decrease, but still 56% supported an expansion). The implication is that support for higher spending was clear in the more modern groups of society (urban, younger, and educated), something that would help this direction to be taken in the future (Alvira & García, 1975).

Education generated the broadest consensus. Primary schooling was not yet universal in Francoist Spain, which caused a lack of opportunities for many individuals and a poorly qualified labour force overall. According to the census of 1960, even though the national literacy rate was 92%, in certain regions close to 20% of the population could still not read and write (Núñez, 2005). During the dictatorship, educational inequality increased: many were left behind, having not even completed primary schooling (24% of those born in 1965), while higher proportions completed secondary and tertiary education (30 and 24% of the same cohort, compared with around 9% in each category for those born in 1950; Núñez, 2005). Spain's human capital had lagged notably behind that of some European neighbours: Spaniards born between 1937 and 1967 completed on average less than eight years of primary education—a level attained in England and France by those born in the late nineteenth century (Núñez, 2005).

Therefore, that Spain needed strong societal investment for improving education levels in the country was hardly contested. This idea was even expressed in conservative circles. For example, the newspaper *ABC*, which represented right-wing and traditional attitudes, wrote in July of 1976 in favour of universal, compulsory, and free education: "*education imparted to all, whose apex must be occupied by the most intellectually capable and not by the most financially endowed*" (author's translation). The budget increases announced, with total education spending planned at 132,000 million pesetas in 1976 (up from 58,000 million in 1971) would fall short of what was needed to meet the objectives set in the education law of 1970. And since it was virtually impossible to obtain resources by diverting funds from other spending areas, "*The only logical solution to increase investment in education lies in the often mentioned tax reform*".[6] A similar argument had been expounded in 1969 by the Francoist minister of public finance Juan José Espinosa San Martín, showing that these attitudes were also held by some people from within the regime: "*Our people want, and it is fair that they want, more schools, better roads, new water supplies and an extensive health network, and for this an efficient and well-equipped Administration is necessary. The trade-off is inevitable. If we want to provide decent public services, we must pay the price*" (cited in Hernández Moyés, 2006, p. 222; author's translation).

Sociological surveys conducted by the *Instituto de Estudios Fiscales* show that education was one of the topics that worried Spaniards the most, at which public efforts should be targeted. For example, in 1971 the "situation of schools" in the country was considered the most serious social problem by respondents (direct taxpayers), second only to unemployment for some social groups (lower classes, those older than 45; García, 1975). Public spending on education attained the highest support, far ahead of other categories such as public works, transport, and defence, and this support was quite homogeneous across social classes (García, 1972). Similar attitudes are found in the survey conducted in 1974, which now aimed to represent all household heads in the country: here, education came second to the price level, considered the most worrying problem—which is quite unsurprising, given the recent spikes in inflation. Sixty-four per cent of those surveyed thought that spending in education should increase, and 31% were willing to pay higher taxes for it, which is the highest score for this question together with the problems of agriculture (Alvira & García, 1975).

This societal consensus was voiced by the main political parties in their programmes for the elections of 1977.[7] Each of them cited the development of education as an urgent need for Spanish society, placing particular emphasis on universalisation of primary schooling and equality of opportunities. For example, the Communist Party of Spain (*Partido Comunista de España*, PCE) stated that: "*The tax reform will provide the means to make the primary, secondary and professional education levels genuinely free, and for an urgent plan for construction of new school buildings*" (author's translation). On the right, the People's Alliance (*Alianza Popular*) pledged to: "*promote education, science and culture as means for personal development as well as factors for national development, which must be available to all Spaniards.* [...] *The preschool and primary education levels will be compulsory and free. The other levels will be made accessible to all social classes through collective societal effort.* [...] *In order to finance collective facilities, extend free education at different levels and expand the scope and financing of social security, it is essential to increase public resources*" (author's translation). Of course, the parties had different views about the extent to which education should be made free, as well as about the precise interpretation of "equality of opportunities". Here, as often, the devil is in the details. But the programmes reflect a basic consensus about the needs for more resources for public education.

Many also wanted an expansion of social spending, which was certainly backward in the European context (Espuelas, 2013; Guillén & León, 2011). According to Comín (2010), "*As soon as democracy was established, Spanish society was quick to reveal its demands for higher social spending*" (p. 41). The *Instituto de Estudios Fiscales* surveys are of little help here, but they do show, for example, that 57% of respondents in 1974 wanted the government to spend more on health and social security, with calls for spending in these areas just below that for agricultural support and education (Alvira & García, 1975). Benefit improvement was certainly one of the key objectives of the labour movement, which was quite active in the final years of the dictatorship despite the lack of freedoms. These demands were made even more urgent by the economic crisis that hit the country in the mid-seventies, with its troublesome combination of inflation and unemployment.

In 1977, political programmes again promised an expansion of social spending. This will be discussed in more detail in Chapter 4, as proposals for social security included important aspects regarding funding. In any case, all parties voiced the need to make the system more universal (for "*all Spaniards*" according to Alianza Popular, or for "*every member of Spanish society, whatever their condition*" in the Socialist's programme), and to expand benefits (which in those days were strongly affected by inflation). The system would thus need more resources, which should not come from social contributions—which were regressive, placed a heavy burden on small firms, and potentially affected employment. State funding of social security therefore had to increase, and even to completely cover some parts of the system.

But there were also, of course, opinions *against* reform. These are well represented in *ABC*, which during the years 1974–1977 opposed redistribution and the need for any tax reform of this kind. The arguments provided were often of a technical nature: an administrative reform should go first, and fiscal effort in the country was already high and could not, or should not, be increased; instead, what was needed was the effective application of the tax regulations already in place: "*The possibilities in our tax system of obtaining higher revenues are considerable, so that these tax reforms are unnecessary*".[8] At the same time, fraud could be combatted through simplification and improved administration and transparency in public expenditure. The main theoretical critique against Fuentes Quintana's reform proposals was that the Spain's tax burden compared with its European neighbours was not so low, taking into account the income level in the country.[9] One contributor to the newspaper typified the anti-fiscal stance: "*Like summer clouds announcing thunder and lightning, for a long time the ordinary and overwhelmed citizen has been sensing the threat of a tax reform*".[10]

In 1976, when talk of tax reform was becoming more frequent, *ABC* criticised the initiatives as populist. Regular contributors were fiercely against the aspiration to use taxation as a channel for the reduction of inequalities. For example, former minister Navarro Rubio argued that reformers were pushing excessively for this solution and that the economic crisis represented a strong reason not to increase the tax burden.[11] He also railed against any need for increasing public spending, and cautioned against the big state: "*Those of us who love freedom cannot agree with the current administrative gigantism. It is a situation that should not be consolidated. The existence of the free world depends on this*".[12]

3.2 The Distribution of the Tax Burden

As mentioned, the answer to "are your taxes very high?" will not be the same for everyone. It will depend on respondents' personal opinions about the desired level of taxation and spending, but also on their actual tax burden, which varied according to position in the income distribution. The Francoist tax system was known to be regressive. We will discuss the evidence for this in Chapter 5, but suffice to say at this point that those at the bottom paid higher taxes, as a percentage of their income, than those at the top.

Economists had their opinions about this, too. The group led by de Torres and Fuentes Quintana wrote that the tax system was excessively regressive because it relied strongly on indirect taxes, which were paid regardless of economic capacity, while direct income taxation was basically non-existent—as well as plagued by fraud. Others did not openly oppose the principle that income taxes were the future of the tax system, or that they should be progressive, but they attached more importance to their impact on incentives and savings. This position was represented in Spain, for example, by José María Naharro Mora (referred to in Chapter 2). The discussion would be a long one in the sphere of public finance. In the eighties, the international "tax reform" movement gave some victories to the latter position.

The press also revealed different opinions about the desired level of progressivity. *Cuadernos para el Diálogo*, a magazine published between 1963 and 1978 with a clearly pro-democratic stance, prominently featured criticism of the tax system during the latter stages of this period. Renowned personalities wrote in *Cuadernos*, making it a good example of progressive-centrist views on many social and political issues. In 1977, opinions published there were clearly amenable to a progressive tax reform. In January of that year the journalist J. Estefanía claimed that the state budget was socially unjust, and that a profound redistributive reform was needed: "*The trend of increasing direct taxes is very slow, and, also, does not automatically achieve a more equitable distribution of the tax burden.* [...] *For example, one of the direct taxes increasing the most is the Labour Tax, about which Spanish workers have repeatedly complained for years.* [...] *It is necessary to eradicate tax evasion starting from above, so that the budget actually becomes an instrument to reduce social differences and achieve greater equality*".[13]

In July 1977 *Cuadernos* published an interview with the new minister of public finance, Francisco Fernández Ordóñez, using a very positive tone. Critiques focused on pressure groups lobbying against the reform (fundamentally from the banking sector), and the acknowledgement that, in spite of tax changes, the bulk of the costs of the economic crisis were falling on workers' shoulders (due to containment of wage increases to fight inflation, as agreed in the Moncloa Pacts). In November 1977, when the first tax reform law passed through Parliament, the editorial took a clear position in defence of the project: "*The enjoyment of democracy is not only* [about] *the exhibition of a Parliament formed by universal suffrage, or laws allowing films to be viewed without prior censorship. It also means enjoying higher distributive justice in the tax burdens and wider development of collective services*". It also stressed that the tax reform was not anti-capitalist but the exact opposite, since it meant reinforcing capitalism in a very critical context—therefore, rejecting it could trigger the radicalisation of voters.[14]

Established in 1976, *El País* soon came to be the most read newspaper in Spain. It contained a diverse range of opinions, but had a clear social-democratic orientation of its own. During 1977 and 1978, *El País* closely monitored the tax reform process, informing its readership about the main debates and bills going through Parliament. Some initiatives from the left were afforded particular attention, such as the insistence on the publication of individual tax data (this will be discussed in Chapter 4). The newspaper's editorials were very favourable to the tax reform, and specifically to the principles of progressivity, generality, and transparency. In July 1977, one editorial stated: "*The tax reform must serve as a stimulus to put in place an effort of national solidarity, and must become the signal that the Government is willing to fight for an equitable society*".[15] Another editorial from April 1979 praised transparency and called for more tax compliance among citizens, while also criticising the fact that the highest burden was still placed on salaried workers: "*Tax evasion is, first of all, an active act of anti-solidarity towards the community. In this regard, the publication of tax returns can become useful to make many taxpayers report and pay more, even if it only is to avoid public shame*".[16]

A series of interviews with members of parliament involved in tax negotiations in 1978 show to what extent the principle of progressivity was generally accepted at the time. Politicians from the centre and left defended the application of this idea. Those on the right were representatives of conservative voters and not so open to progressivity, but this position would only emerge in their proposals about detailed issues (tax exemptions, allowances, or credits), and not in the form of a general challenge to the existence of a progressive income tax.

In this sense, Ramón Trías Fargas, member of the Catalan Minority Group, stated: "*I have maintained since 1963 that strong and progressive taxation is a requisite for liberty and democracy*", but at the same time criticised what he considered to be the excessive rush in the reform process, and a tilt towards equity at the expense of efficiency.[17] Laureano López Rodó from Alianza Popular expressed a similar position: "*In general terms, the philosophy of our project would have been similar to that of UCD* [the Unión de Centro Democrático Party]. *I understand that indeed the income tax must be the king of the system*", which did not preclude him from opposing particular aspects, especially those concerning savings and family treatment.[18]

The same conclusion was reached by Pan-Montojo (1996) when discussing a survey of businessmen from October 1977, in which respondents did not criticise the existing system but acknowledged the need to reform it. In Pan-Montojo's words (p. 286): "*Their resigned answers reveal the political impossibility for its* [the system's] *beneficiaries to openly defend the fiscal status quo, and the absence of a coherent model of taxation, other than that offered by the reformist tradition*".

We now turn towards the general public opinion. Over the last decades, Spaniards have not found their tax system to be fair: well over half of survey respondents would consistently hold this opinion (see Fig. 3.3). As in Figs. 3.1 and 3.2, recall that the representation of the

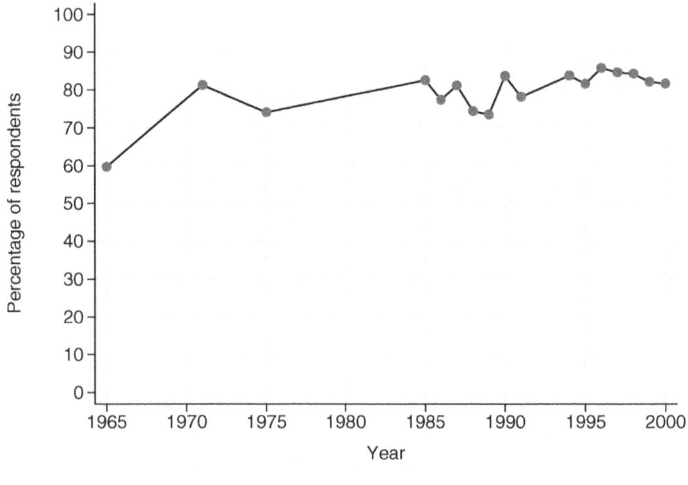

Fig. 3.3 Survey respondents who considered the tax system unfair, 1965–2000 (*Source* Alvira & García, 1976; Strümpel, 1967; Strümpel & Alvira, 1975; and *Centro de Investigaciones Sociológicas* for 1985–2000)

Spanish population in the surveys increased over time. Discontent rose during the last years of the dictatorship—as comparison of the responses from 1965 (60%), 1971 (86%), and 1975 (74%) shows—but the 1971 survey only covered "direct taxpayers". Notably, according to this indicator dissatisfaction seems to have been prevalent, and quite constant, even after the tax reform.

The "unfairness" of the system stemmed from it not being sufficiently progressive. The question posed in the surveys was "*Do you think that, generally, taxes are fairly collected? That is, that those who own more pay more? Or do you think otherwise?*". This was not an optimal question to ask, since it contains the implicit value judgement that a fair tax system is a progressive one (which was the general opinion in public finance thought at the time). On what grounds might a taxpayer have answered in the negative? Does a "no" really mean that respondents wanted greater progressivity? Fortunately, we can discern this from other survey questions and additional evidence.

In 1971, a clear majority of respondents thought that direct taxes were fairer than indirect ones (García, 1975), and 60% of those from a Madrid subsample were in favour of the direct estimation of tax bases rather than objective assessments (Margallo & García, 1971). Both aspects point towards progressivity, since it is direct, personal taxes that make it possible. See Table 3.1 for details about this and related questions from the survey of 1971. It should be noted that, as pointed by García (1975), the universe of this survey was composed mostly of the middle and upper classes, since it is they who were "direct taxpayers"—only around 13% of the country's households. Generally, more progressive views were held by the younger and those from the upper class, something which members of the *Instituto de Estudios Fiscales* interpreted with optimism at the time, because it appeared to bolster the prospects for reform.

In the 1975 survey, the question of progressivity versus proportionality was directly raised, and 89% agreed with the notion of the former while 11% favoured a proportional system. (No regressivity option was provided.) This was a general stance, with very similar percentages of approval across different ages and levels of education. The lowest level of approval of progressivity was 83%, among those with higher income. In addition, 68% of those surveyed supported personal income tax as

Table 3.1 Opinions about fairness of direct and indirect taxation, 1971 (percentage)

	Upper class			Lower class		
	Younger than 45	Older than 45	Total	Younger than 45	Older than 45	Total
Direct taxes are fairer	87	72	79	70	66	67
Indirect taxes hurt the poor	62	48	55	52	39	44
Indirect taxes should be (partly) substituted by direct taxes	69	56	62	53	49	51

Source García (1975)

a good revenue-generating method, but very few respondents answered this question, likely because of a lack of knowledge (Alvira & García, 1976).

Asking people about their support for progressivity in abstract terms, however, has been found to be problematic in previous literature (see the discussions in Bartels, 2005; Edlund, 2003; Singhal, 2013). Given the low education levels prevalent in Spain, as mentioned above, this ought to be approached with caution: many of the respondents may have lacked the basic mathematical skills to adequately answer questions about progressive taxation, even if they subscribed to the principle in itself. Fortunately, a rather straightforward question was asked in 1971 (even if it was only addressed to "direct taxpayers"): "*Considering all your income* [...], *what percentage approximately do you pay in taxes? And what percentage do you think would be fair for you to pay?*".[19]

Figure 3.4 shows the answers. Respondents estimated that they paid between 12 and 17% of their income, with a progressive profile. But everyone wanted to pay less: the "ideal" rates lay between eight and four percentage points below the "perceived" rates. In general, people are not enthusiastic about paying taxes and everyone seems to want their own

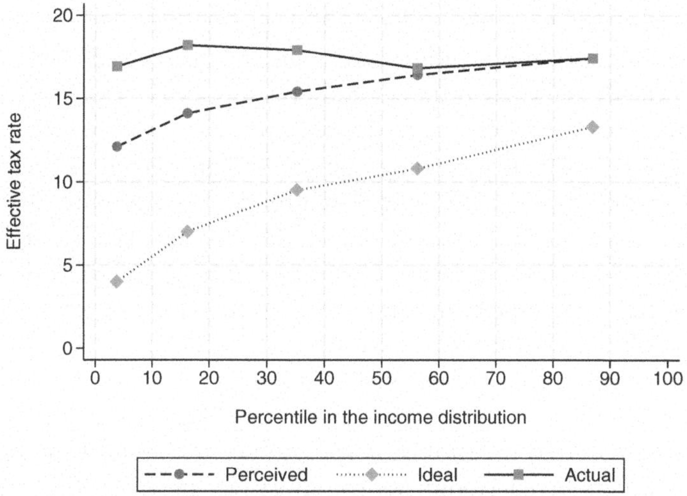

Fig. 3.4 Desired, perceived, and actual distribution of the tax burden (1971) (*Source* Instituto de Estudios Fiscales [1972] and author's calculations. *Notes* The figure does not reflect the whole population, but only certain categories (see text). The survey data was given in income ranges; each group is represented here at the average percentile of observations in their range (for the corresponding social categories). These rates are defined with the denominator including not only market income but also transfers. See Chapter 5 for more details)

part reduced. As noted earlier, this is not a surprising finding, but one that is quite common internationally.

The figure also shows actual effective tax rates at each level (for this purpose, the calculations from Chapter 5 are used).[20] The effective tax rates for this group were basically proportional, with little variation from 17 to 18% (for the whole population, an inverted-U shape is recorded). The figure shows that people high up in the income distribution gave answers that are quite close to their actual tax payments, while those at the bottom under-estimated their contributions. This seems to confirm the suggestion of contemporary analysts that there was acute *fiscal illusion*, and that this was related to the widespread use of indirect taxes. This, however, must be taken with caution, given the small sample size and the fact that the survey was conducted under a dictatorship.

These answers also reflect a demand for greater progressivity, since the "ideal" profile was more progressive than the "perceived" one. This is made especially stark when the desired tax rates are compared with those that were actually in place: the desired reduction was higher at lower income levels, both in percentage points and in percentage terms; the latter is shown in Fig. 3.5. The first group, those around the fourth percentile (with annual income up to 60,000 pesetas) thought they should pay 76% less in taxes. The upper group, on the other hand (around the 87th percentile and with annual income over 240,000 pesetas) wished to reduce their own tax rate by 24%.

As mentioned earlier, people dislike different taxes—and usually, they tend to dislike the ones they themselves pay. Therefore, entrepreneurs and merchants often mentioned corporate tax as the most unfair, while salaried workers hated labour tax the most (Strümpel, 1967, with data from 1965). The dislike of the labour tax is clearly demonstrated in petitions addressed to the fiscal authorities throughout the period. What follows is based on the analysis of 69 petitions dated between 1964 and 1979 that can be found in the Archive of the Ministry of Public Finance, of which 88 per cent referred to the labour tax.[21]

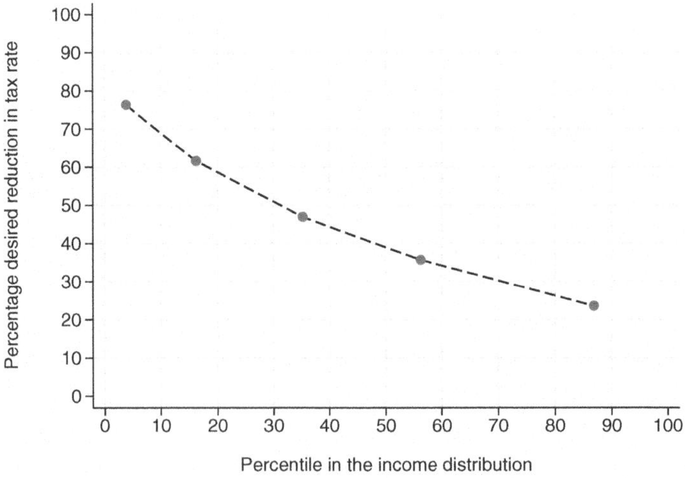

Fig. 3.5 Desired reduction of tax burden (1971) (*Source* Instituto de Estudios Fiscales [1972] and author's calculations. *Notes* Same as Fig. 3.4)

Missives by individuals were very scarce before the transition to democracy, but their number increased considerably from 1977. Some of them were written by highly educated workers, such as doctors, about quite specific issues. But others are a reflection of popular discontent, normally expressed as a petition more than a demand, and frequently focused on inflation (which greatly lowered the real value of the non-taxable threshold) and on the hardship faced by large families. For example, a man from Denia wrote in July 1977: "*I welcome your tax reform, increasing Labour Tax; but as I am a worker with a large family (6 children), I want to ask you to keep in mind these families with your taxes, because it is not the same to have 500,000 ptas and share between 4, than between 8, which is my case*".

Many of the petitions were signed by firms or branches of the official unions (*sindicatos verticales*), and some of these introduce arguments for progressivity. This is the case of a letter written by employees of a building enterprise in March 1977: "*A progressive and fair economic policy requires a deep tax reform, announced so many times and never carried out* [...] *which taxes progressively, and not merely proportionally, the highest wages or incomes*" (author's translation). A year earlier, the president of the national union of metal-sector workers aimed criticism at the tax system: "*We have an unfair and ineffective tax system, and that doesn't mean that the burden workers face is excessive, but that, in fact, capital income is undertaxed*"(author's translation). Of course, the concentration of these complaints on labour tax suggests that lobbying about business taxation was funnelled through other channels and not that it was non-existent.

People might also think the system was unfair not in its intentions but in its effective operation, because of widespread evasion (or tolerance of it). Indeed, tax evasion was a central topic in the surveys, and one to which the reformers of the seventies and eighties attached high importance. However, for the respondents of 1971, this issue was quite far down their list of social problems, and when asked about social sanctions against tax evaders, very few displayed clear attitudes of repudiation (García, 1975). Notably, a rejection of fraud was particularly limited among liberal professionals and managers—precisely those social groups identified by their fellow citizens as being more able and prone to evade (Instituto de Estudios Fiscales, 1972).

Both before and after the reform, the popular perception seems to be that evasion was high and persistent. During the nineties, a growing number of respondents claimed to have been audited, which indicates an improvement in the tax administration's efficiency in this respect. However, they also displayed clear, negative perceptions about the evolution of fraud. One might venture that a decrease in evasion (see Chapter 6) coexisted with growing concern and rejection among the public, to which recent surveys attest.

3.3 Demands for Decentralisation

Decentralisation was one of the big political and administrative changes during the transition to democracy in Spain. The Francoist state was a unitary state, while the new parliamentary democracy re-started the process of granting autonomy to the regions. This was originally devised during the Second Republic to apply only to certain regions with intense nationalist mobilisation, but it ultimately developed into a general system of "autonomous communities". The taxing and spending powers conceded to these autonomous communities made Spain a very *federal* country according to some indicators, even if this term is not used officially.

Specifically, regional autonomy had its precedent in the experiences of the Basque Country, Catalonia, and Galicia during the Second Republic (1931–1936). But there were also two clear precedents during the dictatorship: throughout the period, the provinces of Álava and Navarra maintained a particular fiscal arrangement (Gunther, 1980). In Álava, taxes were collected in two different ways. In the case of most, the provincial authorities had complete autonomy, and transferred to the central state a given sum (the "*cupo*") that was revised every five years (but could not increase by more than the state budget for the same taxes). Other levies (mainly newer ones, such as income tax) were also collected by the provincial authorities, but were subject to state regulations and possible state inspection. Navarra had even greater autonomy in collecting and adjusting taxes within its territory. Furthermore, the "*cupo*" was established in 1941 at 21 million pesetas and *remained fixed in nominal terms* until 1969 (when a variable one was introduced, starting at around 700 million pesetas!). This means, of course, that the contribution of both provinces, but especially Navarra, to the general budget decreased throughout the dictatorship.

In the years preceding the transition, autonomist ideas were usually associated with the left. This is because the dictatorship had been both right-wing and centralist. Demonstrations in Catalonia during the last years of the dictatorship used the slogan "*Libertad, amnistía y estatuto de autonomía*", thus ranking the achievement of territorial autonomy alongside democratisation and the general pardon for political prisoners. The pardon was granted in October 1977 (and also covered repression and crimes against humanity committed by the Francoist authorities, something that has been heavily contested since). The development of autonomy started shortly after the first democratic elections of June 1977, even before the Constitution of 1978 recognised the existence of "nationalities and regions" in the country. According to Aróstegui (1999, p. 293): "*the claim for a different distribution of political power was almost unanimous, with the exception of the most recalcitrant Franco regime*" (author's translation) even if there were substantial differences in opinion about the extent of the autonomy to be granted, and whether it should be granted to some regions or to all.

On the other hand, during the seventies some voices argued against excessive fiscal autonomy. For example, Luis Pérez de Ayala, a professor of public finance and financial law who wrote regular columns for *ABC*, stated in 1977 that these developments could be "very suggestive", but that fiscal autonomy should be limited by the national objectives of economic policy.[22]

But calls for political autonomy were present, to varying degrees, in the main political programmes for the first democratic elections, even if there was less coincidence here than in the case of education or social security. This issue was, in fact, one of the problematic points in the constitutional negotiations during the following year, and was ultimately left unresolved. A good illustration of this is what UCD had to say about "the regions": "*UCD, a coalition which includes several regional parties, recognises the peculiarities of the peoples of Spain and their needs for autonomy. The institutionalisation of the Regions in the manner decided by the* Cortes *and in accordance with the sovereign will of the Spanish people is a fundamental task in the UCD programme*" (author's translation): the wording is very vague, leaving decisions for later. All the main parties recognised these "peculiarities" and the need for "autonomy", even if they clearly had different things in mind. Alianza Popular, for example, stated that "*As Spain is one and diverse, we advocate solutions of institutional autonomy that recognise the geographical and historical existence of the regions and their cultural, economic and social personality*", but added that "*the reform of the State will attend to the solution of the regional problem, without undermining at any time the independence, integrity and political and economic sovereignty of the nation, nor dispensing with the aspirations of the people or establishing unjust privileges*" (author's translation). The tone of the Socialist and Communist parties, especially the former, were much more favourable to the development of autonomous institutions: "*Spain is made up of a series of different nationalities and regions.* […] *Today the peoples of Spain demand the exercise of their right to have their own institutions, and we Socialists share that demand. The PSOE* [the Partido Socialista Obrero Español] *affirms the right to autonomy of the peoples of Spain*" (author's translation).

Of course, the issue of autonomy was even more important for nationalist parties, which predominated in the Basque Country and Catalonia, and prioritised this issue. The Basque Nationalist Party (*Partido Nacionalista Vasco,* PNV) ran during the 1977 Senate elections alongside other groups in a so-called "Autonomous Front" that declared: "*Autonomy. The Basque people have the absolute right to freely decide on their own affairs: economy and finance, labour and social security, justice and law enforcement, education and culture, health, public works, urban planning and all the affairs necessary for our economic, social and cultural development, which can no longer remain in foreign hands*" (Montero García, 2014). Similarly, in Catalonia, various groups came together to form the "Democratic Pact for Catalonia", which also set the establishment of regional autonomy as one of its main goals.

In conclusion, this chapter has shown the existence of a general, albeit basic, consensus about tax reform in the Spain of the mid-seventies. Expert and public opinion were favourable to a reform that increased public revenues, in order to fund more and better public services and social transfers. Many were also in favour of more decentralised management of the tax system, in accordance with the general process of transfer of powers to the regions, which in any case was still far from concrete. And most would adhere to the principle of progressivity in the distribution of the tax burden and with the fact that the income tax needed to be central in the new system.

We can therefore say that there was widespread support for the kind of tax reform designed by the *Instituto de Estudios Fiscales*, which was still on the shelf awaiting its moment. Different social sectors and parties, of course, disagreed on further details, and this would ultimately result in the reform losing momentum after the initial push of 1977–1978. We will discuss the negotiations about these details in Chapter 4.

Notes

1. Alfredo Cerrolaza, "Algunas observaciones sobre nuestro sistema tributario", *Arriba*, 3/4/1954. Quoted in Comín and Martorell (2013, p. 303). Figure 2.1 in Chapter 2 shows tax revenue as a percentage of GDP, and displays the stagnation during the early Franco regime.
2. The concept of "taxpayer" is often used in this way, including by associations. But the rest of the population, even if they do not file, are also taxpayers: they bear the burden of, at least, taxes on their purchases.
3. The discussion of survey results in this chapter is based on the analysis of published aggregated data, since individual observations are not available.
4. In this context, "direct taxpayers" meant business owners (both agrarian and non-agrarian), liberal professionals, firm managers, and public employees. Basically, the definition excluded individuals with no income, or only wage/salary income, except those with high qualifications and earnings (among public employees, only those with tertiary education were included).
5. The Swedes also seemed to think that their taxes were too high, but less so if the survey explicitly compared them to the level of public services. When asked about desired taxes by income level, Swedish respondents also demanded greater progressivity, especially a decrease of taxation on poor households. This, of course, was a very different context from the Spain of the seventies, which makes the coincidence more remarkable.

6. "El futuro de la educación", Editorial in ABC, 2/7/1976, p. 3; author's translation. The text also defended education as a redistribution instrument, preferable to other more "drastic" measures that would be less effective or endanger personal freedom. The system was then recognised as a mechanism preserving social stratification: "*If one thing is currently clear to the vast majority of Spaniards, it is that the education system cannot play, by staying within its present limits – or, even more seriously, by restricting them – at being an element of support for a dominant class, with very strict filters for the promotion of those belonging to other socio-economic strata*".
7. A short presentation of the main parties of the time is made in Chapter 4.
8. "Hojas de alcabala: El porqué y el para qué de una reforma", ABC, 8/10/1974, p. 55; author's translation.
9. As we will see in the next subsection, surveys showed that the tax burden was generally considered to be quite high, but especially for the poorest families, and not for the wealthiest. This point was avoided by the newspaper.
10. "Hojas de alcabala: Nuestro esfuerzo fiscal", ABC, 11/8/1974, p. 43; author's translation.
11. "Teoría de la relatividad fiscal", ABC, 11/6/1976, p. 3; author's translation.
12. "El gasto público", ABC, 15/7/1977, p. 3; author's translation.
13. Cuadernos para el Diálogo, n. 193, 8–14th January 1977; author's translation.
14. Cuadernos para el Diálogo, n. 236, 5–11th November 1977.
15. "La reforma fiscal", El País, Editorial, 31/7/1977; author's translation.
16. "Reforma fiscal y reforma moral", El País, Editorial, 1/4/1979.
17. El País, 2/6/1978; author's translation.
18. El País, 3/6/1978; author's translation.
19. Author's translation from the Spanish: "*Teniendo en cuenta todos sus ingresos* [...], *¿qué porcentaje aproximado viene usted a pagar en conceptos de impuestos? Y ¿qué porcentaje cree usted que le correspondería, en justicia, pagar?*".
20. These rates refer to the year 1970, and specifically to the corresponding socio-economic groups, as far as such correspondence can be established.
21. This sample cannot be considered random nor representative. Letters containing personal data protected by the law were previously removed by the archive staff. Source: General Index 1.851, Box 57.762.
22. "Hojas de alcabala: territorios con régimen especial y política económica", ABC, 18/6/1977, p. 47; author's translation.

References

Alvira, F., & García, J. (1975). Actitudes de los españoles ante el Gasto Público y sentimiento del contribuyente. *Hacienda Pública Española, 34*, 101–145.

Alvira, F., & García, J. (1976). Los españoles opinan sobre la reforma fiscal. *Crónica Tributaria, 16*, 107–126.

Alvira, F., & García, J. (1977). Los españoles y el sistema fiscal. *Hacienda Pública Española, 44*, 235–245.

Alvira, F., & García, J. (1981). Los españoles después de la reforma fiscal. *Hacienda Pública Española, 72*, 243–258.

Alvira, F., & García, J. (1987). Los españoles y la fiscalidad: La pérdida de la ilusión financiera. *Papeles de Economía Española, 30–31*, 90–105.

Alvira, F., García, J., & Delgado, M. L. (2000). *Sociedad, impuestos y gasto público. La perspectiva del contribuyente*. Centro de Investigaciones Sociológicas.

Aróstegui, J. (1999). La transición política y la construcción de la democracia (1975–1996). In J. Martínez (Ed.), *Historia de España. Siglo XX: 1939–1996* (pp. 245–364). Cátedra.

Bartels, L. (2005). Homer gets a tax cut: Inequality and public policy in the American mind. *Perspectives on Politics, 3*(1), 15–31.

Comín, F., & Martorell, M. (2013). *La Hacienda Pública en el franquismo. La guerra y la autarquía (1936–1959)*. Instituto de Estudios Fiscales.

Comín, F. (2010). Los seguros sociales y el Estado del Bienestar en el siglo XX. In J. Pons & J. Silvestre (Eds.), *Los orígenes del Estado del Bienestar en España, 1900–1945: Los seguros de accidentes, vejez, desempleo y enfermedad* (pp. 17–49). Prensas Universitarias de Zaragoza.

Delgado, S. (2007). *Francisco Fernández Ordóñez: Un político para la España necesaria (1930–1992)*. Biblioteca Nueva.

Edlund, J. (2000). Public attitudes towards taxation: Sweden 1981–1997. *Scandinavian Political Studies, 23*(1), 37–65.

Edlund, J. (2003). Attitudes toward taxation: Ignorant and incoherent? *Scandinavian Political Studies, 26*(2), 145–167.

Espuelas, S. (2013). *La evolución del gasto social público en España, 1850–2005* (Vol. 63). Banco de España.

Fuentes Quintana, E. (1978). El estilo tributario latino: Características generales y problemas para su reforma. In J. L. García Delgado & J. Segura (Eds.), *Ciencia social y análisis económico* (pp. 195–279). Tecnos.

García, J. (1972). El Presupuesto y la opinión pública. *Hacienda Pública Española, 19*, 195–213.
García, J. (1975). Crítica popular al sistema tributario español. *Hacienda Pública Española, 34*, 55–99.
Guillén, A. M., & León, M. (2011). *The Spanish welfare state in European context*. Ashgate.
Gunther, R. (1980). *Public Policy in a no-party state. Spanish planning and budgeting in the twilight of the Franquist era.* University of California Press.
Hernández Moyés, A. (2006). *Evolución y determinantes de la fiscalidad franquista*. Universidad Pública de Navarra.
Instituto de Estudios Fiscales. (1972). Actitudes hacia los impuestos de los profesionales liberales, ejecutivos de empresa y funcionarios. *Hacienda Pública Española, 15*, 141–181.
Margallo, M. G., & García, J. (1971). La evasión fiscal en España: Un estudio piloto para su análisis sociológico. *Hacienda Pública Española, 8*, 17–34.
Molinero, C., & Ysàs, P. (1999). Modernización económica e inmovilismo político (1959–1975). In J. A. Martínez (Ed.), *Historia de España. Siglo XX: 1939–1996* (pp. 131–244). Cátedra.
Montero García, M. (2014). El nacionalismo moderado durante la Transición. La conquista de la hegemonía en el País Vasco. *Cuadernos De Historia Contemporánea, 36*, 331–351.
Núñez, C. E. (2005). Educación. In A. Carreras & X. Tafunell (Eds.), *Estadísticas Históricas de España: Siglos XIX y XX* (2nd ed., pp. 157–244). Fundación BBVA.
Pan-Montojo, J. L. (1996). Una larga e inconclusa transición: la reforma tributaria, 1977–1986. In J. Tusell & A. Soto (Eds.), *Historia de la transición, 1975–1986* (pp. 264–304). Alianza.
Singhal, M. (2013). *Quantifying Preferences for Redistribution* (Working Paper).
Strümpel, B. (1967). El español como contribuyente. Actitudes normas y reacciones ante la imposición tributaria. *Revista de Fomento Social, 85*(1), 5–25.
Strümpel, B., & Alvira, F. (1975). Disciplina fiscal y reforma fiscal en una sociedad en cambio. *Hacienda Pública Española, 34*, 21–53.

4

The Political Economy of the Fiscal Transition

In Spanish history, tax changes have normally taken place at times of profound political disruption. Such was the case of the tax reform of 1845 that put in place the country's "liberal" system (Comín, 2010; Fuentes Quintana, 1990). The same pattern repeated itself in the seventies, when a transition to democracy made tax reform possible.

The fact that the fiscal reform took place during the political transition, and in close connection with it, undoubtedly left a mark on what was achieved. It has been argued here that the reform was facilitated by both the pre-existence of both a detailed plan (prepared at the *Instituto de Estudios Fiscales*) and a long-standing demand for higher spending and fairer taxation. The fiscal transition was profound and quick—for the most part. The first law of the new democratic parliament, in October of 1977, fired the starting gun for the tax reform, and the discussion of subsequent proposals for direct taxation coincided with the constitutional talks. This has been called the "period of consensus".

After the Constitution was approved in December 1978, however, the reform lost momentum. Cracks began to emerge in the consensus

© The Author(s), under exclusive license to Springer Nature Switzerland AG 2021
S. Torregrosa Hetland, *The Spanish Fiscal Transition*, Palgrave Studies in Economic History,
https://doi.org/10.1007/978-3-030-79541-2_4

when this important milestone was reached. Spanish society and political parties now had to make uncomfortable decisions about issues that rumbled on below the surface, such as decentralisation or secularisation. The initial tax reform measures, which included the lifting of banking secrecy and the reinforcement of progressive taxation, also began to encounter more heated opposition. According to Pan-Montojo (1996), a fiscal "counter-reform" emerged. The platforms of political parties, which in 1977 had featured general statements that often coincided, were much more concrete and diverse in 1979 and 1982—and proponents of alternative reforms would become more belligerent.

In this context, subsequent steps of the reform plans took longer to reach completion. The introduction of value added tax (VAT) did not arrive until 1986, when Spain joined the European Economic Community (EEC). The development of the tax administration to combat fraud was a long and winding road, and the completion of changes to social security was delayed until 1990.

This chapter explores the reform process, and discusses its determinants. It starts by introducing the political transition and the new "rules of the game" that were then established, particularly the electoral system. This is very important because the first elections created the parliament that negotiated the Constitution, unleashing forces that would shape the new party system. Next, the chapter shows how the economic context underwent considerable changes during the Spanish transition, leaving its mark on the tax reform process. The tax proposals and discussions in Parliament are then reviewed, before the chapter closes with a discussion about the role of pressure groups, which went through a phase of reconfiguration in the first years of democracy.

All in all, it will be argued that several of these factors acted against the establishment of a progressive and redistributive tax system, thus limiting the full satisfaction of popular demand. This is very difficult to prove conclusively, but the historical analysis definitely suggests it.

4.1 Political Transition, Political Parties, and the Electoral System

The basic lines of the political reform process were introduced in Chapter 1. This section will consider how the Spanish transition put in place a system that might have benefited some positions over others. In a comparative piece about the prospects for redistribution after democratisation, Albertus and Menaldo (2014) discussed the importance of the *process* of democratic transition, arguing that the resulting regime would only become redistributive if elite control was effectively challenged by a revolutionary threat. In Spain, democratisation was not the result of a revolution, but only came about after Franco's death in 1975. However, by that time the political elite was no longer a compact bloc, part of it has turned towards a slight reformist agenda.

The opposition was not fully united either, despite the efforts of the Communist Party of Spain (*Partido Comunista de España*, PCE) to achieve a democratic breakout, after which a provisional government of national unity would call for elections. Significant social upheaval occurred throughout the transition at various levels (workers, students, nationalists, etc.), undoubtedly influencing the process of political change.

The usual interpretation, therefore, is that neither Francoists nor the opposition was strong or united enough to impose their views, so a compromise arose. Led from above by Suárez—who had been appointed by the king, Franco's designated successor—the transition process was a political reform that did not openly reject the dictatorship's legal framework, but aimed at reforming it. The strength of the political and social opposition nevertheless made it possible to introduce some changes that led to a clear breakthrough in comparison with the previous regime (Colomer, 1998; Saz, 2010). But were those enough to ensure a democratic tax policy that honoured the redistributive preferences of most Spaniards?

Previous studies suggest parliamentary and proportional political systems result in more redistributive policies than their counterparts. For example, Persson et al. (2000) contended that parliamentary systems would be more redistributive than presidential ones, Persson and

Tabellini (2003) related majoritarian systems to lower social spending, (Alesina et al., 2001) argued that the majoritarian and federal system of the United States worked against redistribution, and Iversen and Soskice (2006) pointed out that proportional electoral systems gave centre-left parties a better chance of taking office. It is crucial to the present argument, therefore, to establish what kind of political system was put in place during the transition to democracy, and whether this acted for or against the realisation of progressive taxation.

But let us first say a little more about the main political parties of the time, since they were the central actors in the process. Some of them had deep roots: they participated in democratic life before the Civil War, and managed to maintain some continuity throughout the dictatorship. This was the case of the Spanish Socialist Workers' Party (*Partido Socialista Obrero Español*, PSOE) and the Communist Party (PCE), as well as the Unified Socialist Party of Catalonia (*Partit Socialista Unificat de Catalunya*, PSUC)—the regional wing of the Communist party. These parties were, of course, weakened by exile and years of operating underground—but in the eyes of many Spaniards, these very experiences gave them legitimacy during and immediately after the transition. During the period, these parties experienced strong tensions between continuity and renovation, and finally underwent a significant ideological overhaul that culminated in the abandonment of Leninism by PCE (1978) and of Marxism by PSOE (1979) (Andrade Blanco, 2012). Even if these two parties played a role in the struggle for democracy in Spain, PCE undoubtedly constituted the "hard core" of the regime's opposition. Nevertheless, as we will see, the Communist party obtained deceiving results in the elections of 1977 and has since had only secondary institutional power. Conversely, PSOE became a central actor in Spanish political life during the transition, and still holds this status today.

Other parties that operated during the transition were newer. Some were formed around informal political groups originated within the Franco regime, and others as an expression of more moderate opposition. Union of the Democratic Centre (*Unión de Centro Democrático*, UCD) was created by Adolfo Suárez, first as a coalition, later as a party representing a wide range of tendencies. Further similar actors were the Social Democratic Party (*Partido Social Demócrata*, PSD) of

Francisco Fernández Ordóñez, the People's Socialist Party (*Partido Socialista Popular*, PSP) of Enrique Tierno Galván, and the People's Alliance (*Alianza Popular*, AP) of Manuel Fraga (this was a conglomeration of the so-called "Magnificent Seven", which included prominent ministers under Franco).[1]

The circle of politically relevant parties is completed with the regionalist parties, which were very influential in Catalonia and the Basque Country, both on the right and the left: Democratic Convergence of Catalonia (*Convergència Democràtica de Catalunya*, CDC), the Basque Nationalist Party (*Partido Nacionalista Vasco*, PNV), the Republican Left of Catalonia (*Esquerra Republicana de Catalunya*, ERC), and the Basque Left (*Euskadiko Ezkerra*, EE). Several additional parties existed at the early stages of the transition, including some at either extreme of the political spectrum. Among the hard left, a few were not even legally registered before the elections of June 1977 (and PCE was only legalised in April, two months before!). Democracy brought about a proliferation of parties, but many of these did not make it into Parliament and were subsequently left on the margins of active politics.[2] The party system was initially quite unstable, subject to considerable reconfiguration and comings-and-goings of politicians—as well as a deep crisis in UCD—but the different organisations had largely stabilised by the mid-eighties.

The first democratic elections of the new democratic regime were held on 15 June 1977. The electoral system was established by a government decree that contained several provisions to reduce representativeness in favour of stability—this was necessary to obtain the "yes" from the old regime *Procuradores*, by assuring them that they would keep some power.[3] In fact, the Parliament was relatively small (350 MPs), and so were electoral districts (provinces instead of regions, with at least two MPs each, which meant that rural areas were overrepresented). In addition, a threshold of 3% of the vote was set for parties to enter Parliament (López Nieto, 1992). Because of this, to this day the Spanish electoral system displays a high level of disproportionality and district malapportionment.

District malapportionment refers to disproportionality in territorial representation, which generally favours less populated regions, with more conservative voters. Samuels and Snyder (2001) compared the extent of malapportionment in different countries in the late nineties, suggesting that this manipulation of electoral representation could in fact favour the chances of democracy in a transitional context, by hurting prospects for future redistribution.[4] The idea is easily applied to Spain, where several studies by political scientists have underlined the interests evident in the design of the electoral system during the transition (Gunther, 1989; Lago & Montero, 2005). Although nominally proportional, in its operation the electoral system is affected by both a majoritarian bias and a conservative bias (meaning that parties on the right benefit more than those on the left from actual non-proportionality).

Samuels and Snyder (2001) showed that Spain's malapportionment value is 9.63% for 1996, sixteenth in a sample of 78 countries.[5] This means that nearly 10% of the parliamentary seats were allocated to districts that would not have them if there were no malapportionment. The value situates Spain alongside several other relatively young democracies, largely in Latin America, while most Western European countries had lower levels of malapportionment (see Table 4.1). I have estimated the malapportionment index corresponding to the first democratic elections of 1977 at 9.29%: the limited, gradual deterioration over

Table 4.1 District malapportionment in Spain and other countries (percentage)

Country	Year	Malapportionment index
Chile	1997	15.09
Spain	1996	9.63
Spain	1977	9.29
Brazil	1998	9.13
France	1998	6.95
Mexico	1997	6.36
United Kingdom	1997	4.56
Greece	1997	4.06
Germany	1994	3.44
Portugal	1995	1.74
Italy	1996	0.82

Source Spain 1977 from Torregrosa-Hetland (2018); rest from Samuels and Snyder (2001)
Note The index is calculated as the sum of differences between all districts' shares of seats and votes, in absolute values, divided by two

time is likely due to the lack of sufficient adjustment to demographic movements.

The Loosemore–Hanby index of disproportionality in parties' outcomes, on which the malapportionment index is based, shows a decreasing time trend, which has to do with the adaptation of parties to the electoral system (see Table 4.1). But in this case the Spanish value of the index is also very high compared to other countries with proportional electoral systems. Gallagher (1991) provided values for a sample of 23 countries, showing the average of the various elections held in the period 1979–1989. Here, Spain is the fifth most disproportionate country, preceded only by countries with plurality systems such as the United Kingdom (see Table 4.2).

During the first years of the new democracy, these disproportionate effects especially benefited Suárez's party, UCD, which consistently obtained a higher share of seats than votes (see Table 4.3). The party won a significant position in the first democratic parliament—even though it

Table 4.2 Loosemore–Hanby index of disproportionality in Spain and other countries (percentage)

	Parties with seats	Including parties without seats
In Spanish general elections, 1977–1986		
1977	15.1	18.8
1979	14.3	17.6
1982	12.2	14.3
1986	10.1	13.2
Other countries, average of various elections held 1979–1989		
	United Kingdom	20.0
	France*	12.2
	Portugal	6.6
	Greece	5.8
	Italy	4.8
	Sweden	2.9
	West Germany	1.4

*France: elections of 1981 and 1986 (double-ballot system)
Source Spain 1977–1986 from Torregrosa-Hetland (2018). Other countries, 1979–1989, from Gallagher (1991)
Note The index is calculated as the sum of differences between all parties' shares in seats and votes, in absolute values, divided by two

Table 4.3 Parties benefiting from electoral rules, 1977–1986

	UCD/AP (since 1982)			PSOE		
	% votes	% seats	Diff	% votes	% seats	Diff
1977	34.5	41.1	6.6	24.4	29.4	5.0
1979	35.1	48.0	12.9	30.5	34.6	4.0
1982	26.5	30.6	4.1	40.8	50.6	9.8
1986	26.1	30.0	3.9	37.9	46.6	8.7

Source Torregrosa-Hetland (2018)
Note In 1982 and 1986, the first columns correspond to electoral coalitions headed by AP, the new dominant party on the right

did not attain an absolute majority, as it had aimed to. UCD was also the most fortunate in 1979. As Gunther et al. (1986) have discussed, the impact of the first election on the party system was very significant. Parties obtaining representation in 1977 not only gained institutional power, but also reinforced their access to public opinion, and—last but not least—obtained funding from the state budget. The ones that did not (and they were many) disappeared or were disadvantaged from then onwards. Thus, the electoral system was an active element in shaping the new party system. And, similarly, given the formative character of this early period, the strong majorities enjoyed by UCD had a lasting impact on public policy.

After 1982, the biggest premiums in terms of parliamentary seats were enjoyed by the PSOE. As can be seen, the Socialist Party won an absolute majority in 1982, which entitled it to initiate welfare state development programmes and to complete the taxation reform, which included the intensification of anti-fraud measures. The party and the context, however, had by then changed in many respects.[6]

4.2 A Changing Economic Context

The economic context was transformed during the Spanish transition (De la Torre & Rubio-Varas, 2021; Trullén, 1993). The author has argued elsewhere that this acted as a restriction against progressive and redistributive tax reform (Torregrosa-Hetland, 2021). This was because of the combination of three rather new elements in the seventies: the growth slowdown, very high inflation, and a rapid process of external opening. While the economic crisis was temporary, and so was the inflation associated with the oil shock, in the medium-term growth rates would be lower than during the "economic miracle" period. The integration of the Spanish economy into the second wave of globalisation also brought about considerable movements of goods, services, and capital across frontiers. This context was very different from the one that accompanied fiscal expansion in Western Europe during the postwar period (Eichengreen, 2007).

Economic growth was on a downward trend from the peak years of convergence with Western Europe. While at the beginning of the sixties the expansion of Spanish GDP per capita was above 7% per year, by the end of the seventies growth had fallen below 3% in real terms (see Fig. 4.1). The energy crisis, as has been discussed elsewhere, is not the only factor behind the slowdown, which was more intense in the countries that had experienced some of the "economic miracles" of the period. Since then, growth has exhibited a long-term average of 2% in real GDP per capita. This is why the expanding sixties were a "lost opportunity"

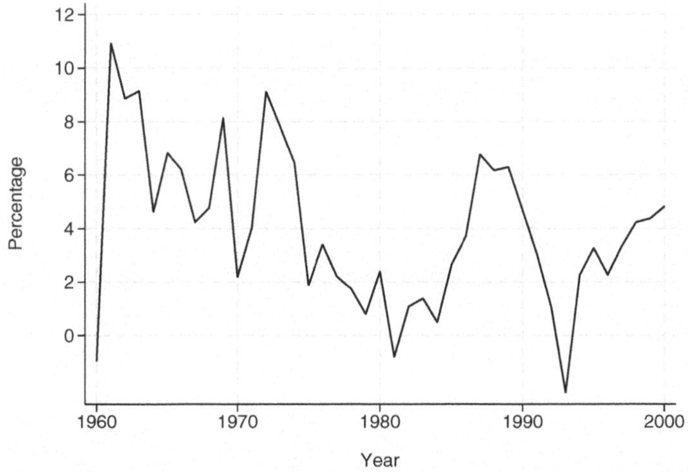

Fig. 4.1 Annual growth in real GDP per capita, 1960–2000 (*Source* Prados de la Escosura, 2017)

for tax reform, since it is easier to redistribute from an increasingly large cake (recall Chapter 2).

The crisis of the seventies and early eighties also had an effect in terms of spending needs: if Spaniards already aspired to an improvement in public services and social benefits in the years leading up to the transition, pressure on the social security system was reinforced by the dramatic increase in unemployment figures. Part of this unemployment has become, decades later, a structural aspect of the Spanish economy, which in turn limits public revenues. The economic crisis, the mature demographic structure of the population, and the large public deficits were unfavourable circumstances that conditioned the construction of the universal social security system in Spain, due to the delay caused by the dictatorship (Comín & Díaz, 2005, p. 894).

Inflation remained very high throughout the seventies and into the mid-eighties, compared to what has been the norm in recent decades (below 5% per year; see Fig. 4.2). This was not, of course, a Spanish particularity, even if price increases were more acute in Spain than in a number of Western European countries (Cuevas & Pons, 2020).[7] The phenomenon also affected much of southern Europe at a time

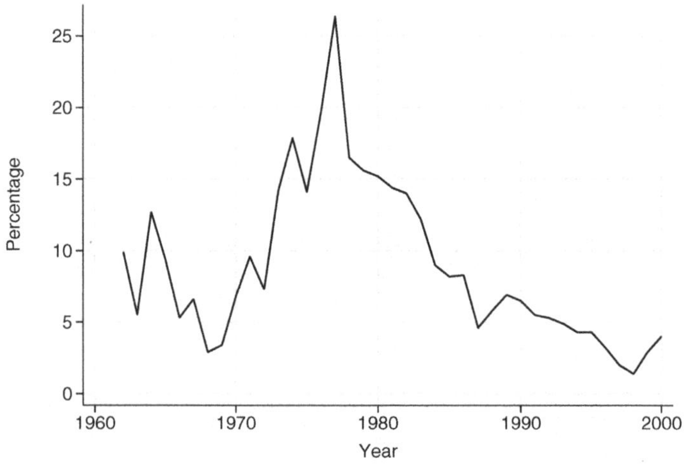

Fig. 4.2 Annual rates of inflation, 1960–2000 (*Source* Calculated using the consumer price index from the *Instituto Nacional de Estadística*)

of continued fiscal underdevelopment. In addition to its depressing effect on living standards, inflation has various connections with public finances. Battilossi (2017) describes the role that inflation and other implicit taxes played in the sustainability of the state deficit between the seventies and nineties. This type of unorthodox financing was progressively restricted in the context of access to the EEC and the associated liberalisation of the financial sector. Another fiscal aspect of price increases is their effect on the collection of taxes that have thresholds set in nominal terms, as is usually the case with income taxes. The Spanish personal income tax of 1978 was soon affected by the phenomenon known as "bracket creep", which meant increases in taxes paid by individuals even in the absence of growth in their real income. Annual inflation was above 10% in the first years of the tax's operation, something that may have had negative effects on its legitimacy at such a crucial period.

Spanish international openness had been on an upward trend ever since the Stabilisation Plan of 1959, favoured by the 1970 preferential agreement with the European Economic Community, and eventually culminating in the country's incorporation into the EEC in 1986 and the subsequent market integration (Carreras & Tafunell, 2018). This is true whether viewed in terms of trade and capital flows or of *de jure* openness (see Fig. 4.3). That economic openness is an obstacle to progressive taxation has long been established in the literature: it arises from the "exit" option given to the owners of mobile tax bases—particularly capital. Open economies will experience tensions arising from the competition for mobile tax bases, leading to downward pressure on them (Bates & Lien, 1985; Genschel, 2002; Persson & Tabellini, 1992). However, openness and the prospect of incorporation into the EEC were probably factors favouring democratisation, since they reduced the economic risks for the elite by warranting the defence of the market economy (Whitehead, 1986).[8]

Notably, and even though tax harmonisation was certainly discussed during the preparations for the common market, the practical results were highly uneven. While there was considerable unification of criteria around indirect taxes (VAT and excises), the same was not achieved when it came to direct taxation (Kopits, 1992); in fact, the issue is still on the

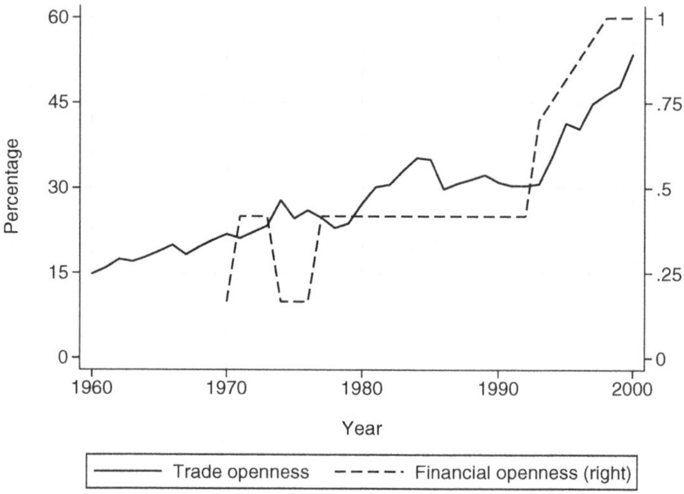

Fig. 4.3 International openness of the Spanish economy, 1960–2000 (*Source* Trade openness from Tena (2005), financial de jure openness from Chinn and Ito [2006])

table for thirty years later, with regard to corporation tax. By contrast, as early as 1991 an agreement was reached to avoid double taxation of dividends across frontiers.

A complete unification of criteria for personal income taxation was never fully on the table. But it was foreseen that, in the absence of automatic information-sharing and/or homogeneous withholding, capital revenues could easily engage in fraud by making use of upcoming liberalisation. This, in turn, would provide the recipients of such kind of income with higher leverage with which to obtain tax privileges, both before and after the lifting of controls in July 1990. Some initiatives were intended to limit these effects. The initial proposal of the European Commission in 1989 was to establish a uniform 15% minimum withholding tax on EC residents' interest income. But this option was abandoned, with the EC stating instead that there would be general "cooperation". Such decisions required unanimity. One interpretation is that interests in countries like the United Kingdom and Luxembourg prevented the adoption of general agreements on automatic information exchange and uniform withholding at source, and this put a hard limit on the possibilities for capital taxation in Spain: *"this situation is forcing, in order to avoid massive outflows of domestic savings, the placement of capital income and capital gains taxation in line with that existing in the rest of the countries in the Community"* (Lasheras, 1990, p. 59; author's translation). The fear of capital flight served as an argument in favour of reducing the maximum rates of income tax—when these rates had only just begun to pay off—and of extending tax privileges on investment.

The slowdown in growth, high inflation, and increasing openness put pressure on the progressivity and revenue capacity of a fiscal system that was still taking its first steps, and whose benefits in terms of public spending would take time to be fully perceived by the population. Although counterfactuals are always complicated, one might assume that Spanish public finances could have been more redistributive if the transition had arrived in 1960. Without the constraints of the critical economic context, twentieth-century taxation might have reached a greater development in the country. The 1977 tax reform model, after all, was beginning to decline internationally when it was introduced in Spain.

4.3 The Reform Process: Party Stances in Parliament

Under the initial plans, the whole tax system should have been overhauled in a couple of years. The reform of direct taxation was supposed to be placed before Parliament in September 1977, and the plans for indirect taxation, in November of the same year. The basic lines of the reform were included in the Moncloa Pacts, signed in October 1977, which referred to the establishment of a "global, personal and progressive" income tax, a corporate tax with less exemptions than the existing one, a system of indirect taxation comparable to that of the countries in the EEC, and equilibrium between the revenue collected by direct and indirect taxes during 1978.

In the end, the proposals for personal income, inheritance, and net wealth taxes came before Parliament in January 1978, while those for corporate tax and indirect taxes did so that June. Table 4.4 presents the

Table 4.4 The process of tax reform: main laws

Law	Publication of initial proposal	Sanction
Urgent tax reform measures	August 1977	November 1977
Personal income tax	January 1978	September 1978
Corporate income tax	July 1978	December 1978
Net wealth tax	January 1978	June 1991
Inheritance tax	January 1978	December 1987
Value added tax	July 1978	August 1985

Source Compiled by author
Notes For the date of the initial proposal, the date of publication in the *Boletín Oficial de las Cortes* is utilised. Approval by the government took place one or more months earlier

main tax initiatives of the period. As can be seen, a substantial part of the reform of direct taxation took place before the end of 1978, such that personal and corporate income taxes were soon in force. However, the remaining direct taxes were bottlenecked by other tasks facing the Public Finance Commission. The net wealth and inheritance tax proposals, as well as that of VAT, did not make it to the plenary session of Parliament until several years later. When the government changed in 1979, and again in 1982, the processes re-started. It should be noted, again, that the discussions about the first tax reform proposals coincided in time with the drafting of the Constitution, which undoubtedly consumed a substantial amount of time and effort. Resulting delays made it possible for those resistant to the reform to fight back and come up with alternative models after 1979.

The Law for Urgent Fiscal Reform Measures

The first proposal of Minister Fernández Ordóñez became the first law to be passed by the new Parliament, urgently processed since it was meant to come into force in 1978. The Law for Urgent Fiscal Reform Measures (LMURF in its Spanish initials) included an ample set of novelties, in an attempt to bridge the gap between the old taxes and the new ones proposed during 1978, as well as to introduce a new kind of relationship between taxpayers and the tax administration. The main changes were the introduction of two transitory taxes (a net wealth tax and a surcharge on high labour income), and a set of anti-evasion measures: tax amnesty, consideration of tax evasion as a fiscal crime, and the lifting of banking secrecy.

With respect to the initial bill, the law as finally approved exhibited an increase in the progressivity of wealth tax rates, and quite closely echoed the policy proposals of the Catalan Socialists. This change, however, was accompanied by a reduction in the revenue capacity of the tax, since rates were reduced for those with under 100 million pesetas in wealth (which applied to the majority of estates), and increased only at the very top, for those with over 500 million. By contrast, the alternative structure put forward by the Communist party was less progressive, but would have yielded higher revenue from the propertied classes.[9] On the other hand, the right-wing AP managed to secure for its voters exemptions from wealth taxation on monuments and significant artworks, and increased deductions for new labour contracts in business taxes (a point it shared with UCD as well as the Basque and Catalan centre-right parties).

The debate in the plenary of Parliament, held on the 25 October 1977, focussed on a couple of especially contested issues. The Socialists pushed for the inclusion of juridical persons in the wealth tax, arguing that leaving them out introduced inequity with respect to sole proprietorships—which was why they had been included in government's first proposal. This point was considered important not because of revenue collection, but because the wealth tax was meant to serve as a registry of estates for the remaining taxes. Responding to this proposal, MP García Añoveros from UCD (who would later be minister of public finance between 1979 and 1982) justified the change because of concerns about double taxation and possible negative impacts on investment. The speeches of Socialist proponents suggest that there was fierce opposition to openly and constructively discussing this issue, which might indicate that external pressures explained the change of opinion within the government.[10] The Socialist proposal was backed by the Communist party, but was nevertheless rejected by 164 votes to 147.

Another matter discussed was when the duty of cooperation of financial entities would start, with regard to the lifting of bank secrecy. The Catalan Socialists, represented by Ernest Lluch, suggested that this principle should come into effect from June 1977, before the law was sanctioned but after the principle had been made public. Indeed, major capital movements were known to have taken place during the year. The Catalan centre-right party CDC argued against this proposal, defending the principle of non-retroactivity. This amendment was also rejected, albeit very narrowly: 147 against 142.

The Taxation of Income, from Individuals and Corporations

Personal income tax was one of the cornerstones of the reform. The government proposal, dated December 1977, was discussed in the Commission between January and May 1978, and sanctioned that September. The processing of this law was quite successful for the government and took place more or less in line with the planned time frame, still during the "period of consensus".

Discussions about this legislative proposal were quite cordial, but still underlined the rifts within the governing party, UCD, whose MPs presented 19% of the amendments to the law (38 out of 202). Taken together, all the parties of the centre-right (which includes UCD) made 70% of the suggested amendments, and their content was more critical than those from the left. This shows that Minister Fernández Ordóñez was situated on the left wing of his own party, UCD (indeed, he would later, in 1982, become a member of PSOE). A faction within UCD was clearly against the income tax proposals, and made their positions known in the press. For example, the professor of economics José Ramón Lasuén wrote in February 1978 that the reform of the income tax was "an economic and political mistake", because it would have very negative effects on savings, something especially serious given the economic crisis.[11]

But a progressive schedule was generally accepted by all parties, at least on paper, and in that sense the proposed rate structure was not discussed much in Parliament. On the other hand, the conservative parties all defended increases in tax credits and allowances, which could be interpreted as a base-voidening strategy. They pushed for increased family allowances (together with the Socialists in this case), as well as greater credits for several kinds of investments, personal expenses, and charitable donations. Some of these measures were accepted, which meant a moderation of the law during its passage through Parliament; indeed, the design of tax credits and allowances profoundly affects the progressivity of a tax, but it does so in a less transparent way.

The same was not the case for the Communist party's proposals or other amendments by the Socialists, such as the elimination or strict limitation of presumptive assessment. Indeed, all income was now to be determined by direct estimation, and without global assessments, although presumptive assessment was kept as an option for small businesses, given their limited administrative capabilities. The thresholds were left to the discretion of government. The executive would also have the power to adapt the schedule and credits by means of a yearly decree. Almost all parties demanded a yearly compulsory adjustment to inflation (which was very high at the time, as mentioned in the previous section). These amendments were not accepted, and inflation finally led to strong bracket creep in the eighties.

When it came to the LMURF and the personal income tax proposals there was considerable controversy over the possibility that the tax administration would be obligated to publish individual fiscal data. The main argument against was that it could facilitate terrorist actions (during these years, the Basque separatist group ETA was highly active). Finally, the requirement was established for both taxes, only to be replaced in 1981 by the publication of aggregate statistics.[12]

The reform of personal income tax was followed soon after by that of corporation tax. The principal novelty in this respect was that the tax base (corporations' profits) was to be established by direct estimation, i.e. based on the accountancy books, and not by objective assessments. Furthermore, schedular taxes, which had functioned as "minimum payments", would disappear for corporations as well, and the tax would instead be based only on total profits. This was a turn away from Navarro Rubio's design, and definitely one towards modernisation.

Corporation tax was now intended to lay on the real economic capacity of firms, alongside the equivalent change in personal income tax.

Both these taxes, indeed, were "complementary", in the words of the minister of public finance, and a good deal of deliberation in Parliament was aimed at ensuring adequate consistency between them. Their combination can generate a "double taxation" of dividends, when business profits are taxed first within the corporation and then, again, through personal income tax following distribution to shareholders. This was limited in Spanish law via deductions in both taxes, as is the case in other countries, but the issue remained a source of complaint for the business community in the years to come (Albi, 2007).

Furthermore, when corporate tax rates are lower than the (maximum) income tax rates, opportunities for avoidance are created. This situation often occurs and indeed did so with the 1978 regulation, in which the rate on corporations was set at 33% (with lower rates for particular groups, like cooperatives), and the top marginal rate for individuals, at 65.51% (for income over 9.8 million pesetas). Individuals could disguise their revenues as corporate income in order to pay less taxes, or to delay payment indefinitely by not distributing dividends. The approach in this case was to establish "fiscal transparency", which meant that some closely held entities had to impute profits (distributed or not) to their shareholders, so that they could be taxed as personal income; they would then not be subject to corporate tax. This mechanism was also set as an option for small companies, which was criticised at the time because it facilitated tax planning (this option was eliminated in 1985, and the whole regime, in 2002).

The parliamentary debates about corporation tax took place in November and December of 1978. The law was finally approved shortly after the referendum over the Constitution, on 14 December 1978. The debates attest to an increase in tension within UCD. For example, the Socialist MP Pablo Castellano said, when commenting on an amendment proposal: "*UCD is the government party, and the government party has to improve government proposals, but be consistent with the government, or the government, consistent with its party*".[13]

An extensively discussed aspect was the tax address of corporations. According to the proposal, as well as in the law finally approved, tax addresses corresponded to a firm's headquarters, from where the business was actually run. According to the UCD MP Jaime García Añoveros, this was convenient for administrative reasons. However, the Socialists argued for the alternative criterion of setting the address to where the majority of a corporation's capital lay, i.e. where its factories were located. This position was backed by the Communist party and the Catalan centre-right. Representing the latter, Ramon Trias Fargas argued that it would be a step towards ascertaining the regional distribution of both revenues and spending, which was of interest for the future financing of autonomous communities.[14] Indeed, the regional "problem" loomed over the whole discussion, with arguments against the excessive centralisation of activity in the Spanish economy.

Derailed Reform: The Taxation of Wealth

The initial net wealth tax introduced in 1977 was meant to be transitory, but it was ultimately in force for fourteen years. A proposal to replace it was introduced to Parliament in January 1978, and prompted greater discussion, around similar issues, than its precedent. The draught law for a new inheritance tax was also presented in January 1978. In both cases, the Commission did not reach an agreement before the government was dissolved for new elections, and a similar process started again in April 1979.

With regard to net wealth tax, the Communist party defended again the need to include juridical persons. Socialists suggested that cadastral values be adjusted yearly, to tackle the widely known problem of their under-valuation, which also affected other taxes. The centre-right, on the other hand, strove for individual instead of joint taxation, an increase in the exempted threshold, and annual adjustment to inflation: all measures geared towards limiting revenue. They also again opposed the publication of individual tax data, because of the terrorist threat: *"Publicising taxpayer lists can encourage kidnappings"*.[15]

In the inheritance tax proposal, the main novelty was greater personalisation according to the wealth recipient, whose pre-existing property would be taken into account to calculate the tax due. This would have the effect of making the tax more progressive. The proposal was rejected by the representatives of the right, namely AP and the Catalan nationalists, who also proposed an increase in exempted thresholds and annual adjustment to inflation. The left-wing parties suggested higher or more progressive rate structures.

Inheritance tax was finally reformed in December 1987, and a new wealth tax was introduced in June 1991, together with the first big reform of personal income tax.

Value Added Tax

Several value added tax proposals were presented to Parliament during the period; the first came in July 1978, and the discussion was reinitiated after the elections in April 1979. This proposal had not yet made it into law before it was withdrawn in 1981 by the government, which instead put forward a new proposal more adjusted to European harmonisation guidelines.

VAT has been considered a "revenue-raising machine", and as such its advantages are many. It is an efficient tax, which may foster compliance in businesses as well as savings with respect to consumption, and represented a remarkable improvement in neutrality when compared to the existing turnover tax. Ultimately, however, at least two factors made it difficult to introduce in Spain at the end of the seventies: the expected impact on price levels (at a time of double-digit inflation) and the fact that it meant putting doing away with undercover export subsidies. In the end, the tax came into force as part of the changes related to accession to the EEC.

The debates about VAT in Parliament are a clear example of special interest politics, with MPs aiming to add complexity to the tax, by granting exemptions, or reduced rates for various industries: for example, health services, insurance, cars, fashion, wine, perfumes, and even shotguns.

Social Security Reform

As mentioned in Chapter 3, by 1977 all parties were also calling for reform of the social security system, for various reasons: excessive complexity and lack of generality, the low level of pensions, and the likely negative effects on employment of the (very regressive) contributions. The lines advocated by AP, UCD, PSOE, and PCE in 1977 were remarkably similar: they tended towards universality, collective control, and increased or total government funding through taxes.[16] This model also appeared in the "Libro Blanco de la Seguridad Social" of April 1977, which was the result of a government-appointed commission. However, during the following years, political programmes would keep mentioning the same issues, because they had not been translated into practice.[17]

The reason is simple. Universalisation and increased pensions, in a context of growing unemployment, needed to be funded with reinforced transfers from the government's general budget. This, however, could scarcely be a reality before the tax reform had paid off in terms of revenue and progressivity.[18] The Social Security reform took off in 1978 with far-reaching institutional changes that brought about improvements in administration: the old *Mutualidades* and the *Instituto Nacional de Previsión* were extinguished, and replaced by new institutions that operated under joint accounting. Benefits were managed by the *Instituto Nacional de la Seguridad Social*, while the reform created some offices for health, social assistance, and employment. In addition, minimum pensions were increased during the following years. But the main reform, whereby the general budget would cover universal healthcare and non-contributory pensions, would not come until 1990. It had to wait for the introduction of VAT, which allowed a reduction in social contributions, and for an improvement of the economic situation. In this sense, Guillén-Rodriguez (2000) has emphasised continuity in the social security system during the transition. The government's participation in funding the system increased (largely due to growing expenditure in unemployment protection), and minimum pensions grew more than higher ones. But the basic characteristics of the regime, with rigidly differentiated categories of workers, were retained and even reinforced.

The contributory system was simplified in 1978, ending the transitory regime that had started in 1972 (Monasterio, 1992). Since 1978, workers would contribute according to their wages, with an upper and lower limit dictated yearly by the government, again for each category. Minimum caps coincided with the national minimum wage. Maximum caps have regressive effects, as they exempt a fraction of higher salaries. The official version was that during the following years the maximum caps would increase especially for the higher-paid categories of workers, thus reducing regressivity. In hindsight, however, this does not seem to have occurred (see Table 4.5): the increase was higher for the upper categories *in absolute terms*, but during 1979–1988 all groups saw their caps increase yearly by very similar percentages: by 1988, they were all at 250% of their 1979 value, with small variation. Between 1989 and 1990 adjustments were made to reduce the actual number of groups (several categories got the same caps). The caps did not increase in real terms in this period (only slightly in 1983): it seems to have been impeded by the crisis (slow growth with high inflation) and the convenience of not pushing up labour costs. As the table shows, they also lagged behind increases in the average wage in most years, which would point to little or no eradication of the regressivity of social contributions—and to the extent that higher wages underwent above-average increases during the decade, regressivity was actually intensifying.

4.4 Pressure Groups

The actions of political parties were constrained by the economic context, but also by the power of organised special interest groups. Here, we consider the positions of business associations and trade unions, which are part of our story.

Indeed, the leaders of the tax reform process cited opposition of de facto powers as a powerful reason for the partial derailment of their plans. Fuentes Quintana asserted in 1996 that "*The reform measures were effectively stopped. A big part of the tax changes were paralysed by vested interests.* [...] *I am certain that there was [business] interference to address what should be done*".[19] Fuentes Quintana resigned in October 1978. His

Table 4.5 Tax caps for social security contributions by categories of workers, 1979–1990

Workers' category	1979	1980	1981	1982	1983	1984	1985	1986	1987	1988	1989	1990
In pesetas per month												
1: Engineers and Graduates	1,06,470	1,24,890	1,40,460	1,54,440	1,87,950	2,14,260	2,29,260	2,47,590	2,59,980	2,67,780	2,75,820	2,91,540
2: Assistants (graduated)	88,200	1,03,440	1,16,430	1,28,010	1,55,790	1,77,600	1,90,030	2,05,230	2,15,490	2,21,940	2,75,820	2,91,540
3: Administrative and workshop heads	76,740	89,970	1,01,280	1,11,390	1,35,540	1,54,530	1,65,350	1,78,590	1,87,530	1,93,170	2,75,820	2,91,540
4: Assistants (not graduated)	67,680	79,530	89,430	98,430	1,19,790	1,36,560	1,46,120	1,57,800	1,65,690	1,70,670	1,75,800	2,91,540
5: Administrative officers	62,850	73,680	82,860	91,110	1,10,880	1,26,390	1,35,240	1,46,070	1,53,360	1,57,950	1,75,800	1,85,820
6: Subordinates	57,360	67,290	75,750	83,400	1,01,490	1,15,710	1,23,810	1,33,710	1,40,400	1,44,600	1,55,520	1,64,400
7: Administrative assistants	57,360	67,290	75,750	83,400	1,01,490	1,15,710	1,23,810	1,33,710	1,40,400	1,44,600	1,55,520	1,64,400
In pesetas per day												
8: 1st and 2nd category officers	2050	2403	2703	2975	3620	4127	4416	4769	5007	5157	5312	5615
9: 3rd and 4th category officers	2000	2344	2637	2902	3620	4026	4308	4653	4886	5033	5184	5615
10: Workmen	1912	2243	2525	2780	3384	3857	4127	4457	4640	4820	5184	5480

(continued)

Table 4.5 (continued)

Workers' category	1979	1980	1981	1982	1983	1984	1985	1986	1987	1988	1989	1990
11: 3rd and 4th year apprentices	1171	1372	1543	1697	2065	2354	2519	2721	2857	2943	3031	3204
12: 1st and 2nd year apprentices	737	864	972	1069	1301	1483	1587	1714	1800	1854	1910	3204
Increase with respect to previous year (mode)	7%	17%	13%	10%	22%	14%	7%	8%	5%	3%	3%	6%
Increase in the average wage	23%	16%	15%	14%	14%	10%	9%	11%	8%	8%	7%	9%

Source Tax caps from *Boletín Oficial del Estado.* Increase in the average wage calculated from Maluquer de Motes and Llonch Casanovas (2005), table 15.25 (total monthly remuneration of industry and service workers, from INE, *Encuesta de Salarios en la Industria y los Servicios*) rapid abandonment of active politics was caused by hard resistance to his economic reform plans, of which the tax measures were only one part: Fuentes was the sponsor of the Moncloa Pacts, which included a whole range of liberalisation measures as well as the stabilisation programme. Some of these were opposed by the banking sector, the energy sector, and fellow members of government, which aimed for a more conservative policy—reflecting the uneasy coexistence of different tendencies inside UCD.[20]

Fernández Ordóñez stayed in government until April 1979, before he was able to conclude his entire tax reform programme; he was substituted for the second term of UCD by Jaime García Añoveros, a man of more conservative positions. Fernández Ordóñez's take on the reactionary resistance to reform was similar to Fuentes Quintana's, and he denounced it in a book published in 1980: *"In Spain, where public spending has not yet reached the levels of industrial countries, and where the tax system has very recently taken its first steps toward justice, a conservative phenomenon has been born, fuelled not only by the international process, but by nostalgia for the past.* [...] *This has strengthened the pressure of conservative forces, from public manifestations against the tax reform and the Moncloa Pacts, to greater control of government policy"* (Fernández Ordóñez, 1980, p. 137; author's translation). This key actor's account of events has been backed, among others, by the historian Juan Pan-Montojo (1996).

The reactions and actions of the business sector vis-à-vis the tax reform were presented with a different perspective by Albi (2007). In his account, "*the initial resistance was rather weak, something to be expected given the low profile of business organisations at the time*" (p. 66; author's translation). In general, the sector accepted the need for reform and for higher public revenues, even if they did complain about the lack of adaptation to the critical economic context. Incipient business organisations spoke loudly against particular features of the reform, especially against the 1977 wealth tax and the procedures of "fiscal transparency" in the income tax law.

Business demands persisted over the years, centred around the reduction of double taxation of dividends, international coordination, and the opposition to compulsory fiscal transparency. They generally argued (as might be expected) for reductions in the burden on firms and a reduction of progressivity, stating that this was better for economic efficiency, especially in an internationally open economy. Furthermore, taxes should be limited because the size of the public sector should also be limited. Some of these arguments were indeed rather old, having featured in the press for decades, but the combination of a long economic crisis and greater international openness, as mentioned earlier, reinvigorated them. Conflict between business interests and the government was intense in the last half of the eighties, but subsequent legislation took up some of their demands (reforms of income tax and wealth tax in 1991, and of corporation tax in 1995). According to Albi (2007), this gave way to more calm and collaborative relations.

The point of departure needs to be taken into account here. Even if there were no autonomous business organisations during Francoism, big firms still had a lot of power, often through personal relationships. In 1974, as many as 77% of ministers and ex-ministers were or had been members of big firm directorates during 1961–1974 (Gunther, 1980, p. 282). Employers' and workers' associations alike were legalised in the spring of 1977, soon giving way to the creation of several business associations: *Confederación Española de Organizaciones Empresariales* (CEOE), *Foment del Treball Nacional* (in Catalonia), and *Instituto de la Empresa Familiar*. CEOE, as a confederation, was the most important, and soon became a prominent voice against progressive tax reform. Its president Carlos Ferrer Salat said in 1977 that "*Because of its contents, this proposal [for general fiscal reform] is going to put an important brake on investment*".[21] On the other hand, owners of small firms were more favourable to the tax changes, since they suffered to some extent from the regressivity of the previous system, through presumptive assessments and the weight of social contributions for labour-intensive enterprises. A small business owner from the metal sector said to the press in June 1977: "*I don't mind the tax reform, what matters to me is that it is done by taking into account the economic capacity of each enterprise and that it prevents the most powerful ones from benefitting. I hope that this democracy makes things go that way*".[22]

One of the biggest concerns of the business sector, indeed, were social contributions. Employers nominally paid around 80% of the total: although the statutory regulation did not necessarily reflect the economic incidence of the tax (see Chapter 5), the relaxation of these contributions was a potentially great relief for business at the time. These demands were included as proposals of the main parties, but, as we have seen, not put into practice immediately. In any case, the lack of a thorough updating of the tax caps was consistent with the position of business.

The banking sector was a needed collaborator for the implementation of the reform. In order to make the taxation of capital income effective, withholding had to be generalised, and information on bank accounts made accessible to the tax administration. But the behaviour of financial institutions was not one of entirely amicable cooperation. The lifting of banking secrecy in November 1977 triggered fierce opposition, based on the argument that personal intimacy was threatened, and that the measure could lead to a reduction of operations and the growth of black markets. *ABC* voiced the concerns of Rafael Termes, president of the bankers' association, who showed willingness to cooperate but complained about the burdensome task of sending information about all their customers.[23] This led to a long court battle, finally settled in 1986 (Castillo, 1994). In the meantime, documents from the General Directorate of Tax Policy from October 1981 show that, although individualised returns were necessary (and had been required by a ministerial order in 1979), "*In practice, Credit Institutions present information about withholdings jointly, without individualisation and identification of recipients*".[24]

Trade unions were also important actors in the transition years. They attained legal status in 1977 after having operated underground during the dictatorship. Between 1980 and 1987, trade unions and employer associations, together with the government, reached a series of social pacts that sought to tackle the economic crisis, focussing on fighting inflation and liberalising the labour market (Mella, 1992). During these years, trade unions were mainly worried about the preservation of the purchasing power of wages and pensions; tax objectives ranked second in their agenda. Furthermore, their power was waning during the eighties, and their membership levels were lower than those in other European countries.

Notes

1. These seven were, in addition to Fraga himself, Licinio de la Fuente, Gonzalo Fernández de la Mora, Laureano López Rodó, Cruz Martínez Esteruelas, Federico Silva Muñoz, and Enrique Thomas de Carranza.
2. According to López Nieto (1992), around 200 parties were registered for the elections of 1977, but soon after only 18% of those were still active.
3. *Procuradores* was the name of members of the Francoist Parliament, a corporative legislative body subordinated to the dictator.
4. This link is explored by Ardanaz and Scartascini (2013) with Latin American data on personal taxation.
5. The ranking is fourth out of twenty if only federal countries are considered.
6. By 1986, the electoral program of PSOE barely considered tax progressivity as an instrument for redistribution, and attention was directed mainly at social expenditure. In spite of this, Fernández-Albertos (2011) considers the long rule of the socialist party (1982–1996) as one of the factors explaining a rather developed redistributive system in Spain. He also mentions in this sense the existence of large, cohesive parties, and proportional representation (without the qualifications underlined here), while, on the contrary, federalism would act against redistribution.
7. Cuevas and Pons (2020) underline that unemployment rates in Spain were also higher than in other Western European countries, and that the financial crisis was also extremely serious.
8. This connects with the ideas of Boix (2003) mentioned in Chapter 1, in that too high redistributive tension could hinder democratisation by undermining elite support for it.
9. In fact, this may be part of the explanation for the distance between the proposal's initial revenue estimate (39,649 million pesetas, of which the government aimed to reach 20,000) and the actual revenues (8589 million in 1978 and over 15,000 in 1979).
10. *"In this case we were told: 'Positions are completely opposed', even though the first draft of the Ministry of Public Finance* [...] *made reference to the wealth tax on corporations"*, words of Enrique Barón Crespo in the *Diario de Sesiones del Congreso de los Diputados*, 25 October 1977, n. 28, p. 1070 (author's translation).
11. *"El proyecto de reforma fiscal, error económico y político"*, published by José Ramón Lasuén in *Informaciones*, 8/2/1978. This MP had submitted an amendment opposing the proposal, which his party made him withdraw.

In his article, he stated that he meant to lead a discussion about the reform, which was not permitted within the party. Lasuén was finally expelled from UCD in September 1978, and he later joined *Alianza Popular*.

12. Lists of taxpayers for 1977 and 1978 were publicly displayed at the Ministry of Public Finance in 1979 and 1980, with the press commenting on some dubious cases. But this data corresponded to the old personal income tax. The regulation was changed to stop publication of the 1979 data (for the new personal income tax) in 1981.
13. Diario de Sesiones del Congreso de los Diputados, n. 144, 13 December 1978, p. 5783.
14. *"On the one hand, although it is not necessary to describe expenditure and revenue, provincially or geographically, it will not hurt to really know who pays and who collects. In other words, regionalised knowledge of these two items is something that interests us a lot and that will interest us a lot when the autonomous regimes are in operation, that is, knowing where taxes are paid and who pays them".* Diario de Sesiones del Congreso de los Diputados, n. 142, Meeting of the Public Finance Commission, 28 November 1978, p. 5600 (author's translation).
15. Words of Laureano López Rodó, from AP, about his amendment to the Wealth Tax in 1978. Archivo del Congreso, Legajo 1698–3: proyecto IPN (author's translation).
16. The parties of the left also insisted on increasing pensions to make them equivalent to the minimum wage, annual adjustment to inflation, and improvement of the conditions of agricultural workers.
17. The main exception was the proposals of the right-wing AP, which by 1982 had evolved towards a two-pillar model, with basic public and complementary private levels (and with private institutions cooperating in the former as well).
18. In the words of the Libro Blanco, the objectives could only be attained *"with more active government involvement. But this leads to the need for a more sufficient and progressive tax system. It would be in vain to base redistributive action on regressive government contributions"* (author's translation).
19. Excerpt of an interview by Andreu Missé, reproduced in (Fuentes Quintana, 2004; author's translation).
20. The interpretation of *El País* was quite clear in this respect: *"The pressures of the financial sector against the reform and the manifestations of the more*

conservative flank of business, along with the manoeuvres to form a big right-wing party outside UCD, undoubtedly frightened the party's political cadres and Suárez himself", *El País*, Editorial of 25/10/1978.

21. *Cuadernos para el Diálogo*, issue 233, 15 to 21 October 1977 (author's translation). These words correspond to a conference about the situation of enterprises organised by the Association for Progress of Direction.
22. *Cuadernos para el Diálogo*, number 216, 18 to 24 June 1977. Retailers from Madrid also complained about presumptive business taxation in 1976 (*"Los comerciantes insisten en el cierre de los sábados", ABC*, 10/11/1976, p. 44; author's translation).
23. ABC, 29/12/1977, p. 51.
24. "*Note on the preliminary draft of the Law sanctioning tax offenses and the information that Credit Institutions must provide*", October 1981, attached to a letter from Victorio Valle, General Director of Tax Policy, to the Minister of Economy and Trade, Juan Antonio García Díez. Archivo General de la Administración, fondo del Ministerio de Hacienda - Dirección General del Tesoro y Política Financiera – índice IDD(1)031.000: 55/15268 (E. 2014).

References

Albertus, M., & Menaldo, V. (2014). Gaming democracy: Elite dominance during transition and the prospects for redistribution. *British Journal of Political Science, 44*(03), 575–603.

Albi, E. (2007). The business community, policy-makers, and tax reform (1977–2004). In J. Martínez-Vázquez & J. F. Sanz-Sanz (Eds.), *Fiscal reform in Spain: Accomplishments and challenges* (pp. 59–97). Edward Elgar.

Alesina, A., Glaeser, E., & Sacerdote, B. (2001). *Why doesn't the US have a European-style welfare state?* NBER Working Paper No. 8524.

Andrade Blanco, J. A. (2012). *El PCE y el PSOE en (la) transición. La evolución ideológica de la izquierda durante el proceso de cambio político.* Siglo XXI España.

Ardanaz, M., & Scartascini, C. (2013). Inequality and personal income taxation. The origins and effects of legislative malapportionment. *Comparative Political Studies, 46*(12), 1636–1663.

Bates, R. H., & Lien, D.-H.D. (1985). A note on taxation, development, and representative democracy. *Politics and Society, 14*, 53–70.
Battilossi, S. (2017). Structural fiscal imbalances, financial repression and sovereign debt sustainability in Southern Europe, 1970s–1990s. In M. Buggeln, M. Daunton, & A. Nützenadel (Eds.), *The political economy of public finance: Taxation, state spending and debt since the 1970s* (pp. 262–298). Cambridge University Press.
Boix, C. (2003). *Democracy and redistribution.* Cambridge University Press.
Carreras, A., & Tafunell, X. (2018). *Entre el Imperio y La Globalización. Historia Económica de la España Contemporánea.* Crítica.
Castillo, J. M. (1994). *El fraude fiscal en España.* Comares.
Chinn, M. D., & Ito, H. (2006). What matters for financial development? Capital controls, institutions, and interactions. *Journal of Development Economics, 81*(1), 163–192.
Colomer, J. M. (1998). *La transición a la democracia: el modelo español.* Anagrama.
Comín, F. (2010). Public finance and the rise of the liberal state in Spain, 1808–1914. In J. L. Cardoso & P. Lains (Eds.), *Paying for the liberal state. The rise of the public finance in nineteenth-century Europe* (pp. 214–250). Cambridge University Press.
Comín, F., & Díaz, D. (2005). Sector público administrativo y estado del bienestar. In A. Carreras & X. Tafunell (Eds.), *Estadísticas Históricas de España. Siglos XIX-XX: Vol. II* (pp. 873–964). Fundación BBVA.
Cuevas, J., & Pons, M. A. (2020). *1977: Hopes fulfilled—Building democracy in turbulent economic times* (pp. 159–194).
De la Torre, J., & Rubio-Varas, M. (Eds.). (2021). *Economía en transición. Del tardofranquismo a la democracia.* Marcial Pons.
Eichengreen, B. (2007). *The European economy since 1945: Coordinated capitalism and beyond*. Princeton University Press.
Fernández-Albertos, J. (2011). The making of egalitarian Spain: Growth, demographics, politics and the income distribution, 1960–1990. *Revista Española De Sociología, 16*, 47–72.
Fernández Ordóñez, F. (1980). *La España necesaria.* Taurus.
Fuentes Quintana, E. (1990). *Las reformas tributarias en España. Teoría, historia y propuestas.* Crítica.
Fuentes Quintana, E. (2004). Los Pactos de la Moncloa y la Constitución de 1978. In E. Fuentes Quintana (Ed.), *Economía y economistas españoles* (Vol. 8, pp. 163–238). Círculo de Lectores.

Gallagher, M. (1991). Proportionality, disproportionality and electoral systems. *Electoral Studies, 10*(1), 33–51.
Genschel, P. (2002). Globalization, tax competition and the welfare state. *Politics and Society, 30*, 245–275.
Guillén-Rodriguez, A. (2000). *La construcción política del sistema sanitario español: de la postguerra a la democracia*. Exlibris Ediciones.
Gunther, R. (1980). *Public policy in a no-party state. Spanish planning and budgeting in the twilight of the Franquist era*. University of California Press.
Gunther, R. (1989). Electoral laws, party systems, and elites: The case of Spain. *American Political Science Review, 83*(3), 835–858.
Gunther, R., Sani, G., & Shabad, G. (1986). *Sistema de partidos políticos en España: génesis y evolución*. CIS - Siglo XXI.
Iversen, T., & Soskice, D. (2006). Electoral institutions and the politics of coalitions. *American Political Science Review, 100*(2), 165–181.
Kopits, G. (1992). Overview. In *Tax harmonization in the European Community* (pp. 1–21). IMF.
Lago, I., & Montero, J. R. (2005). "Todavía no sé quiénes, pero ganaremos": Manipulación política del sistema electoral español. *Zona Abierta, 110*(111), 279–348.
Lasheras, M. A. (1990). Percepción Social y Politica Fiscal en España. Historia de un compromiso. In *Sistema Fiscal y Administración Tributaria. Análisis de dos realidades. España y Argentina* (pp. 43–68). Instituto de Estudios Fiscales.
López Nieto, L. (1992). Las elecciones de la transición. In R. del Águila Tejerina & R. Cotarelo García (Eds.), *Transición política y consolidación democrática, España (1975–1986)* (pp. 77–104). CIS.
Maluquer de Motes, J., & Llonch Casanovas, M. (2005). Trabajo y Relaciones Laborales. In A. Carreras & X. Tafunell (Eds.), *Estadísticas Históricas de España: Siglo XIX-XX* (pp. 1155–1245). Fundación BBVA.
Mella, M. (1992). Los grupos de interés. In R. Cotarelo (Ed.), *Transición política y consolidación democrática. España (1975–1986)*. CIS.
Monasterio, C. (1992). La financiación de las pensiones públicas en España. In *Los sistemas de Seguridad Social y las nuevas realidades sociales* (pp. 207–233). Ministerio de Trabajo y Seguridad Social.
Pan-Montojo, J. L. (1996). Una larga e inconclusa transición: la reforma tributaria, 1977–1986. In J. Tusell & A. Soto (Eds.), *Historia de la transición. 1975–1986* (pp. 264–304). Alianza.
Persson, T., Roland, G., & Tabellini, G. (2000). Comparative politics and public finance. *Journal of Political Economy, 108*(6), 1121–1161.

Persson, T., & Tabellini, G. (1992). The politics of 1992: Fiscal policy and european integration. *Review of Economic Studies, 59*(4), 689–701.
Persson, T., & Tabellini, G. E. (2003). *The economic effects of constitutions*. MIT press.
Prados de la Escosura, L. (2017). *Spanish economic growth, 1850–2015*. Springer International Publishing.
Samuels, D., & Snyder, R. (2001). The value of a vote: Malapportionment in comparative perspective. *British Journal of Political Science, 31*(4), 651–671.
Saz, I. (2010). La lucha por la libertad en España desde una perspectiva comparada (1962–1977). In C. Navajas & D. Iturriaga (Eds.), *Novísima: II Congreso Internacional de Historia de Nuestro Tiempo* (pp. 71–80).
Tena, A. (2005). Sector exterior. In A Carreras & X. Tafunell (Eds.), *Estadísticas históricas de España. Siglos XIX y XX: Vol. II* (pp. 572–643). Fundación BBVA.
Torregrosa-Hetland, S. (2018). Limits to redistribution in late democratic transitions: The case of Spain. In G. Hürlimann, E. Brownlee & E. Ide, *Worlds of taxation. The political economy of taxing, spending, and redistribution since 1945* (pp. 321–347). Palgrave History of Finance.
Torregrosa-Hetland, S. (2021). La reforma fiscal y sus restricciones económicas. In J. De la Torre & M. Rubio-Varas (Eds.), *Economía en Transición. Del tardofranquismo a la democracia* (Chapter 4). Marcial Pons.
Trullén, J. (1993). *Fundamentos económicos de la Transición política española. La política económica de los acuerdos de la Moncloa*. Ministerio de Trabajo y Seguridad Social.
Whitehead, L. (1986). International aspects of democratization. In G. O'Donnell, P. C. Schmitter, & L. Whitehead (Eds.), *Transitions from authoritarian rule* (pp. 3–46). Johns Hopkins University Press.

5

Winners and Losers

When the tax reform was presented to the public in 1977, it was framed as a matter of justice. The reform also aimed at modernisation, facilitation of international integration, and a significant expansion in public revenues. But an objective very much underlined in public discourse was that of fairness: taxation had been considered unfair during the dictatorship, having reflected the archaic power structures in place, and would now be turned on its head. As part of his defence of the first tax reform law in Parliament in October 1977, Minister Francisco Fernández Ordóñez said the following: "*Some sectors have discussed the timing of this reform, which they, once again, consider inappropriate. But* [...] *the tried and tested rule that those who have more, pay more is going to be the golden rule of the new Spanish Treasury*".[1]

In technical terms, this meant progressivity, a concept introduced in Chapter 1. This does not imply that all taxes had to be progressive but that the system as a whole should be, as a result of a change in composition (the expansion of progressive taxes). That is why so much importance was placed on the relative shares of direct and indirect taxation, and the Moncloa Pacts established that they should contribute

© The Author(s), under exclusive license to Springer Nature Switzerland AG 2021

S. Torregrosa Hetland, *The Spanish Fiscal Transition*,
Palgrave Studies in Economic History,
https://doi.org/10.1007/978-3-030-79541-2_5

equally to the budget by 1978. And they did: revenues from direct and indirect taxation almost coincided in the following years (see Fig. 2.5 in Chapter 2), which was celebrated as the first success of the tax reform.

In fact, changes to the tax structure are often used as a first indication of whether a system is progressive. But they only show only an approximate picture: if we really want to know how progressivity changed, who shouldered a higher or a lower burden, we need to look closer. This is because tax incidence *within* these two categories might have changed as well. Furthermore, there were additional changes in the underlying distribution of income, as well as in social contributions. Tax evasion also has distributive impacts that are not neutral; this is taken up in Chapter 6. The remainder of this chapter presents an analysis of how the distribution of the tax burden changed between 1960 and 1990.

Did the tax system in Spain become progressive, as a result of democratisation? The short answer is "yes, but…". The reform undoubtedly transformed Spanish taxation, and followed progressive principles to some extent. It was even written in the Spanish Constitution that "*All will contribute to sustaining public expenditure in accordance with their economic capacity through a fair tax system inspired by the principles of equality and progressivity that in no case will be confiscatory*" (article 31: author's translation). But the effective realisation of these principles proved challenging, and the precise definitions of a "fair tax system" and of what "confiscatory" meant were up for discussion. As we saw Chapter 4, several factors constrained the levels of redistribution. Compromise in Parliament often meant a moderation of proposals before they were passed into law. Resistance to informing the tax administration about capital income meant that this went undertaxed for years, and international openness increased the leverage of capital owners. Furthermore, the persistence of objective methods of assessment was an obstacle to the effective taxation of self-employment and real estate (more on this in Chapter 6).

As a result, convergence with the European core was incomplete in, for example, the revenue levels attained by the personal income tax—the only tax that could have a visible equalising effect on income distribution. Furthermore, and even if all relevant political actors seemed aware that social security contributions were highly regressive, their design did not change much during these years. Finally, the level of tax revenues obviously constrained the level of spending, and thus the redistribution attainable in the form of expenditure. All things considered, it seems that the tax system underwent a transition from a regressive to a somewhat proportional system, and that total redistribution levels (i.e. including the effect of spending) continued to lag behind those of the looked-up-to European neighbours.

5.1 How to Measure Progressivity

But first it is worth delving into methods. How do we measure progressivity? Even if it is a simple concept, it is not so simple to quantify. Some of the issues to consider have no easy answer. Because of this, still today people at different institutions measure progressivity in different ways, which renders comparisons difficult.

Attempts to answer the question "Who pays the taxes?" with any real precision were not possible before the existence of detailed tax and income distribution statistics. The administration of early income taxes provided some of this data, but were limited in scope to the most affluent layers of the population. Information about income across all levels, as well as expenditure (required to evaluate the impact of indirect taxes), only came about with the elaboration of general household budget surveys. These first appeared in the early twentieth century in several rich countries, gradually improving in their representativeness over the following decades. The National Accounts also date from the middle of the past century.

Therefore, early path-breaking studies on tax incidence appeared in this period, notably in the United Kingdom (Barna, 1945; Cartter, 1955; Central Statistical Office, 1962; Nicholson, 1965) and the United States (Colm & Tarasov, 1940; Musgrave et al., 1951, 1974; Pechman & Okner, 1974). The first estimations for these two countries referred to the late thirties: they combined tax revenue statistics with household income distributions, both in a grouped form, to impute tax payments and produce a profile of tax rates over income distribution. Later estimates have made use of individual microdata as this became available.

Interestingly, both in the United Kingdom and the United States, this long tradition of studies has given rise to the production of annual estimates by public bodies: the Office for National Statistics in the former case (since the early sixties) and the Congressional Budget Office in the latter (since 1979—though other agencies and think-tanks also carry out their own estimations).

The basics of this approach are still followed today, in some studies that focus on taxes (Lantz, 2021; Piketty & Saez, 2007), and in others that also encompass public benefits (Barnard et al., 2011; Breceda et al., 2009). Many studies, however, leave aside indirect taxation. This is, one might argue, an important limitation, which stems from the lack of readily comparable information in databases like those of the OECD or the Luxembourg Income Study (Caminada et al., 2017; Whiteford, 2008). Recent work by the World Inequality Database group has attempted to integrate the incidence of taxation into the general framework of the distribution of all national income, in the so-called Distributional National Accounts—a welcome development still unfolding at the time of writing (Piketty et al., 2018). Today, the literature is certainly broad and expanding, but methodological issues remain unresolved.

In Spain, most of the available analyses have focused on specific taxes, and particularly personal income tax (Argimón & Marín, 1989; Onrubia et al., 2007).[2] Several general estimations were conducted in the last years of Franco's dictatorship, in connection with the preparation of reform plans (Instituto de Estudios Fiscales, 1973; Lagares, 1975; Pérez Morales, 1974; Perona, 1972; Valle, 1970, 1974). There is also a study on 1978 (Confederación Española de Cajas de Ahorros, 1978), as well as one for 1990 (Manresa & Calonge, 2001). Finally, a group of scholars supported by the *Fundación de Estudios de Economía Aplicada* (FEDEA) has produced estimates for recent years, which are regularly updated, currently covering the period 2013–2017 (the first report is López Laborda et al., 2016). Regrettably, all these previous estimations are not directly comparable, again due to methodological differences. The present author's work, shown here, provided the first medium/long-term description of the distribution of the tax burden in the country. An earlier version was published in Torregrosa-Hetland (2015c), where the methodology is also more extensively described.

In order to calculate progressivity, one must depart from a distribution of *pre-tax income*, subtract *tax payments*, and obtain a distribution of *post-tax income*. On this basis, it is possible to calculate effective tax rates across the distribution of pre-tax income (tax paid as a percentage of income), as well as indices of progressivity and redistribution that summarise the results. All this is conducted within a yearly benchmark: the analysis will show how taxes affect the distribution of income in different "phases" (defined shortly).[3] So when comparing results across the years, it should be noted that not only did the tax regulations change, but so too did the distributions of income and consumption: the resulting evolution in progressivity will be a joint effect of all these changes.[4]

One of the first problems is that since for most taxes there are no available statistics relating individuals to payments, it is necessary to *impute* them. The economic literature has established that very often the burden of a tax (i.e. the reduction in the economic capacity associated with it) is not borne by the subject legally obliged to pay it. Some taxes are *shifted*: for example, an increase in the tax on petrol would likely lead to an increase in the prices of petrol, so the tax would be borne by consumers (including consumers of goods or services that use petrol as an input). This process of tax shifting might take some time, and generate a whole sequence of economic effects. To what extent different taxes are shifted is the object of the field of tax incidence, which is very well covered in the (now somewhat dated) survey of Fullerton and Metcalf (2002). Regrettably, the matter is not completely clarified for all possible taxes. The most accepted incidence assumptions (see Table 5.1) are followed here, but in the author's earlier work certain alternatives were also used (Torregrosa-Hetland, 2015c).

The estimation of tax payments entails allocating the revenue of each tax using the distribution of the corresponding tax base across households. This means that the procedure relies on the implicit assumption that fraud is uniformly distributed (not that it is non-existent, since real tax revenue, which is affected by fraud, is started with). This has been a necessary simplification which may lead to an overestimation of progressivity, since available evidence points towards tax evasion being concentrated among high incomes (Comín et al., 1995; Torregrosa-Hetland, 2015b, 2020).

Table 5.1 Tax incidence assumptions

Taxes on...	Incidence on...
Income	Income (no shifting)
Wealth	Wealth (no shifting)
Real estate	Occupier
Social contributions	Worker
Corporate profits	34% capital, 33% labour, 33% consumption
Consumption	Consumer
Stamp duties	Purchaser

Source Compiled by author

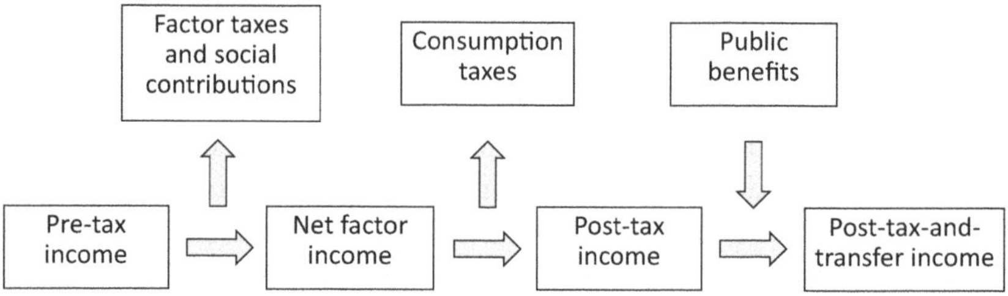

Fig. 5.1 Taxes and phases of income (*Source* Compiled by author)

Figure 5.1 illustrates the procedure. We begin with *pre-tax income*, which corresponds to the sum of income obtained in the market: wages and salaries, revenues from investment, business profits, etc. It also includes some forms of non-monetary income, such as estimates of self-production and rents from owner-occupied housing. Pre-tax income is an important concept, in that it is used here as a reference to the economic capacity of households (it will be the denominator for the tax rates, and also used to rank households).

Factor taxes are those falling on the households' production factors (e.g. wages or capital income), while consumption taxes are paid in the process of acquiring goods or services. This distinction is close to the legal definition of direct and indirect taxes, but does not match it exactly, since consumption taxes include the share of direct taxes of businesses that are shifted onto prices. Finally, post-tax income is a statistical construction, not directly perceived by the households, but necessary for establishing the distributive effects of the tax system. After adding public benefits as well, post-tax-and-transfer income is arrived at. This will reflect the net (monetary) consumption capacity of households, even if it lacks the imputation of non-monetary benefits received through public action, such as education or health, which are outside the scope of this work.

An alternative approach to tax incidence analysis, which has been used by several institutions (for example, the OECD and the Commitment to Equity Institute), is shown in Fig. 5.2. It differs from the present approach in that it imputes some public benefits (notably those with an insurance component: pensions and unemployment benefits) *before* it subtracts taxes, and thus uses different concepts of income. Here, gross income is used as a reference for ranking households. Disposable income is arrived at after subtracting factor taxes but before subtracting consumption taxes. The concept of final income is the same, but the calculated distributive incidence of the system will be different because of the reference income used. Generally, it is expected that inequality of gross income will be lower than that of pre-tax income as defined above.

The decision between these two options is not a simple one, and so some results are presented from both, even though the first is prioritised. The rationale for including public benefits in the reference income is that a substantial part thereof corresponds to capitalisation in pensions of previous labour income, and that those who receive pensions see themselves at similar levels as those with market income of the same magnitude. However, distinguishing what is capitalisation and what is redistribution in pensions is a complex task. Pensions in Spain during the nineties have been shown to be far from actuarially "fair" and highly redistributive (Bandrés & Cuenca, 1996). This is also more consistent, it

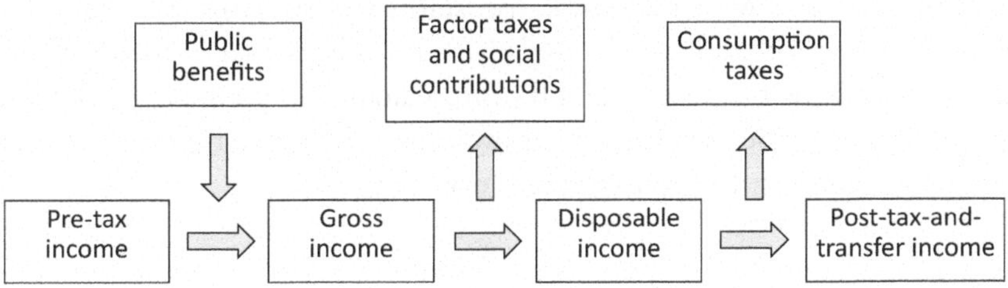

Fig. 5.2 Alternative approach to taxes and phases of income (*Source* Compiled by author)

can be argued, with the fact that public benefits (a) are paid by taxes, and (b) are subject to changes in the political process, so they do not accrue to households in the same way as market income. But there is room for discussion.[5]

Now, a word about the sources. Revenue data corresponding to all levels of public administration is used: central government, social security, and sub-central governments, on an accrual basis. Non-tax public revenue is not included. At the beginning of the period, when there were more taxes and statistics were of a lower quality, a full disaggregation of tax revenue in its components has not been possible, especially for local taxes. All in all, the study covers over 90% of tax revenue in each year. Income tax microdata for 1982 and 1990 from the *Instituto de Estudios Fiscales* is also used, as are additional tax statistics.

For the distribution of income of different kinds, as well as consumption, the Household Budget Surveys (HBSs) for 1973–1974, 1980–1981 and 1990–1991 are employed. In an earlier study by the author, these were adjusted for under-reporting using the corresponding concepts in the National Accounts (Torregrosa-Hetland, 2016). This was necessary because household surveys tend to underestimate income, especially that of self-employment and capital, potentially leading to an underestimation of inequality. For example, in 1973 capital income reported in the survey was 23% of that in the National Accounts, a share that had not increased by 1990 (when it lay at 15%). This contrasts with much better reporting of labour, at 75 and 89% in both years, respectively.

Upon completion of the imputation of taxes, one of the clearer ways to assess whether a system is progressive is to look at the tax rates across the income distribution. Do higher-income individuals pay higher tax rates? For this purpose, we should not use statutory marginal tax rates, but *effective* tax rates, which are defined as tax payments over pre-tax income. A*verage* effective tax rates (AETRs) are calculated for given groups in the income distribution (mostly shown here, in percentiles). These are obtained according to the following formula:

$$AETR = \frac{\sum_{h=1}^{n} (T_h / Y_h) W_h}{\sum_{h=1}^{n} W_h}, \ h = 1 \ldots n,$$

where T_h is total tax payments by household h, Y_h its total pre-tax income, W_h its weight in the calculation (product of sampling weight and the household's real size), and n is the total number of households in the group. If the profile of AETRs is increasing in income, the tax (or the tax system) is progressive (Musgrave & Thin, 1948).

Effective tax rates are most illustrative, but they can show a tax, or a tax system, to be progressive or regressive at different parts of the distribution. In addition, the visual inspection of tax rates might not be enough to determine whether their progressivity increased or decreased between two given years. If one wishes to compare taxes or systems using a single number, the Kakwani index (Kakwani, 1977) can be used, defined as follows:

$$K = C_T - G_T,$$

which is the difference between the concentration of tax payments over income (C_T) and the Gini index of pre-tax income (G_T). The Kakwani index takes the value of 0 for a proportional tax, becomes positive for a progressive tax, and negative in the case of regressivity.

Finally, progressivity will cause redistribution, that is, a reduction in inequality (Chapter 1). Redistribution is measured with the Reynolds-Smolensky index (Reynolds & Smolensky, 1977):

$$RS = G_Y - G_{Y-T},$$

G_Y being the Gini index for Pre-Tax income and G_{Y-T} the corresponding Gini for post-tax income. A tax is redistributive if $RS > 0$. This change in inequality can be decomposed as follows:

$$G_Y - G_{Y-T} = (G_Y - C_{Y-T}) - (G_{Y-T} - C_{Y-T}) = VE - RR,$$

where C_{Y-T} is the concentration of post-tax income with households ranked by pre-tax income. VE captures the vertical effect (redistribution among households with their ranking fixed) and RR is re-ranking (if households get re-ordered, VE overestimates (underestimates) the decline (increase) in inequality caused by taxation).

RS is related to the progressivity index K in the following way:

$$RS = \frac{t}{(1-t)} K - RR$$

This formula illustrates that redistribution (RS) is a combined result of progressivity (K) and the aggregate tax rate (the level effect given by t), as well as possible re-ranking. This relationship is an important one to keep in mind: redistribution and progressivity can move in the same direction (for example, as a result of a tax reform that increases tax rates on high incomes), but they can also move in opposite directions (for example, when rates are increased across the board, leading to lower progressivity but higher redistribution). Similarly, a tax can be very progressive but have very limited effects on the distribution of income, because of t being very small (for example, this is often the case of inheritance taxes).

Households are ranked according to their equivalent pre-tax income (i.e. G_Y always corresponds to this concept, and G_{Y-T} to equivalent pre-tax income minus the tax in question each time). *Equivalising* income before calculating inequality indices follows the standard in the income distribution literature. An equivalence scale is a transformation of household income to obtain an adjusted "per capita" value that takes into account economies of scale within the family (and assumes that all members share their income equally). The classic OECD scale is used, which gives the value of 1 to the first adult, of 0.7 to subsequent adults, and of 0.5 to minors (up to 14 years old). This choice is consistent with the empirical results based on Spanish data (Bosch-Domenech, 1991; Duclos & Mercader-Prats, 1999; Labeaga et al., 2004). Households are then weighted by their real size: this means that the results are given in terms of inequality among individuals, not households, attributing the same importance to all individuals regardless of the family they belong to.

5.2 Who Paid the Taxes?

We are now ready to look into who paid the taxes before, during, and after the tax reform. As a prologue, it should be noted that as a consequence of Navarro Rubio's reforms, regressivity most probably increased during the sixties, likely because of two concurrent changes. On the one hand, the growth of indirect relative to direct taxation: revenue from direct taxes represented 78.5% of that from indirect taxes in 1958, a ratio that fell to 53.5% in 1970. This was probably related to a loss of efficiency in direct taxation, given the generalisation of objective collective assessments, as well as an increase in taxes on international trade due to liberalisation, and growth in luxury tax (probably linked to changes in consumption patterns). Another composition effect arose from the major increase in social contributions, after the reform in 1967. Because these taxes were borne by labour, they had a negative impact on the distribution of net income (despite being the basis for the financing of more generous pensions in the decades to come).

Perona (1972) calculated the distribution of the tax burden in 1965, using the 1964–1965 household survey. In Perona's work, the profile of tax rates was proportionate for most of the distribution, and then regressive at the top. This was the result of the combination of progressive but small direct taxes, regressive indirect taxes, and still small social contributions that had an inverted U shape over the distribution of income. Perona's estimations are not directly comparable with those presented here, because he used "gross income" as a denominator (including transfers), and ranked households by disposable income (as well as other minor differences). However, a comparison of the present estimates for 1970 with those of Perona for 1965, replicating his methodology, shows that the incidence of direct taxes did not change much, while indirect taxes grew over all ranges, and social contributions experienced a very significant increase, affecting the lower income classes in particular (Torregrosa-Hetland, 2015c). Therefore, regressivity in terms of total tax rates was exacerbated.

As a result of the transition to democracy and the tax reform, this evolution changed direction. Average effective tax rates by percentiles are shown in Figs. 5.3, 5.4, and 5.5 for 1970, 1982, and 1990, respectively.[6] The vertical axis is capped in all these figures at 60%. For certain percentiles in the bottom of the distribution, the calculations provide very high effective tax rates, above 100% in some cases. This is because these households barely receive market income, but they pay indirect taxes out of their disposable income, which comes mostly from public benefits. This is one problem circumvented by the alternative framework that places transfers in pre-tax income.

In all years, total tax rates faced by households were higher at the bottom than at the top of the income distribution. This is also the case if we leave aside the very first percentiles, where the above-mentioned "problem" is concentrated. From the second decile upwards, the downward slope is still present right through the period: in 1970 the tax rates fall from 28 to 20%; in 1982, from 44 to 35%; and in 1990, from 70 to 46%. The tax system was regressive: it placed a higher burden on low-income classes. This conclusion is reinforced by a glance at the tail of the distribution: the top 1% paid 16% of their pre-tax income in taxes in

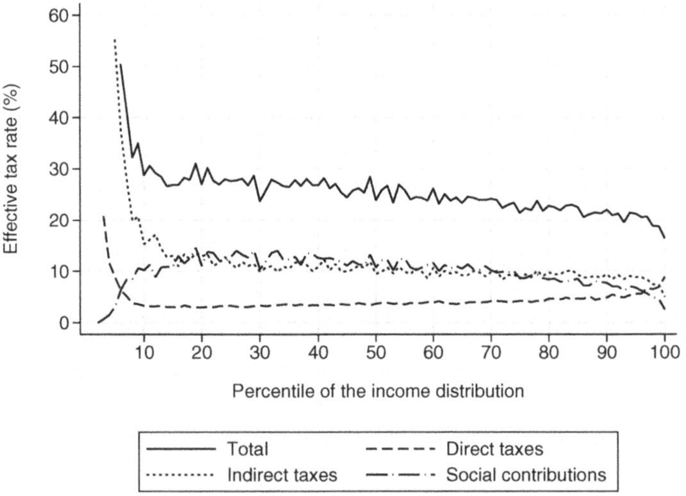

Fig. 5.3 Effective tax rates over income distribution in 1970 (*Source* Author's calculations)

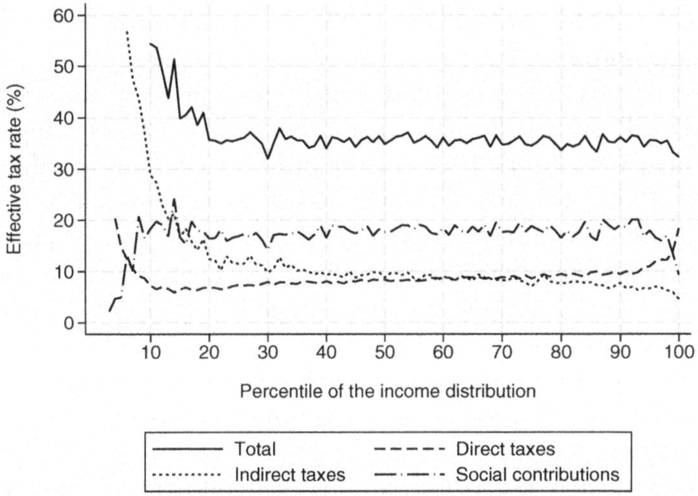

Fig. 5.4 Effective tax rates over income distribution in 1982 (*Source* Author's calculations)

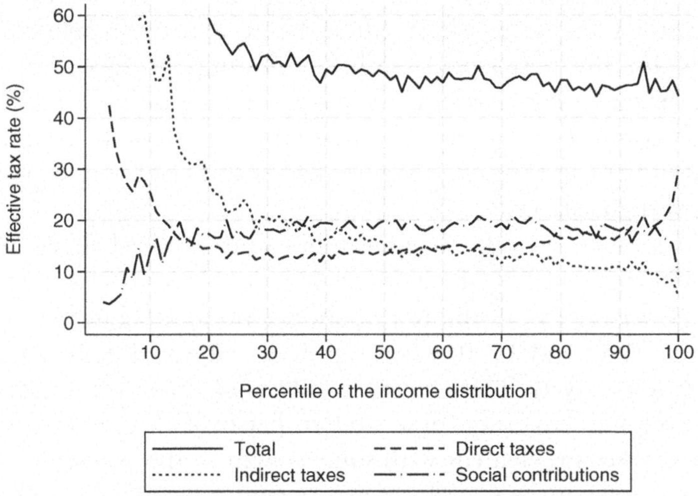

Fig. 5.5 Effective tax rates over income distribution in 1990 (*Source* Author's calculations)

1970, 32% in 1982, and 44% in 1990—i.e. significantly below the rates faced at the bottom.

This result was driven by social contributions and consumption taxes. The latter fell overwhelmingly on the poor, despite mitigating aspects such as luxury tax (until 1986) or the different tax rates in value added tax (since 1986). Initially, the value added tax rates were 6% for foodstuff and other favourably treated goods, 12% for general goods, and 33% for certain sumptuous consumables. The higher rate was abolished in 1992, while the general rate grew progressively up to 21% and the reduced rate was split in two (at present, 4 and 10%). In any case, the regressivity of consumption taxes is a well-established fact internationally, and an unsurprising consequence of consumption being less unequally distributed than income.[7]

With regard to social contributions, their burden was largely determined by the distribution of wages and salaries, but not proportionally. As discussed in previous chapters, the amount to be paid was, up to 1972, assessed upon a legal base set by decree for ten workforce categories, with a regressive effect (these bases were well below salaries, especially for the better-paid workers). During the seventies reforms brought the base progressively closer to real salaries, but never fully. Since 1978, the taxable base has been the salary (but not all of its components), up to an upper cap for each category, which still leaves out a significant portion of high salaries.[8]

Direct taxes, on the other hand, exhibited progressive behaviour.[9] This was already true in 1970, albeit at very low rates (near 6% at the top, but under 4% for almost all the rest of the distribution), but became even more so in 1982 and 1990, when top decile rates had gone up to 12% and 21% respectively. This shows the effects of the reform, particularly the creation and expansion of a modern personal income tax, which is the only progressive element with some weight in the system.[10]

One objective of the tax reform was to converge with more developed Western countries. Was this achieved? Answering this question depends on the availability of comparable historical calculations, which do not abound. Figure 5.6 shows a comparison of Spain with four/two other countries, albeit one restricted to direct taxes and social contributions.[11] Convergence did take place, even if only partially, and was due to changes

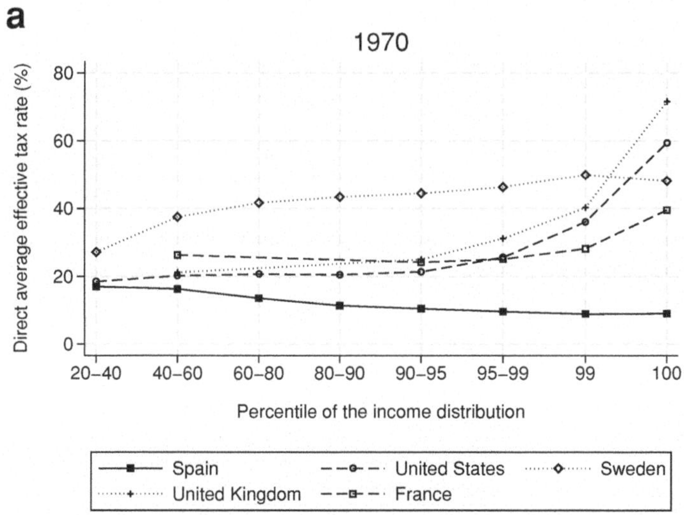

Fig. 5.6 Direct taxes and social contributions in five countries (*Source* For Spain, author's calculations. France, United Kingdom, and United States from Piketty and Saez [2007]. Sweden, from Bengtsson et al. [2016]. *Notes* [1] In the data for France, P40–60 is P0–90. [2] In the data for France, the US, and the UK, the last two values represented are, respectively, those for P99–99.5 and the mean of rates for P99.5–99.9, P99.9–99.99, and P99.99–100. Similarly, for Sweden, the first value is P0–40 and the last two values, P99–99.9 and P99.9–100. This means that the top rates in Spain refer to relatively [slightly] lower percentiles)

from both sides. Spain stood out for its regressivity in 1970 and 1982, but by 1900 looked near-proportional. Meanwhile, both Sweden and the United States had become less progressive. In Spain, higher rates came first to the upper-middle class and later—incompletely—to the top. We can conclude that the evolution towards progressivity, delayed by the dictatorship, did not fully reach the levels seen in these other countries. Spain never got to experience the postwar heyday of progressive taxation.

A recent study for France shows a profile of direct taxation that is very similar to the Spanish one for 1990: starting near 35% at the bottom of the distribution, increasing very smoothly to around 40% in the top percentile, and then with a regressive range at the very top (Bozio et al., 2018).[12] The authors found the total tax system in France to be regressive in 1990 and in the following years, similarly to Spain.

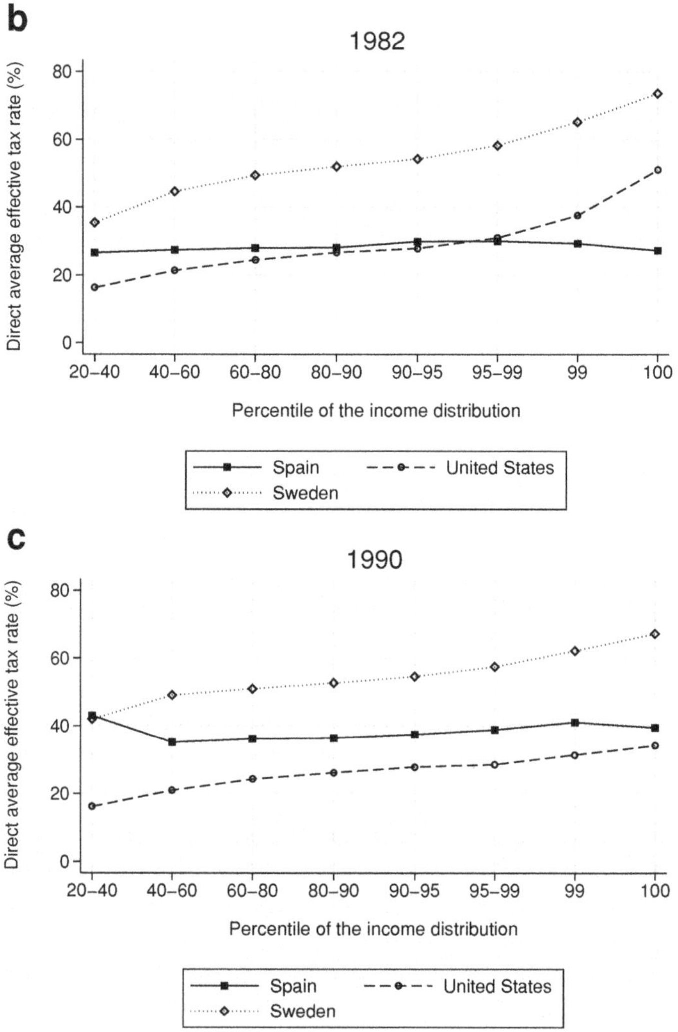

Fig. 5.6 (continued)

Considering the above discussion about the definition of pre-tax income, Fig. 5.7 depicts the total tax rates calculated following the alternative path shown in Fig. 5.2. Here, public benefits (indeed, all transfers) make up part of pre-tax income, used as a denominator for the rates and to rank households.[13] Again, taxation was clearly regressive in 1970, going from nearly 30% at the bottom to 15% at the top. This changed drastically with the reform, giving way to a largely proportional profile in 1982 and 1990, with rates throughout the income distribution of near 30 and 40%, respectively. In both these last years there is a slight positive slope in the curve, but clear regressive effects both at the bottom decile and at the very top. It can be seen that the tax system appears more progressive when public benefits are included in pre-tax income, especially in 1990 (when these benefits were more extensive, given the development of the welfare state!). It could be argued that "reality" lay somewhere between these two estimations, even if the present criterion is to locate it closer to the first than the second. In any case, the system went from being clearly regressive to somewhere between regressive and proportional. It cannot be said to have been progressive as a whole.

The progressivity and redistribution indices in Table 5.2 complement our understanding of the effects of the tax reform. Again, it can be seen that the tax system became less regressive, due to the reform in direct

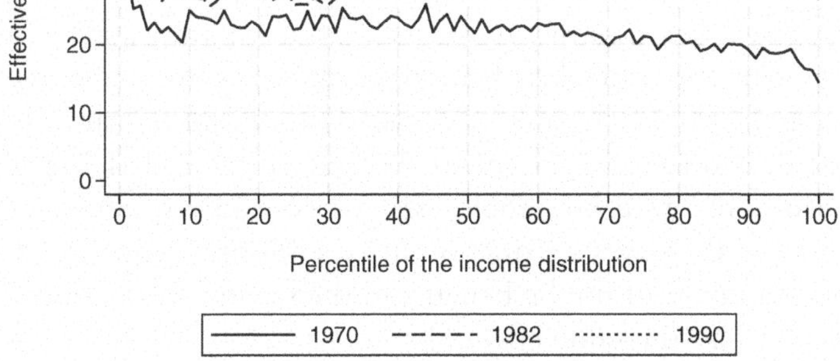

Fig. 5.7 Effective tax rates with benefits as part of pre-tax income, 1970–1990 (*Source* author's calculations. *Note* The vertical axis is also here capped at 60%, which only affects percentile 1 in 1990)

Table 5.2 Progressivity and redistribution indices, 1970–1990

	Direct taxes	Social contributions	Indirect taxes	Total
1970				
Progressivity (Kakwani index)	12.27	−14.79	−12.88	−8.49
Average Effective Tax Rate	4.78	8.88	9.73	23.40
Redistribution (RS index)	0.59	−1.70	−1.63	−3.32
1982				
Progressivity (Kakwani index)	10.40	−3.03	−17.96	−2.74
Average Effective Tax Rate	10.25	16.86	8.53	35.64
Redistribution (RS index)	1.15	−1.10	−1.82	−2.39
1990				
Progressivity (Kakwani index)	7.84	−3.11	−23.55	−4.85
Average Effective Tax Rate	17.57	17.37	13.53	48.46
Redistribution (RS index)	1.47	−1.03	−4.14	−6.67

Source Author's calculations
Notes All indices are multiplied by 100, calculated using pre-tax equivalent income, and weighted by household size. Calculations using 'progres' Stata module by Peichl and Van Kerm (2007)

taxation and the changes in the social security contributory system: the Kakwani index was negative in all years, but became smaller in absolute value. On the other hand, indirect taxes became more regressive, even during the seventies, in the absence of significant reform. This result can be attributed to some extent to changes in the underlying structure of consumption: more households started consuming items subject to luxury tax, and there was a reduction in expenditure inequality (favoured by the development of public benefits in the second sub-period), which, paradoxically, had the same effect.[14]

Aggregate tax rates for each category (total revenue/total pre-tax income) are displayed in the second row to show how direct taxation was powerless to make a positive impact on income distribution, in comparison to the weight of the other components. Social contributions grew a considerably, and consumption taxes were reinforced in 1986: the regressive elements outdid the progressive ones. All in all, this meant that taxation affected an inverse redistribution not only in 1970 but also in 1982 and 1990, during and after the reform. The Reynolds–Smolensky index became larger in absolute value, because of the growth in the tax burden: in 1970 taxation increased the Gini index by around 3.3 points, 2.4 in 1982, and 6.7 in 1990.

These results seem unexpected at first sight. They are at odds with the stated objectives of the reform and the demand for equalisation one would have expected a democratic country to fulfil. There was, in hindsight, no fiscal revolution.

The first stage of the reform, that of direct taxation, was quite successful in expanding redistribution, but faced some significant obstacles. As discussed in Chapter 4, the initial plan did not get fulfilled: it included new inheritance and wealth taxes, a reinforcement of the tax administration for reduction of fraud, and the introduction of value added tax. These further developments were not possible after the breaking of the initial consensus period around 1979, after the Constitution had been passed. The tax reform is connected to the crisis that hit Adolfo Suárez's governing Union of the Democratic Centre (*Unión de Centro Democrático*, UCD), which ultimately led to its division and loss of electoral support.

Internal and external criticism from the right became intense as the tax reform progressed, with increased organisational and lobbying capacity (employers' unions and the growth of the right-wing People's Alliance, *Alianza Popular*). This situation inspired the term "fiscal counter-reform" (Pan-Montojo, 1996). Finally, a second phase of the reform took place after the elections in 1982 brought the social-democratic Spanish Socialist Workers' Party (*Partido Socialista Obrero Español*, PSOE) to the government, where it would remain until 1996. In this regard, Fig. 5.4 represents the first phase of the tax developments; and Fig. 5.5, the results of the first PSOE administrations.

During this period, however, the political and economic context had changed, and support for progressivity was considerably weakened. Significantly, the adjustments made to the income tax schedule during the eighties reduced the number of brackets and cut the top marginal tax rates.[15] This makes it difficult to read changes in tax incidence as a reflection of strongly opposed party positions. Indirect taxation was not only modernised but also reinforced, which especially affected the lower classes at the same time that welfare state transfers and services were expanded. Of relevance to this evolution are the insights of Timmons (2005) about the correspondence between both sides of the budget in a "fiscal contract", as well as Lindert (2004), in that tax progressivity and fiscal redistribution need not go hand in hand. The issue will be explored further in Chapter 8.

To directly assess the effects of taxes (and transfers) on inequality, Table 5.3 displays the Gini index for the previously defined income phases. The difference between the pre-tax and post-tax income Gini indices equals the redistribution index shown above. In 1970, even factor taxes caused inequality to increase (difference between Columns 1 and 2), while in the later years the improvement in the redistributive effect of direct taxation came through. The general impact on post-tax income, nevertheless, was still negative.

Of course, this does not mean that the overall effect of the public sector on the lower classes was extractive. Welfare state development was the other side of the coin to this augmented taxing power. Benefits were extended and public education and health systems were funded, so the expenditure side of the budget allowed for improvements in the income distribution and towards equality of opportunity.

Table 5.3 Taxation and income inequality (Gini index), 1970–1990

Year	Pre-tax income	Net factor income	Post-tax income	Disposable income	Post-tax-and-transfer income
1970	38.04	38.99	41.36	34.66	36.19
1982	42.12	41.51	44.51	32.96	34.49
1990	42.50	40.83	49.17	32.88	37.26

Source Author's calculations
Notes Equivalent income, weighted by household size

5.3 Who Received the Benefits?

Disposable income is normally used to assess the evolution of inequality within a country. This is both because it is readily available from household surveys and because it is the fraction of income that households receive and over which they have direct decision power. Looking at these in Table 5.3, it can be seen that inequality decreased only very slightly during the period (contrary to what some previous and contemporaneous literature, such as Alcaide, 2000, had established—this is discussed further in Chapter 7).

Because the Spanish household budget surveys did not distinguish between private transfers and public benefits before 1990, disposable income adds both components to net factor income at the same time. "Total transfers" therefore may include, for example, remittances sent by emigrants. In any case, the effect on inequality of "total transfers" was to reduce it by around 4 Gini points in 1970, 8.5 in 1982, and 8 in 1990 (this is the difference between the "Net factor income" and "Disposable income" columns in Table 5.3).[16]

It has been argued here that inequality in terms of net consumption capacity is shown by post-tax-and-transfer income, the net results of all the flows taken into account. This final income grew more unevenly distributed over the decades studied, but considerably less than market income (the change was 1.1 vs. 4.5 Gini points respectively). The total tax benefit system had an equalising effect, which reached its maximum in the early eighties: the reduction in inequality was, respectively, 1.7, 7.5, and 4.5 Gini points in 1970, 1982, and 1990. This shows how important it is to consider the joint distributive effects of both sides of the budget in order to have the full picture. In 1990, the Spanish welfare state was more developed than in 1982, but the funding of welfare policies still rested on regressive taxation. Therefore, total redistribution was not expanded between these years. Indeed, a very progressive system of benefits might be turned around by a very regressive system of taxation, and vice versa—and in this sense, overlooking indirect taxes in tax incidence analysis should be avoided.

It was shown in Chapter 3 that increases in public benefits, particularly pensions, were a salient demand in the transition years. So too were unemployment benefits, the need for which exploded during the economic crisis of the seventies and early eighties. Welfare state development was an important societal goal, and for many, taxes were a means towards that end.

Public benefits, indeed, increased greatly during these years. Espuelas (2013) has reconstructed the series of Spanish social spending since 1850, incorporating social security, health and education spending. His data shows that spending on old age and disability protection went from representing around 2% of GDP in the mid-sixties to 10–12% of GDP from the mid-eighties. This was the most important component of social spending. Unemployment spending increased too, from very low levels to between 2 and 4% of GDP for most of the eighties and nineties. On the other hand, family benefits were the weakest part, situated below 1% of GDP. The provision of public health and education services was greatly expanded, with spending in these areas going from nearly 2% of GDP in the last years of Francoism to 5–6% and 4–5%, respectively, in the nineties.

Of course, it is not enough to look at sheer size, in terms of percentage of GDP, because needs changed as well. Spending on unemployment benefits increased because so did the number of unemployed people during the long economic crisis, even if the coverage rate decreased from around 70% in 1976 to 40% in 1983–1984, to grow again in the second half of the eighties (Sanz-Lafuente, 2021, with data from Maluquer de Motes & Llonch Casanovas, 2005, and Toharia, 1998). In 1974, the number of unemployed workers in Spain was 405,500, which represented an unemployment rate of 3%; by 1985, this number had gone up to 3 million and equated to 21.5% of the active population (Nicolau, 2005, Table 2.26).[17] Similarly, the share of people over 65 years of age was also on the increase, albeit only gradually (from 10% in 1970 to 14% in 1991) (Nicolau, 2005, Table 2.24). During the industrial crisis, early retirement and disability pensions were widely used as a way of confronting the unemployment problem.

In any case, in the long run benefits not only increased in size, but they also underwent notable expansion in coverage, towards universalisation and more redistribution (Espuelas, 2013). Low and minimum pensions experienced the higher increases, and coverage of the whole population in the public health system was expanded between 1981 and 1986—previously, this had also depended on previous contribution history. In 1990, a law regulating non-contributory benefits was passed, which represents an important milestone in the Spanish welfare state, in terms of the recognition of these as rights of citizenship. The path towards universalisation is, however, still incomplete: contributory benefits are much more important and generous than the non-contributory ones, and dualism is accentuated by the fact that women are over-represented among the recipients of the latter (León, 2002).

In order to look at the joint effects of taxes and public benefits, Fig. 5.8 plots tax-and-transfer rates, which include transfers as a negative tax. These are averaged by deciles in order to make the trends clearer. Here, deciles with positive rates are net contributors: this started at decile 3 in

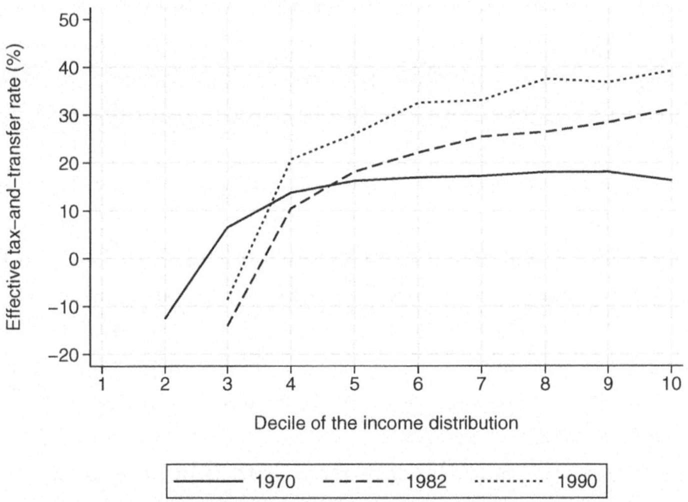

Fig. 5.8 Effective tax-and-transfer rates across the income distribution, 1970–1990 (*Source* Author's calculations. *Notes* Average effective tax-and-transfer rates by deciles. Rates are capped at −20%: for the deciles not shown, transfers make up practically all income. In 1990, a calculation with only public benefits and excluding the rest of transfers is possible, and proves very similar to the total shown. See Torregrosa-Hetland [2015a]. It is possible, however, that private transfers were of more relative importance in earlier years)

1970, and decile 4 in 1982 and 1990. Negative rates mean that, at those levels, people received more money in transfers than they paid in taxes.

Effective tax-and-transfer rates increase with income, meaning that the joint fiscal system did provide redistribution, in each of these years (as shown in Table 5.3). Here too it can be seen that the system in 1970 was clearly less progressive than in later years, since the profile is flatter and crosses the zero line earlier (i.e. households being net contributors back then were poorer than their counterparts in the following decades, both in relative and in absolute terms). Among net-recipient households, the rates were lower in 1982 than in 1990. This is presumably an effect of the increase in tax rates for poorer families that followed the introduction of value added tax, thus reinforcing the convenience of analysing together the distribution of tax payments and what they are financing.[18] At the top, where in 1970 there is a negative-slope stretch, in the following years there is a flat plateau or slightly increasing rates. This was a significant change with respect to the situation during the dictatorship, which is probably due to personal income tax. However, tax-and-transfer progressivity was rather weak beyond the middle of the income scale.

These calculations do not include in-kind benefits (mainly, health and education), which are also usually inequality reducing. Some approaches to the incidence of total social public expenditure can be found in the literature. According to Eduardo Bandrés (1993), in-kind social expenditure would have reduced the Gini index by 3.61 points in 1980, and by 3.99 in 1994 following Calero (2001). These impacts are in any case smaller than those of monetary benefits, which stood between 6 and 15 Gini points in the same studies.[19]

Finally, Spain will again be compared with other countries, this time in terms of total tax-and-transfer redistribution. Figure 5.9 includes the effect of all taxes and transfers/public benefits. Also in this measure, Spain stood clearly behind the United Kingdom and the United States during the whole period 1970–1990, although the gap closed over time.[20] It should be noted that both these countries are usually classified as relatively limited and liberal welfare states, so one should expect higher levels of redistribution in other places in central continental Europe or

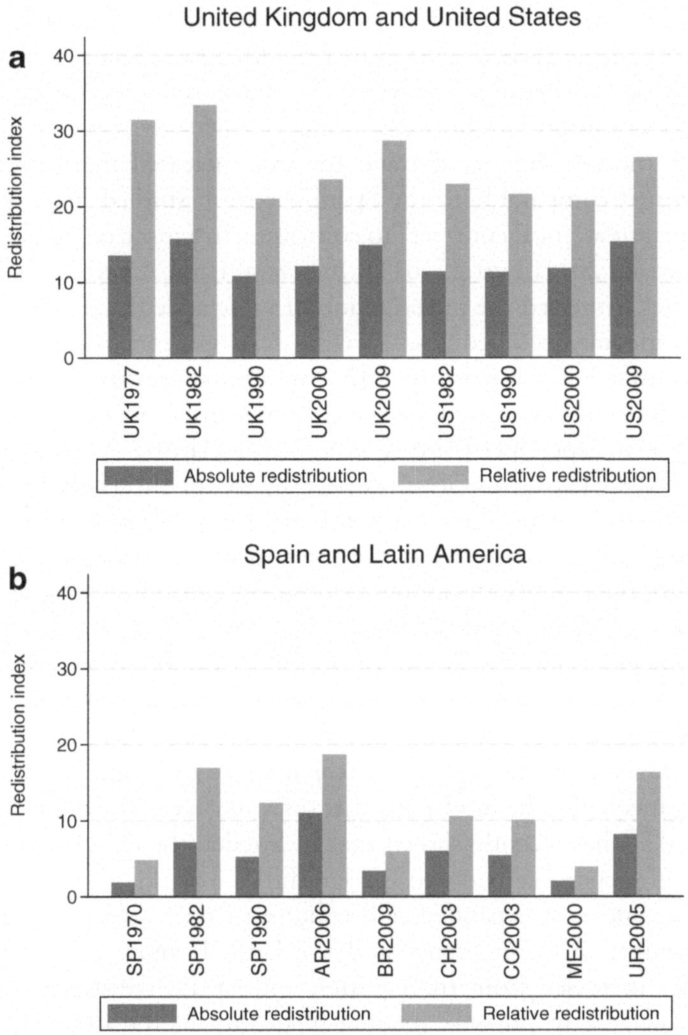

Fig. 5.9 Tax-and-transfer redistribution in several countries (*Sources* For Spain, author's calculations. For Argentina, Cornia et al. [2011]; for Brazil, Lustig [2011]; for Chile, Jorratt [2010]; for Colombia, Barreix et al. [2006]; for Mexico, Goñi et al. [2011], Uruguay, Roca [2010]; United States, Congressional Budget Office [2012]; and United Kingdom, Barnard et al. [2011]. *Notes* SP [Spain], AR [Argentina], BR [Brazil], CH [Chile], CO [Colombia], ME [Mexico], UR [Uruguay], UK [United Kingdom], US [United States of America])

Scandinavia (which was found for 1970 by Hicks & Swank, 1984). Regrettably, no such data is yet available with a historical perspective.[21]

Similarities are stronger between the transitioning Spain and Latin American countries in the early noughties—for example, Chile and Uruguay. Indeed, the recent trend towards increased redistribution in this region is comparable to the Spanish reform studied here, with the search for a new "fiscal contract" to contribute to a more equitable society (Cornia et al., 2011; Lustig, 2011). In several Latin American countries, the eighties witnessed the introduction of value added taxes and the flattening of income tax schedules, as well as developments to strengthen the tax administration, while in the early twenty-first century attempts have been made to increase progressivity: an order of events contrary to that of the Spanish experience (Bird & Zolt, 2014; Martínez-Vázquez, 2007). To what extent Latin American tax reforms will be successful in tackling their high levels of inequality depends on a number of factors, among them their ability to effectively tax top income (Martorano, 2018); in this regard, the region's economies face similar constraints to some of the ones discussed throughout the book.

To conclude: in the Spain of the late twentieth century, fiscal policy impeded the increase in market-given inequality from translating completely into post-tax-and-transfer income. But this was *not* done through taxes, and the process did *not* manage to counteract the trend of rising inequality. In hindsight, this does not seem to be an anomaly. Lantz (2021) has recently shown that in Sweden the tax system became increasingly regressive between the late fifties and the mid-nineties—at the same time as it expanded redistribution from the expenditure side of the budget. Also, in France and the United States, pre-tax income inequality increased from the eighties, and so did redistribution, with a small increase in post-tax income inequality in the former country, but a very significant one in the latter (Bozio et al., 2020).[22] In the United States, however, the tax system itself is progressive, even if less so than in the sixties (Piketty & Saez, 2007; Piketty et al., 2018). The nexus between regressive taxation, inequality, and redistribution deserves further consideration.

Notes

1. *Diario de Sesiones del Congreso de los Diputados*, 25 October 1977, núm. 28, page 1056; author's translation.
2. Other studies have dealt with all of direct contributions (Martínez, 2009), the indirect side of the budget (Argimón et al., 1987; Avellaneda & Sánchez, 2002; Edo Hernández, 1992; Mayo & Salas, 1993), or social contributions (Argimón & González-Páramo, 1987; Castellano, 1977).
3. The annual approach is usual in most of the literature, but there are other options, which tackle related but different questions. Because income levels vary a lot across people's lives, some scholars argued that taking an annual approach would be misleading. The first proposal in this sense was to use "permanent income" as a reference "pre-tax" income, instead of income of the given year; it was obtained with an econometric estimation or proxied by the level of current consumption (Poterba, 1989). Such an approach would be valid in the presence of perfect capital markets; nonetheless, taking this as a baseline assumption seems rather unrealistic. Another approach is to apply a "lifetime" perspective, which means calculating the total amount earned and paid in taxes by individuals through their lives (Davies et al., 1984; Fullerton & Rogers, 1993). The problem in this case is that, given frequent changes in tax policy, if it is done with one year's regulation the exercise only reflects a hypothetical scenario. Thoroughly undertaken, however, a lifetime analysis would allow to disentangle interpersonal from inter-temporal 'life-cycle' redistribution: its results would correspond only to the first one (Bengtsson et al., 2016). In this study, however, we seek to obtain total redistribution, which encompasses not only "from rich to poor" flows, but also "from active to inactive" flows, for example. Income smoothing is, indeed, an important dimension of the welfare state, and as such we want to take it into account. Our results have to be interpreted in this way.
4. Some proposals in the literature have aimed at disentangling both components (Dardanoni & Lambert, 2002; Kasten et al., 1994). The same issue, of course, is present when comparing tax systems in different countries.
5. Particularly, the results of (Bandrés & Cuenca, 1996) for Spain may not hold for other cases, where pension systems might follow capitalization principles to a greater extent.

6. The results presented in this chapter coincide with those in the author's thesis (Torregrosa-Hetland, 2015a), differing only very slightly from the earlier version in Torregrosa-Hetland (2015c).
7. This might be less so in developing countries with high informality, where the poor spend more in informal providers than the rich, as recently pointed out by Bachas et al. (2020).
8. A good description of the Social Security contributory system can be found in Monasterio (1992).
9. The first decile is an exception here, as a result of low pre-tax income combined with the shifting of real estate and corporation taxes on the prices of goods.
10. The income tax, however, was affected during the eighties by significant fiscal drag, which made it less progressive (by bringing up mostly the rates of taxpayers at the bottom), but also more redistributive (because of the increase in the average tax rate). See e.g. Salas (1997).
11. The Spanish data includes the personal income tax (for 1970: taxes on labour and capital income), social contributions, and taxes on corporations, inheritance and wealth. Corporate taxation is not considered in the calculations for France, the United Kingdom, and Sweden. AETRs for Spain shown in the figure are different from my baseline results because, out of coherence, the weighting unit is the household and pre-tax income excludes imputations from owner-occupied housing.
12. We refer to the effective tax rates showed in Fig. 5a. "Taxes paid by factor income percentile, France 1990". This figure uses a similar income concept as a reference, even if it only includes the working population.
13. Another way to circumvent the problem of households with no market income is to restrict the analysis to active households (i.e., those where the "main breadwinner" is active). This I have done as well, even if the resulting graphs are not shown in the book. In this case, both 1970 and 1990 display regressive profiles, and 1982 looks basically proportional; we do not find here tax rates above 60%. In essence, what this procedure implies is to disregard the lower deciles from our baseline representation.
14. The Gini index for total consumption among individuals was 35.1 in 1970 and had gone down to 33.1 by 1982 and 32.1 by 1990. Increasing regressivity in indirect taxation was already observed by Argimón et al. (1987) when comparing their results for 1980 with those for 1965. A similar observation on increasing negative impact of indirect taxation was made for the case of the UK in the eighties and nineties by Glennerster (2006).

15. There were 28 brackets in 1978 (a maximum of 34 in 1982), which were brought down to sixteen in 1988. At the same time, the top marginal tax rate was set at 56%, while it had earlier been set at above 68%.
16. In 1990, public benefits were 89.5% of total transfers received by households according to the HBSs. This percentage was likely lower in earlier years, in which case "redistribution" shown by the Gini indices will be overestimated, with the bias probably decreasing over time.
17. A new maximum was attained in 1994, with 3.9 million unemployed and a 24% unemployment rate. Similar heights have been reached again during the recent Great Recession, peaking at 26% in 2013 (data from INE).
18. In fact, and quite surprisingly, if the mean post-tax-and-transfer real income by deciles between 1982 and 1990 are compared, it can be seen that the poorest households actually *lost* net purchasing power during the decade. This does not seem to be so when looking at disposable income figures, but it becomes apparent once indirect taxation is taken into account.
19. The cited works carry out an imputation of monetary public transfers that goes far beyond the simple exercise performed here.
20. The comparison with the United States is affected by the fact that general sales taxes collected by individual states are not included in the data. Nevertheless, these have relatively low rates, generally well below 10%. It should also be mentioned that in-kind transfers might change the conclusion; see Garfinkel et al. (2006).
21. One might compare the estimations for Spain shown here with those from Caminada et al. (2017), limiting ourselves to redistribution by income taxes, workers' social contributions, and social transfers. For this concept, the average redistribution index (RS) of the fifteen developed countries in Caminada et al. (2017) is 15.2 around 1985 and 17.2 around 1997. The corresponding values in the Spanish data would be 8.9 and 10.6 for 1982 and 1990 respectively (it almost corresponds to the difference in inequality between pre-tax income and disposable income in Table 5.3). Spanish redistribution therefore lied clearly behind.
22. This comparison has to be made with caution, given that Bozio et al. (2020) use a broader concept of pre-tax income than the studies for Spain and Sweden.

References

Alcaide, J. (2000). La renta nacional de España y su distribución. Serie años 1898 a 1998. In J. V. Fuertes (Ed.), *1900–2000. Historia de un esfuerzo colectivo: cómo España superó el pesimismo y la pobreza* (pp. 741–810). Fundación BSCH.

Argimón, I., & González-Páramo, J. M. (1987). *Traslación e incidencia de las cotizaciones sociales por niveles de renta en España, 1980–1984* (Documentos de Trabajo FIES, 1/1987).

Argimón, I., González-Páramo, J. M., & Salas, R. (1987). ¿Quién pagaba los impuestos indirectos en España? Un ejercicio de reparto de la carga impositiva indirecta en 1980. *Hacienda Pública Española, 104*, 99–127.

Argimón, I., & Marín, J. (1989). *La progresividad de la imposición sobre la renta* (Estudios Económicos, 43, Servicio de Estudios del Banco de España).

Avellaneda, P. A., & Sánchez, J. (2002). Incidencia personal de la imposición indirecta: una estimación para España. *Cuadernos de Ciencias Económicas y Empresariales, 43*, 77–122.

Bachas, P., Gadenne, L., & Jensen, A. (2020). *Informality, consumption taxes and redistribution* (No. 9267; Policy Research Working Paper).

Bandrés, E. (1993). La eficacia redistributiva de los gastos sociales. Una aplicación al caso español (1980–1990). In *I Simposio sobre Igualdad y Distribución de la Renta y Riqueza: Vol. VII* (pp. 123–172). Fundación Argentaria.

Bandrés, E, & Cuenca, A. (1996). Análisis y evaluación del contenido redistributivo de las pensiones públicas en España. In *II Simposio sobre Igualdad y Distribución de la Renta y la Riqueza: Vols. VII, Secto*. Fundación Argentaria.

Barna, T. (1945). *Redistribution of income through public finance in 1937*. Oxford University Press.

Barnard, A., Howell, S., & Smith, R. (2011). *The effects of taxes and benefits on household income, 2009/10*.

Barreix, A., Roca, J., & Villela, L. (Eds.). (2006). *La equidad fiscal en los países andinos*. BID-Eurosocial.

Bengtsson, N., Holmlund, B., & Waldenström, D. (2016). Lifetime versus annual tax-and-transfer progressivity: Sweden, 1968–2009. *The Scandinavian Journal of Economics, 118*(4), 619–645.

Bird, R. M., & Zolt, E. M. (2014). Taxation and inequality in the Americas: Changing the fiscal contract? In *Taxation and Development: The Weakest Link?* Edward Elgar Publishing.

Bosch-Domenech, A. (1991). Economies of scale, location, age, and sex discrimination in household demand. *European Economic Review, 35*, 1589–1595.

Bozio, A., Garbinti, B., Goupille-Lebret, J., Guillot, M., & Piketty, T. (2018). *Inequality and redistribution in France, 1990–2018: Evidence from post-tax distributional national accounts (DINA)* (2018/10; WID. World Working Paper Series).

Bozio, A., Garbinti, B., Goupille-Lebret, J., Guillot, M., & Piketty, T. (2020). *Predistribution vs. redistribution: Evidence from France and the U.S* (2020/22; World Inequality Lab—Working Paper).

Breceda, K., Rigolini, J., & Saavedra, J. (2009). Latin America and the social contract: Patterns of social spending and taxation. *Population and Development Review, 35*(4), 721–748.

Calero, J. (2001). *La incidencia distributiva del gasto público social. Análisis general y tratamiento específico de la incidencia distributiva entre grupos sociales y entre grupos de edad* (Papeles de Trabajo, Instituto de Estudios Fiscales, Issue 20/01).

Caminada, K., Wang, J., Goudswaard, K., & Wang, C. (2017). *Income inequality and fiscal redistribution in 47 LIS-countries, 1967–2014* (LIS Working papers 724).

Cartter, A. M. (1955). *The redistribution of income in post war Britain.* Yale University Press.

Castellano, F. (1977). Distribución por niveles de ingreso de la cuota patronal de la Seguridad Social en España. *Investigaciones Económicas, 2*(1), 103–124.

Central Statistical Office. (1962). The incidence of taxes and social service benefits on different groups of households. *Economic Trends, 109*(November), 90–105.

Colm, G., & Tarasov, H. (1940). *Who pays the taxes.*

Comín, F., Pan-Montojo, J., Pro, J., Vallejo, R., & Zafra, J. (1995). *La práctica fiscal en la España contemporánea. Una historia de la Administración tributaria (1800–1990).* Instituto de Estudios Fiscales.

Confederación Española de Cajas de Ahorros. (1978). El sector público de cara a 1978. Los efectos redistributivos del Presupuesto. *Coyuntura Económica, 13*, 33–40.

Congressional Budget Office. (2012). *The distribution of household income and federal taxes, 2008 and 2009* (Issue 4441).

Cornia, G. A., Gómez-Sabaini, J. C., & Martorano, B. (2011). *A new fiscal pact, tax policy changes and income inequality. Latin America during the last decade* (Issue 2011/70).

Dardanoni, V., & Lambert, P. J. (2002). Progressivity comparisons. *Journal of Public Economics, 86*(1), 99–122.

Davies, J., St-Hilaire, F., & Whalley, J. (1984). Some calculations of lifetime tax incidence. *The American Economic Review, 74*(4), 633–649.

Duclos, J.-Y., & Mercader-Prats, M. (1999). Household needs and poverty: With application to Spain and the U.K. *Review of Income and Wealth, 45*(1), 77–98.

Edo Hernández, V. (1992). *Análisis económico de los impuestos sobre consumos específicos*. Universidad Complutense de Madrid.

Espuelas, S. (2013). *La evolución del gasto social público en España, 1850–2005* (Vol. 63). Banco de España.

Fullerton, D., & Rogers, D. L. (1993). *Who bears the lifetime tax burden?* Brookings Institution.

Fullerton, D., & Metcalf, G. E. (2002). Tax incidence. In *Handbooks in economics* (Vol. 4). Elsevier Science, North-Holland.

Garfinkel, I., Rainwater, L., & Smeeding, T. M. (2006). A re-examination of welfare states and inequality in rich nations: How in-kind transfers and indirect taxes change the story. *Journal of Policy Analysis and Management, 25*(4), 897–919.

Glennerster, H. (2006). *Tibor Barna: The redistributive impact of taxes and social policies in the UK: 1937–2005*. CASE LSE STICERD Research Paper No. CASE115, London School of Economics.

Goñi, E., López, H., & Servén, L. (2011). Fiscal Redistribution and Income Inequality in Latin America. *World Development, 39*(9), 1558–1569.

Hicks, A., & Swank, D. H. (1984). Governmental redistribution in rich capitalist democracies. *Policy Studies Journal, 13*(2), 265–286.

Instituto de Estudios Fiscales. (1973). *Informe sobre el sistema tributario español*. IEF.

Jorratt, M. (2010). Equidad Fiscal en Chile: Un Análisis de la Incidencia Distributiva de los Impuestos y el Gasto Social. In *Equidad Fiscal en Brasil, Chile, Paraguay y Uruguay*. BID – Eurosocial.

Kakwani, N. C. (1977). Measurement of tax progressivity: An international comparison. *Economic Journal, 87*(345), 71–80.

Kasten, R., Sammartino, F., & Toder, E. (1994). Trends in federal tax progressivity, 1980–93. In J. Slemrod (Ed.), *Tax progressivity and income inequality* (pp. 9–50). Cambridge University Press.

Labeaga, J. M., Preston, I., & Sanchis-Llopis, J. A. (2004). Demanda y escalas de equivalencia: Evidencia para España. *Cuadernos Económicos Del ICE, 68*, 63–87.

Lagares, M. J. (1975). La distribución de la carga tributaria en España: Algunos datos de interés para la política fiscal. *Hacienda Pública Española, 33*, 141–159.

Lantz, G. (2021). Letting the masses pay for the welfare state: Tax regressivity in postwar Sweden. *European Review of Economic History, 25*(1), 160–179.

León, M. (2002). Towards the individualization of social rights: Hidden familialistic practices in Spanish social policy. *South European Society and Politics, 7*(3), 53–80.

Lindert, P. H. (2004). *Growing public*. Cambridge University Press.

López Laborda, J., Marín, C., & Onrubia, J. (2016). *Observatorio sobre el reparto de los impuestos entre los hogares españoles. Primer informe* (2016/21; Estudios Sobre La Economía Española).

Lustig, N. (2011). *Fiscal policy and income redistribution in Latin America: challenging the conventional wisdom* (Issues 2011–227).

Maluquer de Motes, J., & Llonch Casanovas, M. (2005). Trabajo y Relaciones Laborales. In A. Carreras & X. Tafunell (Eds.), *Estadísticas Históricas de España: Siglos XIX y XX* (2nd ed., pp. 1155–1245). Fundación BBVA.

Manresa, A., & Calonge, S. (2001). La incidencia impositiva y la redistribución de la renta en España: Un análisis empírico. *Papeles De Economía Española, 88*, 216–229.

Martínez-Vázquez, J. (2007). The Spanish tax reform: Overview and lessons. In J. Martínez-Vázquez & J. F. Sanz Sanz (Eds.), *Fiscal reform in Spain: Accomplishments and challenges* (pp. 532–553). Edward Elgar.

Martínez, R. (2009). Sector público y redistribución. *Temas Actuales De Economía, 4*, 411–440.

Martorano, B. (2018). Taxation and inequality in developing countries: Lessons from the recent experience of Latin America. *Journal of International Development, 30*(2), 256–273.

Mayo, R., & Salas, R. (1993). Progresividad del IVA y los impuestos especiales. Incidencia de las pautas de gasto. *I Simposio Sobre Igualdad y Distribución de La Renta y Riqueza*, 25–61.

Monasterio, C. (1992). La financiación de las pensiones públicas en España. In *Los sistemas de Seguridad Social y las nuevas realidades sociales* (pp. 207–233). Ministerio de Trabajo y Seguridad Social.

Musgrave, R. A., Carroll, J. J., Cook, L. D., & Frane, L. (1951). Distribution of tax payments by income groups: A case study for 1948. *National Tax Journal, 4*, 1–53.

Musgrave, R. A., & Thin, T. (1948). Income tax progression, 1929–1948. *The Journal of Political Economy, 56*(6), 498–514.

Musgrave, R. A., Case, K. E., & Leonard, H. (1974). The Distribution of fiscal burdens and benefits. *Public Finance Quarterly, 2*(3), 259–311.
Nicholson, J. L. (1965). *Redistribution of income in the United Kingdom in 1959, 1957 and 1953*. Bowes and Bowes.
Nicolau, R. (2005). Población, salud y actividad. In A. Carreras & X. Tafunell (Eds.), *Estadísticas Históricas de España: Siglo XIX-XX* (pp. 77–154). Fundación BBVA.
Onrubia, J., Rodado, M. C., Díaz, S., & Pérez, C. (2007). Progresividad y redistribución a través del IRPF español: Un análisis de bienestar social para el periodo 1982–1998. *Hacienda Pública Española, 183*, 81–124.
Pan-Montojo, J. L. (1996). Una larga e inconclusa transición: la reforma tributaria, 1977–1986. In J. Tusell & A. Soto (Eds.), *Historia de la transición. 1975–1986* (pp. 264–304). Alianza.
Pechman, J., & Okner, B. (1974). *Who bears the tax burden?* Brookings Institution.
Peichl, A., & van Kerm, P. (2007). *PROGRES: Stata module to measure distributive effects of an income tax.* Statistical Software Components S456867, Boston College Department of Economics.
Pérez Morales, L. C. (1974). Distribución de la carga tributaria por escalones de renta. *Hacienda Pública Española, 26*, 15–24.
Perona, D. (1972). *La distribución de la carga tributaria en España*. Instituto de Estudios Fiscales.
Piketty, T., & Saez, E. (2007). How progressive is the U.S. federal tax system? A historical and international perspective. *Journal of Economic Perspectives, 21*(1), 3–24.
Piketty, T., Saez, E., & Zucman, G. (2018). Distributional national accounts: Methods and estimates for the United States. *Quarterly Journal of Economics, 133*(2), 553–609.
Poterba, J. (1989). Lifetime incidence and the distributional burden of excise taxes. *American Economic Review, 79*(2), 325–330.
Reynolds, M., & Smolensky, E. (1977). *Public expenditure, taxes and the distribution of income: The United States, 1950, 1961, 1970*. Academic Press.
Roca, J. (2010). Equidad Fiscal en Uruguay. Cuánto y cómo modifica el Estado el bienestar de los uruguayos. In *Equidad Fiscal en Brasil, Chile, Paraguay y Uruguay*. BID – Eurosocial.
Salas, R. (1997). Distribución de la renta y redistribución a través del IRPF en España. *Hacienda Pública Española, 140*, 165–174.

Sanz-Lafuente, G. (2021). 'Pacto social' y lucha obrera: trabajadores en Transición. Chapter 3 in J. De la Torre & M. Rubio-Varas (Eds.), *Economía en Transición. Del tardofranquismo a la democracia*. Marcial Pons.

Timmons, J. (2005). The fiscal contract: States, taxes, and public services. *World Politics, 57*, 530–576.

Toharia, L. (1998). El sistema español de protección por desempleo. *Areas: Revista Internacional de Ciencias Sociales, 18*, 43–68.

Torregrosa-Hetland, S. (2015a). *Tax system and redistribution: The Spanish fiscal transition (1960–1990)*. PhD thesis, University of Barcelona.

Torregrosa-Hetland, S. (2015b). *Bypassing progressive taxation: Fraud and base erosion in the Spanish income tax, 1970–2001* (IEB Working Papers, 2015/31).

Torregrosa-Hetland, S. (2015c). Did democracy bring redistribution? Insights from the Spanish tax system (1960–1990). *European Review of Economic History, 3*(19), 294–315.

Torregrosa-Hetland, S. (2016). Sticky income inequality in the Spanish transition (1973–1990). *Revista De Historia Economica—Journal of Iberian and Latin American Economic History, 34*(1), 39–80.

Torregrosa-Hetland, S. (2020). Inequality in tax evasion: The case of the Spanish income tax. *Applied Economic Analysis, 28*(83), 89–109.

Valle, V. (1970). El reparto de la carga tributaria por niveles de renta: Un ejercicio práctico referido a España. *Hacienda Pública Española, 5*, 15–31.

Valle, V. (1974). La distribución de la carga monetaria de los impuestos. Una aplicación de la hipótesis de Pechman-Okner. *Hacienda Pública Española, 26*, 75–80.

Whiteford, P. (2008). How much redistribution do governments achieve? The role of cash transfers and household taxes, growing unequal: income distribution and poverty in OECD countries. In *Growing unequal? Income distribution and poverty in OECD countries* (pp. 97–121). OECD Publishing.

6

Bypassing the Progressive Income Tax

This story about tax reform is to some extent also the story about the introduction of income tax. This is because income tax was a fundamental component of the twentieth century tax toolkit in developed countries: it provided a significant share of revenues, occupied a pivotal place in the debate, and played a central role in redistribution. Income tax has also been considered essential according to "fiscal contract" interpretations of the tax system, since payments of this kind can be more salient to taxpayers, and therefore form the basis for tax citizenship.

The classic income tax of the mid-twentieth century rested on two pillars: generality and the use of a comprehensive income definition. The former meant that the tax would affect all citizens above a given income threshold, without excluding on, for example, occupational grounds. The latter meant that a broad concept of income would be used—the closest possible to the famous (among economists) Haig-Simons definition, which equated total income to consumption plus change in net worth during the year. Both these traits made income tax follow the "ability to pay" principle introduced in Chapter 1. In this way, the income tax of the twentieth century would be fundamentally different from *ancien*

© The Author(s), under exclusive license to Springer Nature Switzerland AG 2021
S. Torregrosa Hetland, *The Spanish Fiscal Transition*, Palgrave Studies in Economic History,
https://doi.org/10.1007/978-3-030-79541-2_6

régime taxation, the realm of privileges, and also from nineteenth century schedular taxes (which targeted each revenue source independently and differently). Income taxes also began to take into account personal and family circumstances, and, soon after, to use progressive scales (see, for example, Scheve & Stasavage, 2016). With these ingredients, they could become an instrument for the effective reduction of economic inequality—which, indeed, they have been argued to be (Onrubia et al., 2007; Roine et al., 2009).

However, in the presence of fraud and base erosion, real-life income taxes might differ considerably from the expectations placed on them. Fraud in a broad sense not only reduces tax revenue, thereby imposing heavier spending constraints on the government; it also represents a net loss for society because of the effort expended on concealment and punishment activities, and affects equity across taxpayers. Because of this, it can also negatively affect the legitimacy of the tax system: who wants to pay their income taxes when others are not doing so?

Tax evasion has received increased public and academic attention in recent years, notably in the work of Gabriel Zucman (2013, 2014). The public finance literature has long discussed the factors affecting fraud—something taken up here, with specific reference to Spain, in the next section. Recently, advances have been made in the quantification of something as inherently elusive as tax evasion. The latest studies make use of detailed microdata, including those from recent tax haven leaks (Alstadsæter et al., 2019; Johannesen, 2014; Johannesen & Zucman, 2014). For countries and periods where this information is not available, other methods have been used, often based on the comparison of reported magnitudes with macroeconomic flows. In the case of Spain, there have been studies on corporation tax (Almunia & Lopez-Rodriguez, 2012; Truyols, 1994), value added tax (de Enterría et al., 1998; Díaz & Romero, 1994), and others. Tax evasion was recognised as one of the main problems in the pre-reform tax system, but also criticised as a fundamental unresolved issue after 1978 (Comín, 2007a; Fuentes Quintana, 1990). Even today, Spain often ranks high in comparative international estimates of tax evasion or of the underground economy.

This chapter reviews existing estimates of (broadly defined) tax evasion in Spanish income tax, and presents some new estimates for the post-reform period. Because evasion was high, persistent, and unequally distributed, it is argued here that Spain barely had a fully operational "classic" income tax in the years after 1978—and therefore missed the chance to deploy this crucial redistributive instrument in the way that more developed Western countries did in the postwar era. Indeed, Spain *bypassed* modern income tax to some extent. By the early twenty-first century, globalisation had facilitated both international tax evasion schemes and the creation of tax privileges for capital. This constrained the full development of "classic" income taxes in latecomer countries—not only Spain but others too, mostly in the Global South. Initiatives to ensure the taxation of income in a globalised world are now emerging, but they have yet to bear fruit.

6.1 The Pillars of Compliance: Coercion, Consent… and Information

Why do people pay taxes? The answer to this question is complex and nuanced, but ultimately hinges on a combination of two poles: coercion and consent. Payment of taxes is, of course, compulsory, so there is some degree of coercion to do so. But coercion is not the whole story: after all, no tax administration in the world can uncover every tax offence, nor enforce every possible punishment. People also pay taxes because they choose to. In other words, they are "willing to pay".

The first economic theory of tax evasion was based on the concept of coercion, considering that individuals paid taxes because they were *deterred* out of evasion by the threat of sanctions (Allingham & Sandmo, 1972). In this model, individuals decide to what extent they will report their income, taking into account the risk of detection if they choose to evade, as well as the penalties that they would face. Their objective is simply to minimize total tax payment (to maximize their own final income). Allingham and Sandmo's study prompted an abundance of explorations of how income level and marginal tax rates would affect evasion. People on higher income might face greater incentives to evade, and the same might be true of those subject to higher tax rates, but the outcomes depend on the attitudes of each individual in face of risk.

In Spain, the deterrence model was applied by Lagares (1974) to show that, given the limited sanctions, meagre probabilities of detection, and rather high interest rates in the economy, the rational choice for a risk-neutral individual would be *not* to declare one's income. This would have remained the optimal strategy in 1986, according to Castillo (1994). The point of these studies was to show that deterrence was very weak under the old Spanish income tax. According to Lagares, the sanctions imposed were usually below 200% of the evaded tax, and would be automatically halved if the taxpayer accepted the assessment. Income could not be investigated after five years.

Certainly, if taxation relies on deterrence, a properly functioning tax inspection system becomes essential. But throughout Spanish history tax inspection had been hampered by an acute lack of material and human resources, and was confronting an activity—fraud—that had long enjoyed a level of social prestige vis-a-vis unfair taxation, or was at least not the object of strong disapproval (as shown in Chapter 3). Historically, inspection had dealt with each tax separately: this might have had some logic within the nineteenth-century system of schedular taxes, but it paved the way for discoordination, and was an obstacle to the joint consideration of income within the modern income taxes on both individuals and corporations.

Once established, however, the corporative structure of inspection was difficult to overcome, as different groups were often protective of their competences (Toboso Sánchez, 2007). Furthermore, during Francoism, some inspectors did not even work in this role full time, but also performed other technical activities for the state. The task of inspectors was not made easy by widespread double-accounting practices, or even absence of accounting books. Finally, the number of inspectors remained essentially unchanged between 1940 and 1972 (or at least increased less than the workload). Inspectors of corporations and income from labour and capital were generally thought to give "*favourable treatment to groups with higher income*" (Toboso Sánchez, 2007, p. 62; author's translation). When it was detected that an inspector had received bribes, they were not expelled or punished, but invited to leave the civil service and move to the private sector—where they would be welcomed.

In September 1977, tax inspection was reorganised in an attempt to better coordinate efforts: administrative division would in future stem from tasks instead of taxes. However, inspection personnel were not sufficiently expanded, with a total number in 1981 still below that of 1972 (Comín, 2007b). According to Comín, inspection and the fight against fraud in general were among the aspects of the tax reform project that were not fully developed. Avoidance also remained possible, by using the fiscal transparency scheme to the taxpayer's benefit, or by planning when to realise capital losses against income from other sources. The plans to develop tax inspection were resumed by Spain's social-democratic governments after 1985, through a vigorous computerisation process and a policy aimed at increasing staff numbers. The latter proved difficult initially, as during the eighties the administration kept losing highly qualified employees to the private sector, where salaries were higher: the 853 inspectors active in 1981 had dwindled to 606 by 1989 (Pan-Montojo, 2007).

We can therefore conclude that coercion, or deterrence, was not a particularly powerful force in the Spanish tax system until at least the eighties. Anecdotal evidence suggests that it was harsher on the poor. But, in fact, people not only pay taxes because they fear an inspector will come knocking at their door: more recent work has paid attention to other possible factors behind compliance, notably tax morale (Luttmer & Singhal, 2014). Tax morale can involve an implicit motivation to pay taxes, to "do the right thing", or it can stem from consent with the tax system and the state more generally. Levi (1988) wrote about "quasi-voluntary compliance" as the basis of the fiscal contract: compliance being decided by the taxpayer, in the presence both of some deterrence and some agreement with the fairness and adequacy of the fiscal exchange. The question of consent has inspired a recent strand of work on fiscal sociology and historical institutionalism (Bergman & Steinmo, 2018; Martin et al., 2009). Besley et al. (2019) have recently combined deterrence and tax morale with the existence of social norms.

The reader has probably noticed that the lines of thought around coercion and consent rest on the implicit assumption that taxpayers decide how much to report. Decisions might be based on whether they think they will be caught if they "misbehave", or on how much they agree that society benefits from everyone paying taxes. But in any case the taxpayer makes a *reporting decision.* In the real world, however, many individuals do not make especially free income-tax reporting decisions, since they receive a pre-filled tax return that shows just how much the tax administration already knows about their income. This knowledge comes from third-party reporting. This may be only reporting, or it may include withholding, but the effect is the same: some income is known by the tax administration beforehand, while other income is not—which ultimately means that some people are able to cheat, and others are not (Kleven et al., 2011). In many contexts, income from labour is better controlled than income from capital.

This distinction is crucial for the remainder of the chapter. Moreover, lack of information goes a long way to explaining the historically high levels of fraud in Spanish personal income taxes. It also made the tax highly unequal: while those who received formal wages were bound to comply due to withholding at the source, when it came to other sources of income the tax administration's ignorance was so notorious that it motivated the establishment of collective presumptive assessment as late as 1957–1964. The government thus recognised that it was unable to monitor taxpayers' income, despite the creation, already in 1940, of a "Registry of Income and Wealth". In accordance with this registry, banks, stock exchange agents, and other actors had to report on their clients' operations and assets; but a lofty title is not usually enough in itself to ensure effectiveness, and third-party information was far from a reality in Francoist Spain. As seen in Chapter 4, resistance was hard when banking secrecy was abolished in 1977.

So how did evasion vary across income levels? Individuals on higher income evaded the most, which partly derives from the incidence of third-party reporting. Other factors might of course contribute to this pattern. In the presence of some fixed costs associated with hiding income, more-affluent individuals are expected to under-report to a greater degree. In addition, tax morale might be higher among the middle class, in terms of demand for public spending (while the rich could sometimes "opt out").

Some previous studies on other countries have attested to this pattern. Johns and Slemrod (2010) used data from a programme of random audits in the United States, which has existed with some form since the eighties, and found that evasion reached its maximum levels among the top percentiles—partially as a result of income composition, but not exclusively. Similar conclusions were obtained by Feldman and Slemrod (2007), who estimated under-reporting using un-audited data (the same method followed below): evasion was found to increase with income levels, for several income sources. Under-reporting rates increasing with income have also been found, for example, in Alm et al. (1991), Benedek and Lelkes (2011), and Leventi et al. (2013).

6.2 The Struggle for Generality in Spanish Income Taxation

The path towards general income taxation in Spain was slow and full of backward steps. Initially, as shown in Chapter 2, generality was not even pursued, which is evident in the high threshold in the original income tax. Only the very rich were expected to pay this tax, as with early income taxes in other Western countries. But there was also, additionally, a persistent lack of compliance. The generalisation process is shown in Table 6.1 based on the number of returns, returns with positive tax due, and the relationship of both with the number of households in the country.[1] Returns are related to households instead of individuals since this was a "family tax", or more accurately a "household head tax", for most of the period. The combined income of spouses was jointly considered, where applicable, until an option for separate taxation was introduced in 1989.

Consistent with income growth and some decreases in the threshold—especially in real terms—filing gradually became more widespread until coverage was practically complete by the late eighties. Several turning points correspond to major reforms of the tax in 1954, 1967, and 1978. The number of actual taxpayers dropped after Navarro Rubio's reform, which came into effect in 1967 (this data was also shown in Fig. 2.3). The tax was then filed to an increasing extent, but less than

Table 6.1 Generality of personal income taxation in Spain (1933–2000)

Period	Returns	Taxpayers	Taxpayers/returns (%)	Households	Returns/household (%)	Taxpayers/household (%)
1933–1954	19	7	55	6.124	0.3	0.1
1955–1967	211	65	31	7.779	2.7	0.8
1968–1979	956	77	7	9.508	9.6	0.8
1980–1990	7.641	6.020	75	11.140	68.2	53.2
1991–1900	13.776	11.286	81	12.310	111.8	91.4

Source Torregrosa-Hetland (2015a)
Notes All data is expressed in thousands and averaged over the periods in the first column. From 1983, the data corresponds only to the autonomous communities under the common fiscal regime (i.e. excluding the Basque Country and Navarra)

10% of taxpayers actually paid something as a result: the remainder had already fulfilled their obligations by way of schedular taxes. This meant, as noted in Chapter 2, that revenue collection through *general* tax was insignificant, so its progressive rates did not apply to most.

Under the modern personal income tax, on the other hand, 80–90% of tax filers had positive tax due, which meant 50–60% of households. During the nineties the tax attained generality, with returns actually outnumbering households (because of separate taxation). Here again, part of the shortfall was due to people falling below the threshold, but also to failure to comply with the system.

The results of tax inspection activity can shed some light on evasion—even if it only shows “the tip of the iceberg”, and its trends do not necessarily coincide with those of actual fraud. Figure 6.1 shows uncovered tax evasion: evaded tax due is shown as a percentage of the total tax

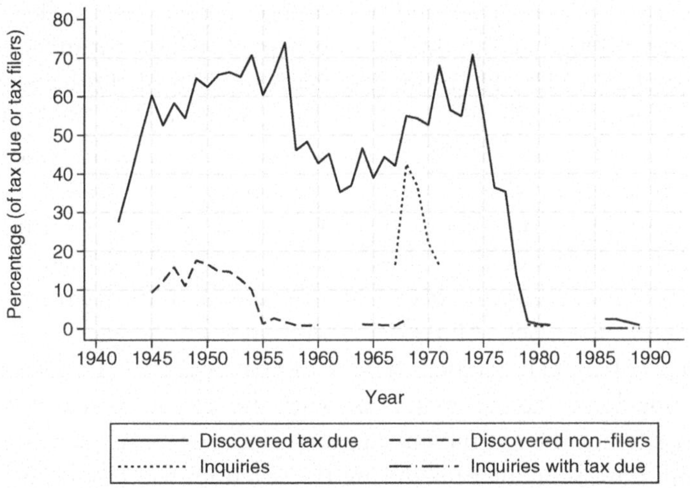

Fig. 6.1 Results of inspection of personal income tax (1942–1990) (*Source* Torregrosa-Hetland [2015a]. *Notes* "Discovered tax due" is that obtained by inspection, and is shown as percentage of each year's total tax due. "Discovered non-filers" are individuals who did not present a return and were caught; they are displayed as a percentage of each year's number of filers. "Inquiries" represents the total number of formal investigations [which refer both to filers and non-filers], while "Inquiries with tax due" is the number of those which resulted in a positive amount to pay for the taxpayer. Inquiries are also shown as a percentage of each year's filers)

due for the corresponding year (which does not imply that all uncovered tax was ultimately paid). The figure fluctuated around a staggering 50% of revenue, showing that there was indeed cause for concern. The relative decrease in the sixties is associated, according to Gota Losada (1970), who collected the early data, with the use of presumptive assessment in several of the income components, which were thus no longer subject to inspection. It should therefore *not* be taken as an indicator of improvement. The same evolution is mirrored in the series of discovered non-filers: in the forties, their number was around 15% that of tax filers, and dropped to below 2% after 1955; this may be related to the re-introduction of some objective criteria for subjection to the tax, such as dwellings, vehicles owned, or number of servants, whose usage had been sidelined following the Civil War.

All indicates that recorded evasion was indeed only the tip of the iceberg. The economist Manuel de Torres (referred to in Chapter 2) wrote in 1954 that only around 500 million pesetas were collected, out of 1500 or 2000 that should have been paid, which meant a compliance rate of 25–33%. He estimated that only 5% of those required to submit returns actually did so (cited in Comín et al., 1995). An estimate by Gota Losada (1970) for 1965 situated filing compliance below 8%. He compared a distribution of taxpayers, which included 146,932 households with income above 100,000 pesetas, with the distribution of household income calculated by Alcaide (1967), where there were 1.7 million households earning over 120,000 pesetas. With regard to underreporting of tax bases, Albi (1975) obtained the staggering figure of 78% for 1971 (which equated to 33% of Spain's GDP). This calculation jointly considered the old income tax with the schedular taxes that made up its base (since the old income tax was a super-tax). As mentioned, the most important schedular tax during the seventies was labour tax, which could be considered the real precedent to the current personal income tax. Fraud here was estimated to be around 56% in 1964–1972 (Santos Peñas, 1975).[2]

With the introduction of modern income tax, a profound change was expected. The 1977 Law of Urgent Fiscal Reform Measures granted an amnesty on both income and corporation taxes. Taxpayers could, during the first half of 1978, correct their tax returns for 1976 (i.e. the last they had filed before the reform) without incurring any sanction whatsoever, while the tax administration would not be able to use that information to investigate earlier years.[3] According to the minister of public finance, the tax amnesty was a success, in that "*more than 70 percent of the corporations and a higher percentage of income-tax payers have regularised their tax situation. This has meant, in terms of this last tax, the doubling in a single year of its usual collection*".[4] Indeed, in 1977 the revenue from income tax had been 12,018 million pesetas and in 1978 it went up to 24,405.

Did this mean that there had been a "fresh start", and that tax morale would guide Spanish taxpayers to comply with their obligations in the future? On one hand, compliance with the new tax was soon higher than with its predecessor: around 59% of obliged households filed a return in 1979, up from 20% two years earlier (according to Alcaide, 1980, 1981). In addition, reported income was 21% that of real estimated household income in 1977, and 61% that of 1979. This data does signal an improvement, but also the continued existence of significant evasion.[5] In a random sample of returns from 1979, 27.5% were found to be fraudulent, with the percentage of tax evaders increasing with income (Fuentes Quintana, 1990).

In Fig. 6.1, it can be seen that both detected tax evaders and their corresponding tax due decreased after 1978. This is the result of the intense growth in both denominators with the introduction of the modern tax. In terms of GDP (Fig. 6.2), evaded tax detected through inspection remained around 0.10%, while tax revenue, as a percentage of GDP, multiplied by a factor of 28 between 1958–1978 and 1979–1990. It has already been mentioned that the number of tax inspectors remained largely stagnant throughout the first decade after the reform. The new tax required more resources for control, which were not found—so the tip of the iceberg remained a tip, probably even a smaller one.

During the eighties, the government appointed expert commissions to estimate evasion of several taxes; the results for the Commission dedicated to income tax are shown in Table 6.2. Compliance was found to be below 70% across all categories, but had increased over the period. Between 52 and 64% of those legally obliged to file actually did so, and

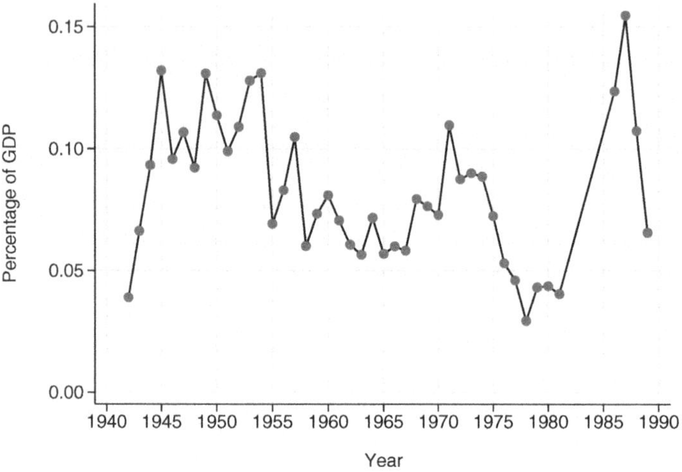

Fig. 6.2 Tax due detected by inspection of personal income tax (1942–1990), as a percentage of GDP (*Sources* Same as Fig. 6.1, with GDP from Prados de la Escosura [2017])

Table 6.2 Compliance with Spanish income tax according to the Commission (1979–1986)

Year	Filing (%)	Tax base reporting		
		Total (%)	Labour (%)	Other (%)
1979	52	43	54	22
1980	57	48	62	24
1981	56	49	63	25
1982	56	50	65	25
1983	59	51	67	23
1984	59	51	67	25
1985	61	52	69	26
1986	64	55	71	3

Source Comisión para el Estudio del Fraude en el IRPF (1988)
Note Excluding the Basque Country—only Álava in 1979–1980, and Navarre

43–55% of total taxable income in the country was reported.[6] Unsurprisingly, labour income was better reported than non-labour income, at 71 and 30%, respectively, in 1986 (a different estimate in fact situates compliance in the case of labour income at 88.4% in 1987 and 93.8% in 1990; Díaz & Fernández, 1993).[7] Similarly, Díaz and Melis (1993) performed a (rough) calculation of evasion in entrepreneurial income in 1989, situating it at around half of the real tax base.[8]

The *Comisión para el Estudio del Fraude en el IRPF* produced results for the period 1979–1986, after which it was wound up. According to its head, M.J. Lagares, "*It was not easy* [...] *to present the results obtained, because these showed a reality far from what had been expected by the Tax Administration, still divorced from the actual magnitudes of our national income, and from what could have pleased politicians*" (Lagares, 1999, p. 606). For more recent years, other studies have found lower rates of evasion. Esteller-Moré (2011) situated compliance in 1993–2000 at 80% in terms of the total tax base. In 2008, according to Domínguez-Barrero et al. (2016), under-reporting of non-wage income stood at 40–55%. However, the distributive implications of evasion have not yet received the attention they deserve.

6.3 Evasion and Inequality After the Tax Reform

This section presents the author's estimates of evasion of Spanish personal income tax after 1979, and discusses their implications for progressivity and redistribution. The estimates of evasion combine two methodologies: an analysis of discrepancy using the National Accounts, and an econometric exercise based on the relationship of reported charitable donations with the composition of income in tax returns. Here, only a brief presentation of the methods is offered; further details can be found in Torregrosa-Hetland (2015b).

We approach fraud in a very broad sense, which combines three distinct components. The first is non-filing: some individuals, legally obliged to pay taxes, fail to do so. This was a problem of considerable magnitude in Spain throughout most of the twentieth century. Second, those who do file a tax return can also escape some of taxation by means of (legal) under-assessment and (illegal) under-reporting. Both are jointly studied here, since the data does not allow them to be disentangled. Of course, only under-reporting is fraud from a legal point of view, but there is an extensive grey area between the two concepts. For our purposes, both under-assessment and under-reporting limit the capacity of income tax to act as a general contribution falling on all income.

In Spain, legal under-assessment arises most notably in self-employment activities under a certain threshold, which can make use of presumptive taxation, and in imputed income of owner-occupied housing, which are included in the tax base as a percentage of the cadastral value of dwellings. Both procedures result in taxable values considerably below real economic values, which has been known for a long time (Durán-Cabré & Esteller-Moré, 2010; Naredo, 1993). Tax privileges for capital income act essentially in the same way. Also, because of the special treatment given to collective investment institutions, which was reinforced in 1985 and 1992 (Carbajo Vasco, 1991), mobile capital income can be shifted into these arrangements, thereby lowering the burden on the "personal income" of recipients. Some other forms of avoidance might also be detected by our econometric estimation, but are less likely to be captured by the discrepancy exercise.

The *discrepancy approach* relies on the comparison of macro-magnitudes derived from tax returns with those from the National Accounts or household surveys. It is a straightforward and quite well-established method for calculating tax evasion in the broadest sense, and has been widely applied, for example, in Italy (Bernardi & Bernasconi, 1997; Fiorio & D'Amuri, 2005; Marino & Zizza, 2012). The idea is that the National Accounts provide the "real" magnitudes, so that the ratio between tax and national accounting data can estimate compliance. Household surveys are used to establish what percentage of the population is above the filing threshold, or to investigate reporting behaviour by income levels. In this literature, responses to household surveys are considered more truthful than tax returns, since the incentive to conceal income for tax reasons is not present in an anonymous interview.

For this exercise, the Spanish National Accounts, the income tax returns microdata (which the *Instituto de Estudios Fiscales* has provided since 1982), and the Household Budget Surveys undertaken by the *Instituto Nacional de Estadistica* (INE) have been used. These were previously adjusted to the National Accounts in Torregrosa-Hetland (2016).[9] What is crucial in this method is to homogenise the categories and population covered in the numerator and the denominator. The same categories of income need to be identifiable, which in this case restricts the analysis to total income, labour income, self-employment income, and capital income.[10] The results presented are for 1982 and 1990, corresponding to the modern income tax, and also for 1971, based on statistics for the old tax.

Figure 6.3 presents the aggregate compliance rates for the four income types considered. A remarkable increase took place in terms of the total tax base, but evasion was still nearly 20% in 1990, after eleven years of existence of the modern tax. There are also persistent differences across sources of income: labour income was the most correctly reported throughout, self-employment compliance started low but underwent a significant improvement, while capital income was always subject to the highest degree of deceitful behaviour. It should be borne in mind that wages were withheld at source, even in 1971 (within the formal economy!): the 17% compliance estimated for that year indicates that many wage-earning taxpayers failed to make a return, and thus escaped

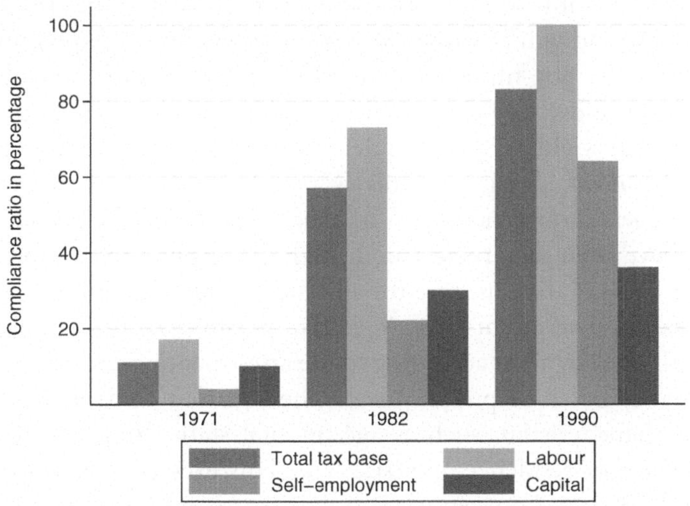

Fig. 6.3 Aggregate discrepancy between tax returns and National Accounts (1971–1990) (*Source* Torregrosa-Hetland [2015a], based on tax statistics, household budget surveys, and the National Accounts. See the source for methodological details)

the progressive tax, but they would probably have paid labour tax anyway.[11]

The second estimation is an *econometric approach* that follows, with some modifications, the method of Feldman and Slemrod (2007), which, in turn, was based on Pissarides and Weber's (1989) insight about relative under-reporting in household surveys: the self-employed were shown to be untruthful reporters of their income, because of their seemingly higher expenditure on food relative to (reliable) wage-earners. In Feldman and Slemrod's method, the truthful category is no longer a type of individual, but an income source (labour), and the expenditure item—which might be related to the level of income but in principle not to its composition—is charitable donations. Charitable donations are deductible in both the United States (deduced from the tax base) and Spain (deduced from the tax due), as well as many other countries, which means that taxpayers report their donations when filing their return (donations are also controlled by third-party reporting).

One might think of many characteristics that determine the income share that an individual wishes to give to others, but it is plausible that this decision is not influenced by whether the income was obtained in wages, business revenues, or interest. This allows estimation of an equation that yields relative under-reporting for all income sources, *relative to labour*. In a way, this is to ask if people with non-wage income appear "too generous to be true". The following six sources of income have been discerned: labour, movable capital, fixed capital, self-employment, negative income (of all kinds), and other income (mostly, capital gains). For recent years, it is also possible to further sub-divide within self-employment according to the assessment procedure employed (accountancy-based or presumptive). The equation controls for a set of personal characteristics, such as age, marital status, number of dependants, region of residence, city size, etc. This exercise is performed for 1982 and 2001; in between, certain data issues preclude successful estimation. The procedure includes a control for sample selection, which was not present in the original Feldman and Slemrod model, because in Spain the share of tax returns with donations is much lower than in the United States: 3% in 1982 and 14% in 2001.[12] Again, all methodological details are covered in Torregrosa-Hetland (2015b) and in Torregrosa-Hetland (2020), where the method is applied to the years 2001–2004.

Table 6.3 shows the results. Estimated compliance rates are nearly 50% for all non-labour income in 1982. By 2001, compliance had improved for almost all categories, approaching 90% in self-employment and 74% in fixed capital—but the reporting of movable capital income remained stagnant.[13] In 2001 (when the number of observations is higher), it has been possible to discern compliance for the bottom 90% of the distribution and the top decile, making use of a dummy variable. This shows that *within* several income types as well, evasion was concentrated at the top.

The results of the discrepancy and the econometric estimation are consistent with each other and allow the story of income tax evasion in late twentieth century Spain to be reconstructed. In 1982, aggregate non-labour income was concealed by around 70% of its true value (see Fig. 6.3)—but almost half of that fraud was due to non-filers. Those who did file declared non-labour revenues of around a half of what they actually earned, on average. While total compliance increased over the years, the aggregate behaviour of filers appears to have been more stable, which points to extension of filing as a significant part of the improvements made during the eighties.

The increase in compliance was most notable in the case of self-employment, while capital income displayed the lowest rates throughout. The favourable evolution in self-employment income is related to the

Table 6.3 Compliance rates by income source, 1982 and 2001 (percentages)

	1982	2001		
	Baseline	Baseline	Bottom90	Top10
Movable capital	56	53	61	47
Fixed capital	52	74	–	51
Self-employment	53	–	–	–
Self-empl. Direct	–	88	–	82
Self-empl. Standard	–	–	–	53
Other incomes	48	–	58	–

Source Author's calculations. Disaggregated results by income level for 2001 come from Torregrosa-Hetland (2020)

introduction of value added tax in 1986 (which encouraged the reporting of activity in order to claim back taxes paid on purchases), and, second, to a reform of the presumptive taxation system in 1991, in response to rampant under-assessment in the original regime.[14] It might also be suggested that a "learning" process took place after the introduction of the modern tax, in the context of the greater legitimacy that the system gained under democracy.

As regards fixed capital income, there were two potentially opposing changes. On the one hand, imputed rent from main residences were no longer subject to tax after a reform in 1998 (this "loophole" would push down estimated compliance). On the other, withholding was introduced for rental income in the same year (but this obligation concerned only tenant institutions and not individuals, given the associated compliance costs), and cadastral values were updated during the nineties.[15]

The persistently low values obtained for movable capital might seem harder to explain, considering the improvements in collaboration by the financial sector. But these improvements were slow to appear. Regulation in 1985 tried to reinforce the reporting of this income, acknowledging that labour had a disproportionate weight in the aggregate tax base until that point, due to unequal compliance. However, the banking sector found ways to avoid fiscal transparency, creating several opaque instruments that had considerable success during the second half of the decade.[16] It is remarkable that the state itself issued one opaque public debt asset, the *pagarés del Tesoro*, which it swapped in 1991 for another kind of anonymous debt (*deuda pública especial*) granting complete impunity.[17] In this way, the government conceded amnesty to black money, in exchange for finance below the market price. The persistence of low compliance rates well after these episodes may point to the role of financial sophistication and avoidance, including international mobility and use of tax havens. Piketty (2003) provides similar insights for the case of France.[18]

The present results for filers in 2001 can be compared with those of Domínguez-Barrero et al. (2016) for 2008, who estimated compliance at 60% for movable capital, 70% for fixed capital, and 65% for self-employment under direct estimation (78% under presumptive assessment). These levels are similar to those obtained for 2001 when the method of Domínguez et al. is replicated, meaning that compliance improved in the last two decades of the twentieth century and then stagnated. Domínguez-Barrero et al. (2017) applied a similar method to the years 2005–2008 and found that compliance decreased for all income sources, except movable capital, in which there was some improvement.

But it has been shown here that evasion was more prevalent in non-labour income, which will probably have an impact on inequality. To assess this, each observation in the tax microdata is imputed to the average behaviour obtained for each source of income. This allows for calculation of "real" income, and for their comparison with reported income, showing again that income concealment was concentrated at the top. Both for 1982 and 2001, compliance is estimated at over 90% for taxpayers in the bottom half of the distribution (above 95% in 2001); at the top decile, on the contrary, it fell to 81% in 1982 and 89% in 2001. Further up, at the top percentile, compliance is estimated at 64 and 80%, respectively.[19]

The three different scenarios shown in Table 6.4 illustrate the impacts of evasion on inequality. The first column, "Original", shows the distributive impacts of the tax as calculated with reported income and actual tax payments (i.e. the original data). In the presence of fraud, these indicators are a miscalculation of real progressivity. The other

Table 6.4 Impact of fraud on tax progressivity and inequality

	1982			2001		
	Original	Corrected	No fraud	Original	Corrected	No fraud
Pre-tax Gini	33.3	35.7	35.7	37.5	39.6	39.6
Post-tax Gini	30.7	34.0	31.8	32.3	35.2	33.7
Average tax rate	11.7	10.1	14.5	15.8	14.8	17.3
Redistribution	2.6	1.7	3.9	5.2	4.4	5.9
Progressivity	20.3	15.8	23.5	28.3	25.9	28.5
Tax rate top 10%	15.9	12.9	19.1	23.8	21.2	25.8
Tax rate top 1%	22.7	14.8	33.5	34.0	27.2	36.7

Source Author's calculations. The data for 2001 corresponds to the disaggregated estimates by income level, published in Torregrosa-Hetland (2020)

columns use "real" income, obtained by factoring up the reported revenues according to the estimated compliance rates. The "Corrected" column represents the actual behaviour of the tax, with "real", factored-up income in combination with actual tax payments (which derive from reported decisions). Furthermore, in a "No fraud" scenario, the distribution of the tax burden and thus the reduction in inequality would have been very different: the full reporting of real income would have given way to alternative simulated (higher) tax payments.

Using the difference between the "Original" and "Corrected" columns, it can be seen that real inequality would be around 10% higher than it appears in the reported data, and a similar bias is found in the average tax rate. The redistribution estimates are the most affected: the tax would reduce inequality by nearly 1 Gini point less each year: 1.7 instead of 2.6 in 1982, and 4.4 instead of 5.2 in 2001 (which, given the stickiness of the Gini index, is quite a difference). This was because of the impact on both the tax rate and on progressivity—a very negative and significant impact that, on the other hand, clearly decreased over these decades.

Without evasion, personal income tax would have behaved in a notably different way. The "No fraud" column shows that, as expected from the progressive rate schedule, the taxation of high income would have been much greater with full compliance. The top 1% of taxpayers paid 14.8% of their income in income tax in 1982, but they should have paid, according to their real income, 33.5%! Similarly, in 2001 they should have paid 36.7% instead of 27.2%, a difference of ten percentage points. Again, the impact of fraud was more intense and more unequalising in the eighties, but still in 2001 redistribution would have been 1.5 Gini points higher if income sheltering were eradicated.[20]

A natural question that arises next is whether Spain was at all peculiar in this respect. Are its evasion rates high in comparison with similar countries? Fig. 6.4 explores this question by showing several estimates of compliance, in relation to the level of GDP per capita corresponding to each one. Some estimates refer to the total tax base (in circles) and others to total tax liability (in diamonds). Under a progressive tax, we would expect the latter to be lower than the former: for example, if 20% of the total tax base is evaded, this could correspond to 25% of potential

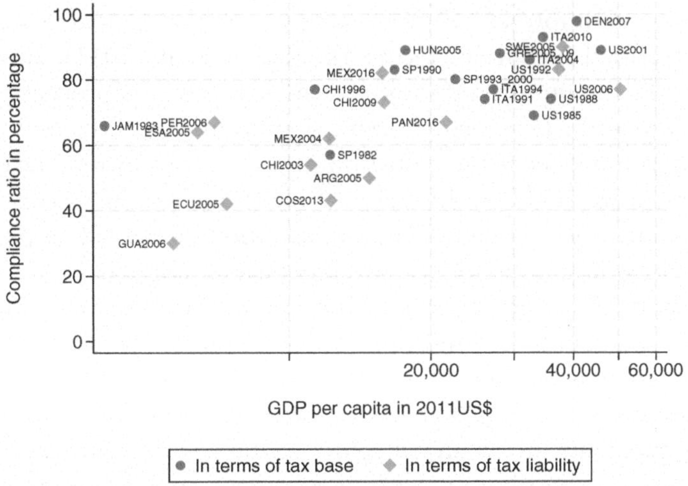

Fig. 6.4 Tax compliance in personal income tax, Spain and other countries (*Sources* For Spain, author's calculations and Esteller-Moré [2011]. Remaining countries from Albarea et al. [2020], Alm et al. [1991], Benedek & Lelkes [2011], Bernardi [1996], Bernardi & Bernasconi [1997], Black et al. [2012], Engel et al. [1999], Gómez-Sabaini & Morán [2020], Internal Revenue Service [1996], Jiménez et al. [2010], Johns & Slemrod [2010], Kleven et al. [2011], Leventi et al. [2013], Marino & Zizza [2012], and Swedish National Tax Agency [2008])

tax payments (because including real income in the tax would probably activate higher tax rates, and also if affluent people evaded the most).

Spain in 1982 was comparable to several Latin American countries in the early noughties. It does exhibit a very low level of compliance, considering that these other estimates refer to tax liability, which may be related to the fact that income tax was a recently introduced tax and was indeed under-performing. Spain in 1990 is close to Mexico in 2016 or, closer to home, Italy in the early nineties. Many estimates for European countries in the literature refer to higher GDP levels, something which clearly affects the comparison since compliance tends to increase with economic development.

Most Western countries with GDP per capita above 2011 US$30,000 display compliance levels of or above 80%. The same countries, however, had compliance rates *for self-employment income* between 60 and 80% in the same studies. These numbers are found not only for Spain, but also for small informal business suppliers in the United States, and for self-reported income in Denmark (Kleven et al., 2011). And more importantly, the numbers do not present any visible improvement with economic growth. This suggests that a significant part of the evolution in aggregate compliance is the reduction in the share of income taxed with presumptive methods or through self-reporting, which usually occurs with economic development. The formalisation of salaried employment and growing firm size favours tax compliance (Kleven et al., 2016). Indeed, both the wage-earner rate and average firm size were comparatively low in Spain in the mid-seventies but increased thereafter, towards convergence with Europe.[21]

To summarise, this chapter has reviewed the slow and twisting path towards generality in Spain's income taxation. The principle that all citizens should contribute according to their economic means was not followed for much of the twentieth century, during which progressive personal taxation only targeted very rich households, and was severely limited by non-filing and under-reporting. The nature of the problem changed with the reform of 1978: the tax was now intended to capture all income and treat it equally, but resistance was hard and the tax administration was weak. Many did not file, and those who did reported income well below their real value on average. This was particularly true of self-employment and capital income, which means that it was high income that mostly escaped the tax.

Given legislative, administrative, and economic developments, compliance improved over the following decades, especially with regard to self-employment income. Better administration and the extension of third-party reporting are probably a large part of the explanation, but they have been partly counteracted by an increase in capital mobility, avoidance schemes, and the development of tax privileges, which can be seen as a "white-collar" substitute for outright evasion. In this sense, Spanish income tax—similarly to others—violates the principles of generality and comprehensiveness, limiting redistribution. This, of course, affects the performance of the whole tax system, and indeed of the tax-and-transfer scheme in general.

Notes

1. Under the old tax regime, returns with no positive tax due correspond to individuals who did not pay any personal income tax in addition to schedular taxation; Column (2) therefore represents more closely the concept of "taxpayer" than Column (1). For the modern tax (after 1979), Column (2) still represents real taxpayers: those with positive tax due, which does not necessarily mean that they made a payment during filing season.
2. This general estimate conceals acute differences between categories of workers: 5.6% for civil servants; industry workers, 28.5%; service workers, 43.1%; and professionals, 71.0%. This relates to our discussion about the different extents to which reporting decisions are voluntary.
3. Tax amnesties are often used in combination with tax reform. This was also the case of Spain in 1991, when 36,257 complementary returns were filed, with corresponding total evaded tax of nearly 20,000 million pesetas (Pérez Pérez, 1992).
4. These words correspond to the debate in the plenary of Congress about corporation tax, on 13 December 1978. *Diario de Sesiones de las Cortes*, Núm. 144, p. 5752.
5. Over 6 million pesetas, the returns/households ratio was below 8% and 19% in 1977 and 1979, respectively. This does not necessarily mean that the wealthiest families did not file a return, but that they probably did not report a significant share of their income. It should also be noted that the comparison is complicated by the differences between the super-tax of 1977 and the modern income tax of 1979: in 1977, many low-income households may have paid their share through schedular taxation and simply not filed a return for income tax—which may not have increased their tax due anyway!
6. Because of their distinct systems of tax administration, the commission could not include Navarra and the Basque country in its study. Using the same methodology, Sasigain (1993) found slightly higher levels of compliance in the Basque country during 1983–89 (60–64% in total).
7. This estimate is based on a different source, the withholding data from firms (*Estadística Anual de Retenedores*). This allows salaries to be disentangled from pensions, and for the scope to be limited probably more accurately to those obligated to file a return. Díaz and Fernández (1993) attributed the difference in the results precisely to the latter. However, it is

also true that the coverage of the source was 85%, and that the commission study would subsume the effect of non-filing, making the lower results lower expected.

8. If the average wage reported in tax were imputed to taxpayers with this kind of revenue, and the minimum wage were imputed to their relatives working with them, business income would be estimated at more than double the reported magnitudes. The authors state that this approximation "*yields an index of concealment equal to the average index obtained by the Tax Inspection in the sample investigation that served as a base for the establishment of assessments for the reform of presumptive taxation*" (p. 189).
9. Income in the HBSs are always given in net terms, so gross revenues can only be obtained after imputation of the tax paid, which was tackled in Chapter 5. The data does not include Ceuta, Melilla, the Canary Islands, and the regions with charter tax regimes (Basque Country and Navarra).
10. Labour income includes pensions in 1990, but this data is not available in the HBSs for previous years. Pensions are thus added from other sources for the aggregate discrepancy in 1982. Several nonmonetary items are included: imputed income from owner-occupied housing (in capital income), in-kind compensation (in labour income), and self-supply (in self-employment income). Offshore unreported revenues will not show up in this calculation, to the extent that they are not present in the National Accounts either.
11. This is also part of the reason why the estimate shows lower compliance than that performed by Albi (1975) for the same year; he considered income reported for schedular taxes, while the present results only refer to the super-tax.
12. A two-step Heckman estimation is used: first, a Probit model is run to explain the "donating or not" behaviour, and the results are used to include an additional variable in the main equation, which would reduce the selection bias. The "instrument" (the variable used in the Probit estimation, but not in the main equation) is a wealth dummy, indicating whether there are capital gains in the return, i.e., intended to capture status. In 1982, regional dummies have also been excluded from the second equation, to attain higher precision in the estimates and since they were not significant.
13. The behaviour of the self-employed in 2001 under presumptive taxation (including agrarian activities) cannot be statistically distinguished from total compliance. This may be surprising for readers familiar with the Spanish context, but it may be derived from the relatively low number of observations for these categories.

14. In the 1978 law, the method for presumptive taxation was the *estimación objetiva singular*, based on turnover. The 1991 reform introduced the *estimación por signos, índices y módulos*, which uses parameters such as the number of employees or the situation or size of the business premises. This system seems to have improved the reporting of entrepreneurial income, but is still fiercely criticised. Presumptive taxation was applied to 8% of the taxpayers in 1982, 14% in 1990, and 11% in 2001–2028, 74, and 52%, respectively, of those with some business income reported (calculations based on the tax microdata).
15. This update operation was highly controversial and triggered considerable opposition (these values are also the basis for other housing taxes, fundamentally a local real estate tax). It came to be known as "*catastrazo*", which carried an implication of an authoritarian policy, treating taxpayers unfairly. See the parallels with the reforms of property taxation in the United States (Martin, 2008).
16. Notably, the "*primas únicas*" and "*cesiones de crédito*." See Castillo (1994) and Esteve (1990).
17. The identity of the holders would only be known to the government at the time of expiration, in 1997, when the tax crime could no longer be prosecuted. On these events, see López-Laborda and Rodrigo Sauco (2003).
18. He reports a falling ratio of dividends in tax returns to those in the National Accounts over the period 1927–1995, and relates it to the development of funded pension plans and retirement saving accounts.
19. Using the results from the discrepancy analysis, similarly decreasing compliance rates would be obtained along the income distribution for 1990 and 1982, but those for 1982 are generally at lower levels. Since this exercise is probably less reliable, it is not reported here; it can be found in Torregrosa-Hetland (2015b).
20. Of course, such a result is highly implausible. The exercise serves as an indication of the extent of the distortion, and not as a credible policy objective. Furthermore, the government surely took into account the existence of fraud when designing tax schedules. The estimated tax gap in terms of tax liability is between 1 and 2% of GDP—and it is a lower-bound, since regions with particular fiscal regimes are not included. This is close to the difference in income tax revenue between Spain and other Western European countries (see Chapter 7).

21. The share of employed workers in the overall workforce, according to the OECD database, was around 75% in Spain in the mid-seventies and grew to nearly 85% thirty years later (in wealthier economies it was around 90%). At the same time, small and medium-sized firms decreased considerably as a share of total employment (from 92% in 1986 to 79% in 1998, which is still a high value in comparative terms; data from Tafunell, 2005, p. 721).

References

Albarea, A., Bernasconi, M., Marenzi, A., & Rizzi, D. (2020). Income underreporting and tax evasion in Italy: Estimates and distributional effects. *Review of Income and Wealth, 66*(4), 904–930.

Albi, E. (1975). *Impuesto sobre la renta y equidad: el caso español*. Instituto de Estudios Fiscales.

Alcaide, A. (1980). Análisis estadístico del Impuesto General sobre la Renta de las Personas Físicas en España. *Hacienda Pública Española, 64*, 17–72.

Alcaide, A. (1981). Análisis del IRPF en 1979. Distribución de contribuyentes por niveles de renta y regiones geográficas. *Hacienda Pública Española, 72*, 215–241.

Alcaide, J. (1967). La renta nacional en España y su distribución. *Revista Sindical de Estadística, 86*.

Allingham, M. G., & Sandmo, A. (1972). Income tax evasion: A theoretical analysis. *Journal of Public Economics, 1*, 323–338.

Alm, J., Bahl, R., & Murray, M. N. (1991). Tax base erosion in developing countries. *Economic Development and Cultural Change, 39*(4), 849–872.

Almunia, M., & Lopez-Rodriguez, D. (2012). *The efficiency costs of tax enforcement: Evidence from a panel of Spanish firms* (Issue 44153).

Alstadsæter, A., Johannesen, N., & Zucman, G. (2019). Tax evasion and inequality. *American Economic Review, 109*(6), 2073–2103.

Benedek, D., & Lelkes, O. (2011). The distributional implications of income under-reporting in Hungary. *Fiscal Studies, 32*(4), 539–560.

Bergman, M., & Steinmo, S. H. (2018). Taxation and consent. In S. H. Steinmo (Ed.), *The leap of faith: The fiscal foundations of successful government in Europe and America* (Vol. 1). Oxford University Press.

Bernardi, L. (1996). L'Irpef: Un'introduzione al dibattito. In A. Fossati & S. Giannini (Eds.), *I nuovi sistemi tributari* (pp. 17–48). Angeli.

Bernardi, L., & Bernasconi, M. (1997). L'evasione fiscale in Italia: Evidenze empiriche. *Il Fisco, 38*, 19–36.

Besley, T., Jensen, A., & Persson, T. (2019). *Norms, enforcement, and tax evasion* (No. 25575; NBER Working Paper Series).

Black, T., Bloomquist, K., Emblom, E., Johns, A., Plumley, A., & Stuk, E. (2012). *Federal tax compliance research: Tax year 2006 tax gap estimation.*

Carbajo Vasco, D. (1991). La nueva fiscalidad de las instituciones de inversión colectiva. *Impuestos, Revista De Doctrina, Legislación y Jurisprudencia, 7*, 193–201.

Castillo, J. M. (1994). *El fraude fiscal en España.* Comares.

Comín, F. (2007a). Reaching a political consensus for tax reform in Spain: The Moncloa Pacts, joining the European Union and the rest of the journey. In J. Martínez Vázquez & J. F. Sanz Sanz (Eds.), *Fiscal reform in Spain. Accomplishments and challenges* (pp. 8–57). Edward Elgar.

Comín, F. (2007b). Reforma tributaria y reforma de la inspección durante la transición a la democracia en España. In J. Pan-Montojo (Ed.), *Los inspectores de Hacienda en España: Una mirada histórica* (pp. 85–124). Centro de Estudios Financieros/APIFE-APIHA.

Comín, F., Pan-Montojo, J., Pro, J., Vallejo, R., & Zafra, J. (1995). *La práctica fiscal en la España contemporánea. Una historia de la Administración tributaria (1800–1990).*

Comisión para el Estudio del Fraude en el IRPF. (1988). *Evaluación final del fraude en el IRPF en los ejercicios 1979 a 1986*. Instituto de Estudios Fiscales.

Gómez de Enterría, P., Melis, F., & Romero, D. (1998). *Evaluación del cumplimiento en el IVA: revisión de las estimaciones años 1990 a 1994.* Papeles de Trabajo, 18. Instituto de Estudios Fiscales.

Díaz, C., & Fernández, R. (1993). El fraude en las rentas del trabajo: Salarios y pensiones. *Cuadernos De Actualidad, 7*, 268–274.

Díaz, C., & Melis, F. (1993). La distribución sectorial y personal de la renta de las empresas personales. *I Simposio Sobre Igualdad y Distribución De La Renta y La Riqueza, II*, 171–198.

Díaz, C., & Romero, D. (1994). *Evolución del fraude sobre el valor añadido. Serie 1986–1992* (Issue 4).

Domínguez-Barrero, F., López-Laborda, J., & Rodrigo-Sauco, F. (2016). El hueco que deja el diablo: Una estimación del fraude en el IRPF con microdatos tributarios. *Revista De Economía Aplicada, 23*(68), 81–102.

Domínguez-Barrero, F., López-Laborda, J., & Rodrigo-Sauco, F. (2017). Tax evasion in Spanish Personal Income Tax by income sources, 2005–2008: From the synthetic to the dual tax. *European Journal of Law and Economics, 44*(1), 47–65.

Durán-Cabré, J. M., & Esteller-Moré, A. (2010). Tax data for wealth concentration analysis: An application to Spanish wealth tax. *Review of Income and Wealth, 56*(3), 620–631.

Engel, E., Galetovic, A., & Raddatz, C. (1999). Taxes and income distribution in Chile: Some unpleasant redistributive arithmetic. *Journal of Development Economics, 59*(1), 155–192.

Esteller-Moré, A. (2011). Is the tax administration just a money machine? Empirical evidence on redistributive politics. *Economics of Governance, 12*(3), 275–299.

Esteve, N. (1990). *Análisis del fraude fiscal procedente de las pólizas de seguros de prima única y las cesiones de crédito* (Issue 20).

Feldman, N. E., & Slemrod, J. (2007). Estimating tax noncompliance with evidence from unaudited tax returns. *The Economic Journal, 117*(518), 327–352.

Fiorio, C. V., & D'Amuri, F. (2005). Workers' tax evasion in Italy. *Giornale Degli Economisti, 64*(2–3), 247–270.

Fuentes Quintana, E. (1990). *Las reformas tributarias en España. Teoría, historia y propuestas.* Crítica.

Gómez-Sabaini, J. C., & Morán, D. (2020). *Estrategias para abordar la evasión tributaria en América Latina y el Caribe* (No. 215; Macroeconomía Del Desarrollo).

Gota Losada, A. (1970). La realidad de la imposición personal sobre la renta. *Hacienda Pública Española, 3*, 17–41.

Internal Revenue Service. (1996). *Federal tax compliance research: Individual income tax gap estimates for 1985, 1988, and 1992.*

Jiménez, J. P., Gómez-Sabaini, J. C., & Podestà, A. (2010). *Evasión y equidad en América Latina.*

Johannesen, N. (2014). Tax evasion and Swiss bank deposits. *Journal of Public Economics, 111*, 46–62.

Johannesen, N., & Zucman, G. (2014). The end of bank secrecy? An evaluation of the G20 tax haven crackdown. *American Economic Journal: Economic Policy, 6*(1), 65–91.

Johns, A., & Slemrod, J. (2010). The distribution of income tax noncompliance. *National Tax Journal, 63*, 397–418.

Kleven, H. J., Knudsen, M. B., Kreiner, C. T., Pedersen, S., & Saez, E. (2011). Unwilling or unable to cheat? Evidence from a randomized tax audit experiment in Denmark. *Econometrica, 79*(3), 651–692.

Kleven, H. J., Kreiner, C. T., & Saez, E. (2016). Why can modern governments tax so much? An agency model of firms as fiscal intermediaries. *Economica, 83*(330), 219–246.

Lagares, M. J. (1974). Hacia una teoría de la evasión tributaria. *Hacienda Pública Española, 28*, 37–54.

Lagares, M. J. (1999). La Hacienda Pública en las Facultades de Ciencias Económicas y en la sociedad española durante la segunda mitad del siglo XX. In E. Fuentes Quintana (Ed.), *Economía y economistas españoles* (Vol. 7, pp. 571–617). Galaxia Gutenberg.

Leventi, C., Matsaganis, M., & Flevotomou, M. (2013). *Distributional implications of tax evasion and the crisis in Greece* (No. EM17/13). EUROMOD Working Paper.

Levi, M. (1988). *Of rule and revenue*. University of California Press.

López-Laborda, J., & Rodrigo Sauco, F. (2003). Tax amnesties and income tax compliance: The case of Spain. *Fiscal Studies, 24*(1), 73–96.

Luttmer, E. F. P., & Singhal, M. (2014). Tax morale. *Journal of Economic Perspectives, 28*(4), 149–168.

Marino, M. R., & Zizza, R. (2012). The personal income tax evasion in Italy: An estimate by taxpayer's type. In M. Pickhardt & A. Prinz (Eds.), *Tax evasion and the shadow economy* (pp. 33–60). Edward Elgar.

Martin, I. W. (2008). *The permanent tax revolt: How the property tax transformed American politics*. Cambridge University Press.

Martin, I. W., Mehrotra, A. K., & Prasad, M. (2009). *The new fiscal sociology: Taxation in comparative and historical perspective*. Cambridge University Press.

Naredo, J. M. (1993). Composición y distribución de la riqueza de los hogares españoles. In *I Simposio sobre Igualdad y Distribución de la Renta y la Riqueza* (pp. 7–80). Fundación Argentaria.

Onrubia, J., Rodado, M. C., Díaz, S., & Pérez, C. (2007). Progresividad y redistribución a través del IRPF español: Un análisis de bienestar social para el periodo 1982–1998. *Hacienda Pública Española, 183*, 81–124.

Pan-Montojo, J. (2007). La organización, la formación y las tareas profesionales de los inspectores, 1977–2007. In J. Pan-Montojo (Ed.), *Los inspectores de Hacienda en España: Una mirada histórica2* (pp. 125–150). Centro de Estudios Financieros/APIFE-APIHA.

Pérez Pérez, J. A. (1992). La regularización fiscal y sus implicaciones económicas. *Cuadernos De Actualidad, 4*, 109–117.
Piketty, T. (2003). Income inequality in France, 1901–1998. *Journal of Political Economy, 111*(5), 1004–1042.
Pissarides, C. A., & Weber, G. (1989). An expenditure-based estimate of Britain's Black economy. *Journal of Public Economics, 39*(1), 17–32.
Prados de la Escosura, L. (2017). *Spanish economic growth, 1850–2015*. Springer International Publishing.
Roine, J., Vlachos, J., & Waldenström, D. (2009). The long-run determinants of inequality: What can we learn from top income data? *Journal of Public Economics, 93*(7–8), 974–988.
Santos Peñas, J. (1975). Presión impositiva sobre las rentas de trabajo en España. *Hacienda Pública Española, 37*, 41–60.
Sasigain, F. J. (1993). Aproximación al fraude en el Impuesto sobre la Renta de las Personas Físicas en el País Vasco. *Ekonomiaz: Revista Vasca de Economía, 25*, 251–292.
Scheve, K., & Stasavage, D. (2016). *Taxing the rich: A history of fiscal fairness in the United States and Europe*. Princeton University Press.
Swedish National Tax Agency. (2008). *Tax gap map for Sweden: How was it created and how can it be used?*
Tafunell, X. (2005). Empresa y bolsa. In A. Carreras & X. Tafunell (Eds.), *Estadísticas Históricas de España. Siglos XIX–XX* (2nd ed., pp. 707–833). Fundación BBVA.
Toboso Sánchez, P. (2007). La fragmentación corporativa de la inspección fiscal en el franquismo. In J. Pan-Montojo (Ed.), *Los inspectores de Hacienda en España: Una mirada histórica* (pp. 57–84). Centro de Estudios Financieros/APIFE-APIHA.
Torregrosa-Hetland, S. (2015a). *Tax system and redistribution: The Spanish fiscal transition (1960–1990)*. PhD thesis, University of Barcelona.
Torregrosa-Hetland, S. (2015b). *Bypassing progressive taxation: Fraud and base erosion in the Spanish income tax, 1970–2001* (IEB Working Papers, *2015/31*).
Torregrosa-Hetland, S. (2016). Sticky income inequality in the Spanish transition (1973–1990). *Revista De Historia Economica—Journal of Iberian and Latin American Economic History, 34*(1), 39–80.
Torregrosa-Hetland, S. (2020). Inequality in tax evasion: The case of the Spanish income tax. *Applied Economic Analysis, 28*(83), 89–109.
Truyols, M. A. (1994). El Impuesto sobre Sociedades en términos de Contabilidad Nacional. *Hacienda Pública Española, 130*, 127–150.

Zucman, G. (2013). The missing wealth of nations: Are Europe and the US net debtors or net creditors? *The Quarterly Journal of Economics, 128*(3), 1321–1364.

Zucman, G. (2014). Taxing across borders: Tracking personal wealth and corporate profits. *Journal of Economic Perspectives, 28*(4), 121–148.

7

An Assessment of the Tax Reform

It was noted earlier that the objectives of tax reform were to raise more revenue, in a fairer and more efficient way. The intention was to follow the lead of Western European countries not only to become more modern, but also to better prepare for eventual integration into the European Economic Community and the future common market. Voices calling for decentralisation would soon be heard, and the devolution of competencies during the political transition was associated with the transfer of resources and some power to tax.

This improved tax system should facilitate and be facilitated by increased taxpayer acceptance. At the time of the reform, great importance was placed on the creation of a "new beginning" in relations between tax collector and taxpayers, to mark a departure from the general public rejection of the previous system.

This chapter will attempt an assessment of the tax reforms from the point of view of modernisation and Europeanisation, fiscal decentralisation, and social legitimacy. More space is dedicated to the objective of being "fair" or progressive in Chapters 5 and 6, but the chapter will end

© The Author(s), under exclusive license to Springer Nature Switzerland AG 2021
S. Torregrosa Hetland, *The Spanish Fiscal Transition*, Palgrave Studies in Economic History, https://doi.org/10.1007/978-3-030-79541-2_7

by looking at the evolution of income inequality, which is affected by tax-and-transfer policies along with several other factors.

7.1 Modernisation and Convergence

The Spanish tax system was certainly modernised between 1977 and 1990. During Francoism, a gap had opened and expanded between Spanish and Western European taxation. The structure in Spain had become obsolete. The country lagged behind in terms of total tax revenue over GDP, and also of the proportion raised through general income and consumption taxes, which are undoubtedly the modern components in a contemporary tax system (remember Table 2.2). By 1990, some years after completing the reform, the situation had fundamentally changed. Table 7.1 shows the same indicators as Table 2.2, but for twenty years later. By then, Spain was raising 32% of its GDP in taxes, which denoted a considerable albeit incomplete convergence with other Western European countries. Looking at the composition of revenue, Spanish taxation was quite similar in terms of what was raised by social contributions and value added tax, but was still below in terms of personal income tax (joined in this case by neighbouring France).

In subsequent years, the tax structure has remained remarkably stable. Table 7.1 also shows data for 2018, the latest available in the OECD database at the time of writing (and which excludes the immediate effects of the housing bubble in Spain, the Great Recession, and the recent and ongoing Covid-19 crisis). The average EU-14 country by then raised 39.4% of GDP in taxes, with personal income tax and social contributions accounting for similar proportions (10.5 and 10.6% of GDP, respectively) followed by value added tax (7.5% of GDP). Some differences between the different countries can be seen (for example, the smaller share of social contributions in the United Kingdom, which relates to its "basic–coverage" pension system), but they all largely adhere to a similar model. Spain does conform to this structure in general terms, but still in 2018 there remained a stubborn gap, in relation to the EU-14 average, of five points of GDP in total tax revenue. This need not be a problem if there is nothing fundamentally better about having a

Table 7.1 Selected taxes as a percentage of GDP in Spain and other Western European countries, 1990 and 2018

	Total tax revenue	Personal income tax	General consumption tax	Social security contributions
1990				
Sweden	49.4	19.0	7.3	13.5
United Kingdom	32.9	9.7	5.5	5.6
France	41.2	4.4	7.6	18.1
Germany	34.8	9.6	5.8	13.0
Italy	36.4	9.6	5.3	12.0
Spain	32.2	7.2	5.2	11.4
EU-14	37.1	10.6	6.7	10.2
2018				
Sweden	43.9	12.7	9.3	9.7
United Kingdom	33.5	9.1	7.0	6.4
France	46.1	9.5	7.2	16.1
Germany	38.2	10.4	7.0	14.4
Italy	42.1	10.8	6.2	13.1
Spain	34.4	7.6	6.6	11.6
EU-14	39.4	10.5	7.5	10.6

Sources OECD Statistics, except for Spain 1990, from Torregrosa-Hetland (2015) with GDP from Prados de la Escosura (2017)
Notes Countries in descending order by total tax revenue in 1970. EU-14 includes all countries in EU-15 except for Spain

higher level of tax revenue, but given economic integration, Spanish citizens seem to expect the state to deliver a similar level and quality of public goods and services as their fellow Europeans receive, which poses a conflict with the country's lower tax take.[1]

In terms of the tax structure, the share of social contributions, which was extremely high in Spain at the end of Francoism (remember: half of total tax revenues), has been in retreat, and is now at the same level as in other continental European countries such as Italy and France. Conversely, the share of value added tax has increased, and is also approaching the European norm: it represented 16% of tax revenues in 1990, and 19% in 2018 (the same as the average for the EU-14). The contribution of personal income taxation has stayed remarkably stable: it was 22% in 1990, and remains at the same value almost thirty years later.

This is an anomaly in the European context, shared only with France and a few other countries not shown in the table (like Portugal and Greece). As seen in Chapter 6, part of this gap can be explained by tax evasion (especially since it was concentrated on the high-income individuals), but not all of it.

That taxation in Spain expanded and managed to bring higher revenue streams into the hands of the government is therefore undeniable. But was this increase a *sufficient* increase? A common view among experts was that Spain's performance was "*uneven* [...] *but in the long run a rather successful one*" (Martínez-Vázquez, 2007, p. 535). Indeed, if sufficiency is considered from the point of view of deficit and debt, the initial insufficiencies were not acute in historical terms, and were later remedied. Public budgets were subject to deficits during the first years of democracy, because of the need to catch up and confront serious gaps in infrastructure and social spending, for which, as noted, the demands during the transition rang loud and clear. Not unexpectedly, deficits reached maximums in periods of economic crisis, when unemployment was very high, in the mid-eighties and mid-nineties. But they were not extraordinary if considered alongside previous episodes in Spanish history, particularly 1870 and 1915–1921 (when the country was at war with Cuba and Morocco, respectively); in all these years, the public deficit of the central government lay between 5 and 6% of GDP. A new maximum was reached later, in 2009, of 11.1% of GDP in terms of general government (Comín, 2012).

Public debt lay at very low levels at the end of the dictatorship, given low deficits and the containment of debt through financial repression and inflation.[2] Under democracy, debt initially accumulated, reaching the OECD average in the mid-nineties; it was later reduced, in order to meet the Maastricht criteria for joining the European monetary union. In terms of public debt over GDP, higher levels, well over 100%, had been reached in the late nineteenth century. Importantly, democratic Spain was late to stop using unorthodox methods for public debt financing, including the inflationary tax and financial repression: "*Responsible public debt management was set as a goal by the Spanish government in 1978 but it was not actually implemented until 1987, a year after Spain became a member of the EEC*" (Comín, 2012, p. 383; see as well Cuevas &

Pons, 2021). During the eighties, income from seigniorage and financial repression were estimated by Repullo (1992) as an average of 1.7% of GDP, but fiscal deficits led to money creation for most of the period until 1998, according to Escario et al. (2011).

One might also define *sufficiency*, in this context, as the attainment of a level of public revenues that is adequate to provide a given standard of goods and services. Spain spends less than other European countries, for example, on R&D policies and social assistance. The gap in welfare spending is attributed by some (notably, Navarro, 2006) to the long shadow of the dictatorship. From a different standpoint, Conde-Ruiz et al. (2015) have argued that Spain currently has a structural deficit of around 3% of GDP, which should be fought by increasing revenues. Both these positions qualify the assessment of the tax reform with respect to sufficiency.

Finally, the *flexibility* of the fiscal system is considered here as a sign of modernisation. As discussed in Chapter 2, one of the characteristics of Spanish taxation through the early twentieth century was rigidity. To be even more illustrative, some taxes were said to be petrified: even if economic activity was visibly on the increase, yields stayed stubbornly low. This ought to be remedied by way of a system with progressive elements, direct assessment of the tax bases, and social security spending (particularly on unemployment). Automatic stabilisers such as these would allow not only the long-term growth of revenue in line with the economy, but also the public budget to act counter-cyclically, as expected by Keynesian thought.[3] Furthermore, discretionary fiscal decisions went in the same direction, from being mainly pro-cyclical throughout most of Francoism to counter-cyclical during its final stages and in the first decades of democracy (Battilossi et al., 2013).[4] Several associated innovations as part of the transition tax reform were the improved budgeting techniques, better coordination of investment, models for forecasting tax revenue, and the adoption of programme budgeting.

However, tax administration was signalled by many as one of the deficits of the reform. Without a renewed administration, some aspects of the tax legislation were worth little more than the paper they were written on. This, it has been argued here, was the case of personal income tax, whose high levels of evasion can partly be attributed to lack of adequate flows of automatic information and control. Jorge Onrubia's interpretation is that the reform of the tax administration was known to be important, but left for later, since the fundamental reform of taxes had to be done first: "*the reforms in tax policy jumped ahead of the existing capabilities in tax administration, but with a clear sequence established for the administrative reforms that were to follow*" (Onrubia, 2007, p. 12). This has also been highlighted by Martínez-Vázquez (2007) as one of the things that were actually done right: reform of taxes had to come before the reform of administration, because attempting better enforcement of an unfair and inefficient system would have been counterproductive (even though that was precisely what conservative circles advocated in the mid-seventies!). However, in the plans of Fuentes Quintana, Fernández Ordóñez, and their team, tax administration reform was an important step to be taken, but got delayed much more than initially foreseen due to the resistance and the weakness of divided UCD governments after 1978.

The tax administration was reinforced after 1985, when social-democratic governments enjoyed a strong majority, and after official studies of tax evasion had shown the need for vigorous action. New offices were opened throughout Spain (during Francoism, the structure had been limited basically to one office in each province capital), the structure of administration and inspection was reformed (with specialisation by functions instead of taxes), computerisation was undertaken, and personnel numbers were increased (Castillo, 1994; Onrubia, 2007; Pan-Montojo, 2007). In 1977, the tax administration personnel amounted to around 9000 people, a number that had risen barely to 11,600 in 1982—when the processing of 6.5 million income tax returns with scant technical resources was very labour-intensive! During the next five years, the number almost doubled, reaching 22,500 by 1987 (Onrubia, 2007).

In 1991, an autonomous tax agency was created, the *Agencia Estatal de la Administración Tributaria* (AEAT), tasked with introducing greater efficiency, as well as more flexible operations than those of the public sector overall (particularly, the ability to pay higher wages to inspectors). The AEAT was empowered to act against fraud and reduce administrative costs, including taxpayer assistance (following the model of tax administration as a *service*), which it was hoped would facilitate voluntary compliance. Nonetheless, Onrubia (2007) has shown how, compared with other Western European countries, insufficiencies in terms of personnel, simplicity, and organisation were still significant even into the early twenty-first century. Furthermore, according to the same author, tax decentralisation gave rise to some coordination problems – and it is precisely to the question of tax decentralisation that we now move.

7.2 Fiscal Federalism and Its Discontents

A Spanish tax expert wrote in 2007 that "*the issue of the financing central government versus the regions is today still the centre of political disputes*" (Albi, 2007, p. 65). Indeed, Emilio Albi experienced the whole process, in his own words, as an "active witness". His appreciation of the tensions surrounding fiscal decentralisation was true in 2007, and is still so in 2020. At time of writing, the Spanish press is filled with pages about a recent agreement between the government and a regional party on a degree of regional tax harmonisation.

During the transition to democracy, decentralisation was demanded by a significant section of the Spanish population, and accepted by much of the rest—as mentioned in Chapter 3. However, it proved difficult to settle on the details: whether decentralisation should be administrative or political, up to what level, and for which regions. This was one aspect that generated rather a lot of discussion during constitutional talks (Colomer, 1998). But as early as 1977–1978, early versions of the future regional institutions were created throughout Spain under the name *preautonomías*, and were normally coordinated by the members of parliament corresponding to each region (Aróstegui, 1999).

The Constitution of December 1978 gave Spain the status of "autonomic state", which in essence is quite similar to a federal state, but without actually using that name. Under this system, all regions would have elective executives and parliaments, which are assigned certain competencies in the Constitution as well as in their respective "statutes of autonomy" (*estatutos de autonomía*). These agreements were approved between 1979 and 1983 for the different autonomous communities (except for the cities of Ceuta and Melilla, whose *estatutos* date from 1995). Even if regional identities were stronger in some areas than in others, the decision was made to provide almost all regions with the same kind of basic arrangement—a policy that was famously called "*café para todos*" ("coffee for everyone") by the then minister for the regions, Manuel Clavero. However, greater autonomy was given to the Basque Country and Navarre, which already had some particularities during Francoism (although in the case of the Basque country this was true only of Álava, one of its three provinces). These two communities were given specific "charter systems" (*regímenes forales*), while the rest operate under the "common regime" (*régimen común*).

The process of devolution was gradual, unfolding over a couple of decades, but was quicker in some regions than in others. According to López Laborda and Monasterio (2007), some differences persist, but not many. The central state retains control of foreign relations, financial and banking regulation, general economic planning, and social security, among others. Autonomous communities are responsible for town and country planning, housing, culture, and, importantly, healthcare and education. These are two of the main pillars of the welfare state, and those in which the Spanish system is more "universal" and less "Bismarckian" (Guillén & León, 2011). Health and education are "shared" competencies, in the sense that the central state is responsible for general regulation, establishing a basic level that has to be provided in all communities.

Common regime autonomous communities were first financed with lump-sum grants that were supposed to cover the costs of policies assigned during the year of the devolution, according to the "effective cost method" (López Laborda & Monasterio, 2007). Health expenditure was an exception to this point, as was, in part, education. Later, it was agreed that the level of funding should result from a consideration of variable characteristics that determine the costs of providing the same level of goods and services in every region (population, area, age structure, etc.). The basic provisions were established in the Autonomous Communities Financing Act of 1980 (*Ley Orgánica de Financiación de las Comunidades Autónomas*, LOFCA), which established that the autonomous communities would be given revenues of different types:

not only transfers from the general budget (and, later, the European Union), but also a share of existing central taxes, and the possibility of raising additional taxes of their own (with some limitations).[5] They were also given the authority to collect fees, and resort to public debt (even if this was also limited, especially after the Maastricht Treaty of 1991).[6]

Starting in 1982, the state "ceded" the first taxes to the communities. These taxes were regulated at the central level, but collected by the autonomous communities. This was the case of wealth tax, inheritance tax, capital transfer tax and stamp duties, gaming taxes, vehicles excise, and hydrocarbons and electricity taxes. Later, in 1996, autonomous communities were also given 30% of the revenue of the income tax in their territory, together with some regulatory powers. Their regulatory capacity was increased in 2002, when the communities also started to receive a share of the revenue generated by value added tax and excise duties within their territories (Monasterio, 2002). Regulatory capacity paved the way for differentiation. Because autonomous communities can change their part of the income tax schedule, as well as create additional tax credits and allowances, they can end up collecting more or less than their initial share of the tax raised locally (which was set at 50% in 2009).

The Basque Country and Navarra function under "charter regimes", which represent the continuation of the special arrangements of Álava and Navarra under Francoism (see Chapter 3), and their extension to the other Basque provinces of Guipúzcoa and Vizcaya in the initial years of democracy. The charter regimes entail near total tax autonomy, except for social contributions, import duties (which are now set at European level), value added tax, and excises. The last two are administered by these communities but cannot be reformed, as they are harmonised at the European level.

Both charter communities make annual transfers to the central state, which in principle are supposed to cover the cost of centrally provided services. The calculation of these quotas is revised every five years, with growth determined by that of the equivalent taxes in the common regime. This method means that the charter regions do not participate in regional equalisation schemes—despite being among the richest in the country. At the same time, charter regimes have generally used their regulatory powers to reduce the tax burden, through, for example, more generous allowances and tax credits for corporations, as well as lower tax rates (López Laborda & Monasterio, 2007, p. 443).

The theory of fiscal federalism posits that some decentralisation can be beneficial by allowing public policies to be more responsive to public preferences, which can vary across the territory. It is important, however, to reach an optimal design of where different responsibilities for taxing and spending should lie (Oates, 1999). In practice, fiscal decentralisation in Spain has encountered some problems. The final part of this section briefly discusses three: the disequilibrium between spending and revenue, the "race to the bottom" dynamics, and inequality between territories.

The process of decentralisation in Spain was first one of devolution of competencies, and only later, and incompletely, entailed the capacity for autonomous communities to generate their own public revenues (in common regime autonomous communities). In 2004, regional taxes represented almost 55% of the non-financial revenues of these communities, while grants, including the equalisation scheme, made up the rest (López Laborda & Monasterio, 2007). Relatedly, in the early noughties regional and local authorities in Spain were responsible for around 50% of total public expenditure, but their share of revenues was just 30% (Martínez-Vázquez, 2007). This mismatch between the decentralisation of revenue collection and spending has been deemed a problem by the economic literature, in that it could lead to lack of accountability and irresponsible behaviour, or to decisions being strongly conditioned by political criteria.

Another potential problem associated with fiscal decentralisation is that of tax competition. A tax differentiation process within a country reproduces some of the challenges of international taxation in the absence of harmonisation, with respect to mobile taxable bases. It may open up the possibility for taxpayers to avoid or evade taxes by establishing themselves, in reality or in fiction, in different territories. The different administrations could then engage in a "race to the bottom" dynamic to capture such mobile factors of production—something which has been widely discussed in Spain in recent years, both with respect to the charter regimes and within the common regime communities. For example, since 2008, the autonomous community of Madrid has completely credited the payment of the wealth tax, and has therefore been called a "tax haven"—as recent research has tended to confirm (Agrawal et al., 2020).

According to Rodríguez Cabrero (2011), decentralisation brought services closer to citizens, and facilitated a learning process—but also increased regional inequalities. This is especially true with respect to the charter regions, which are outside the equalisation system—and have been deemed by some to be an "original sin" (Martínez-Vázquez, 2007, p. 550). The desired level of regional solidarity is the subject of considerable controversy in Spain. During the last decades, the calculation of "fiscal balances" for the communities (i.e. the difference between what is paid in taxes and what is spent in each territory) has been used to support or oppose the grievances of some of them, notably Catalonia (Bosch et al., 2010; de La Fuente et al., 2014; Uriel, 2003).

7.3 Public Opinion and Legitimacy

The tax reform sought to bring about a shift in the prevalent attitudes of the Spanish public towards taxation. In the seventies, the available evidence suggested that the system was considered unfair and burdensome: even if taxes were low in macroeconomic terms, they were not low for everyone, and came with high compliance costs (recall Chapter 3). In relation to this, evasion was not condemned all that firmly. The tax reformers wanted this to change. A fair tax system would *need* taxpayers to report their income and activities truthfully, and would also *prompt* them to do so by promising fair treatment and more public goods and services. Were they successful in this respect? Did the new tax system gain in legitimacy?

On the one hand, the public continue to say that the system is unfair, at a remarkably stable rate of around 80% between 1985 and 2000—recall Fig. 3.3. But after some years, there was a reduction in those who considered taxes to be too high (Fig. 3.1), and a positive trend in how they perceived the balance between the taxes paid and the services they received in return (Fig. 3.2). However, in 1995, 96% thought that the government should take measures to reduce what they perceived as intense income differences, while 88% judged actual redistribution policies to be non-existent or ineffective (Centro de Investigaciones sobre la Realidad Social, 1995).

Demand for redistribution was comparatively high in Spain. Using data from 1999, Fernández-Albertos (2011) found that it was the highest among all non-ex-communist states in a sample of 25 countries. In Spain, support for redistribution was "virtually universal"; even among the 15% with the highest income, nearly 79% were in favour of government action to reduce inequalities. The author linked this result to the fact that even top-earning individuals felt they would benefit from greater equality; indeed, this was borne out by a survey conducted in 1993, and more recent research has shown that people generally underestimate inequality in the societies where they live, and consider their own position to be more typical than it actually is (Cruces et al., 2013; Hvidberg et al., 2020; Fernández-Albertos & Kuo, 2018). In the early twenty-first century, Spaniards were avowedly opposed to any cuts in welfare state services (Del Pino, 2005). In comparison with their French, German, and Italian counterparts, Spanish people appear more amenable to an expansion in taxes and benefits—30% of respondents, versus 14 to 17% in other countries (Boeri et al., 2001)—which is consistent with the incomplete convergence of Spain to the Western European core.

General demand for progressivity was also shown in a survey from 1991. Respondents stated that families with modest and middle income paid too much in taxes, while the richest or big businessmen paid too little—and people on high income were actually more likely to answer that taxes were not fair (Centro de Investigaciones Sociológicas, 1991). Similarly, in a study of seven OECD countries in 1996, Spain was the country with the most people who were clearly in favour of progressivity in personal income taxation: 86% said so, and 63% gave strictly progressive answers when asked in monetary terms about desired tax payments in several income levels (the general averages were 87 and 38%, respectively, for all countries) (Singhal, 2013).[7] Singhal's study focused on personal income taxation (including income taxes as well as social contributions paid by workers), and therefore fell short of considering the total tax system. It showed that responses tended to reflect the steepness (progressivity) of the income tax schedules in place, but not their levels: ideal rates were a bit lower than actual rates, showing that people might not be fully aware of the public need for resources. Although this was a general result, it was also applicable to Spain. Thus, it is difficult to sustain that respondents in the mid-nineties favoured a strong increase (or decrease) in the progressivity of direct personal taxation. Their dissatisfaction may have reflected other aspects of the system, such as the regressivity of indirect taxes, the unequal impact of fraud, or inefficiency in the use of public revenues.

During the eighties, the perception of high taxes was still prevalent. Indeed, during this decade, the increase in taxation appears to have made a clearer and more immediate impact than the improvement in public services. Building the welfare state took time, particularly given the very low starting point. Furthermore, new taxpayers were brought into the income tax net every year, in part due to inflation, which made taxation heavier *and more visible* among lower-middle income classes.[8] This seems to have strongly affected the legitimacy of the tax, given that increases outstripped real earnings for several years (a point made by Lagares, 1990).

Similarly, tax evasion has been persistent in the eyes of citizens, and an increasing cause for criticism—even though actual tax evasion, as found by several studies, has decreased (see Chapter 6). Figure 7.1 shows some responses to questions about fraud in public opinion surveys. There is considerable stability in the respondents' perceptions about the fiscal behaviour of their acquaintances: around 30% of respondents thought that most of them cheated to some extent in their taxes (although a similar proportion thought that their relations filed correctly for the most part). When the question is framed as whether there is an improvement in general terms of "fewer people trying to evade", the trend is towards a more negative perception of fiscal behaviour. At the same time, respondents have become more critical towards the performance of the tax administration in preventing fraud, even if there is some increase in the number of people who have undergone a tax audit.

The increased criticism coexisting with a decrease in fraud seems to be caused by an improvement in tax morale after democratisation. Fraud was widely indulged in during the early seventies, but was progressively rejected in later decades. Using data from the World Values Survey

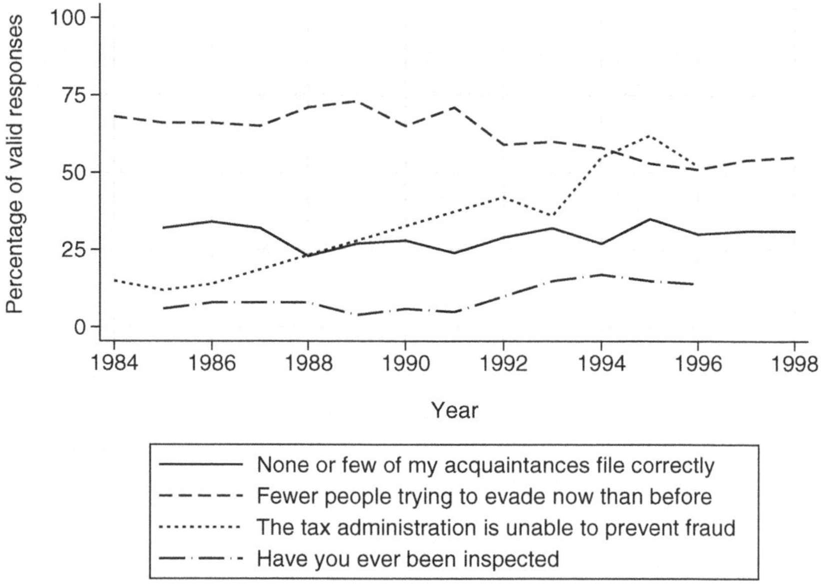

Fig. 7.1 Perceptions of fraud after the tax reform (*Source* Alvira et al., 2000)

and the European Values Survey, Martínez-Vazquez and Torgler (2009) showed that in 1981 around half of the population considered cheating on taxes to be "never justified", while fourteen years later this number had gone up to around 70%. Their analysis also indicated that tax morale was higher among the lower class: "*Being in the upper class rather than the lower class reduces the probability of stating that tax evasion is never justifiable by 7.2 percentage points*" (Martínez-Vazquez & Torgler, 2009, p. 12).

The same data pointed to a decline in tax morale between 1995 and 1999. Possible reasons for this, according to the authors, were high unemployment and welfare state retrenchment during the crisis of the mid-nineties, corruption scandals during the later PSOE governments, and further tax reforms that might have generated, again, a perception of unfairness. Indeed, economic distress and growing public indebtedness gave rise to an image of poor fiscal management and squandering. This was shown in the early nineties in a study conducted by the *Instituto de Estudios Fiscales* (Díaz García & Delgado Lobo, 1994), in which

68 people were interviewed from different social groups: journalists, tax consultants, representatives from business organisations, financial institutions and trade unions, small and medium businessmen, liberal professionals, workers, and pensioners. Most interviewees agreed that the tax burden was high in relation to the level and quality of public services, which the authors linked to the economic situation. For example, one small businessman said that "*taxes are wasted on some things and in others, they skimp a lot. Then nothing is noticeable. I feel cheated when I have to pay taxes*", while a worker was of the opinion that "*we have a tax system that has been increasing since approximately 1980 to date in very large progressions and the services provided by the State are practically the same*". Rejection of fraud was categorical across all groups, even if attitudes were more forgiving for small businessmen in economic distress.

But what do Spanish people actually know about the taxes they pay? This issue has been recently investigated by Foremny (2020) with respect to personal income taxes. He showed that survey respondents still tend to overestimate the taxes they pay, and are also "*mostly unaware that the autonomous communities have a substantial degree of autonomy to change the tax rates*". His work also demonstrated that Spanish people remain in favour of redistribution and a (more) progressive tax system; for example, about 80% think that the poor should pay less tax. Foremny's conclusion after an experiment is that, when provided with additional information, citizens are *even more* in favour of redistribution and progressivity.

7.4 Inequality: Unresolved Business?

Transitions from dictatorship to democracy have been expected to bring about a decrease in income inequality, as discussed in Chapter 1. Democracies would be more inclined to favour the lower classes, compared to (right-wing) dictatorships, as political economy theory has discussed. They would do this via labour market regulation, welfare state benefits, and progressive taxation, among other strategies.

The tax system has been the focus of this book, but inequality is of course also affected by many other factors and policies. One distinction that has been used lately is between "pre-distribution" and "redistribution": the distribution of income obtained in the market, *and* the changes thereto through taxes and transfers. The former, the distribution of market income, depends crucially on the education system and labour market institutions, among others, and is something we have taken here as given. The relative emphasis on one or the other of these two concepts, in relation to reducing inequality, has changed over time. In Spain of the seventies, some believed that trying to change the distribution of market income was more conflictive (which might not be surprising in a period of intense labour unrest), and therefore put a lot of emphasis on redistributing through the tax-and-transfer system. This was, for example, the opinion of Fernández Ordóñez: that the high inequality of the mid-seventies "*required action on both the tax system and the public expenditure side. Tax policy has always seemed to me less dangerous for the functioning of the system than the reduction of the range that occurs in salary negotiation* [...]. *Those who attack tax progressivity and spending for equity in the Budget are closing the path to the least unsettling mechanism for meeting the demands of justice, and are forcing the debate on the distribution of income to move to the much more problematic sphere of the company*" (Fernández Ordóñez, 1980, pp. 135–136, author's translation).

Today, however, several experts underline that efforts to reduce inequality should consider both dimensions (which are often intertwined in any case), and have put forth pre-distribution policy proposals along with ideas for tax and benefit reform (Atkinson, 2018; Bozio et al., 2020; Stiglitz, 2012).[9] Redistribution might face powerful constraints. But importantly, while the impacts of redistribution are generally almost immediate (i.e. taxing high income this year will reduce net income, and potentially fund higher benefits, in the same year or soon after), pre-distribution is often a matter of longer time periods (especially when considering the roles of inheritance and education; see e.g. Cowell et al., 2018).

The Spanish transition (1976–1982) is an interesting case in the context of this discussion. The early years of the new democracy were hit by the oil crises, industrial restructuring, and an unprecedented and dramatic increase in unemployment, as well as coinciding with intensified international integration. In this sense, transformations in the economy could have pushed inequality to higher levels, as opposed to the effects of welfare state development made possible by democratisation. So which force prevailed? Was democratisation a strong enough driver of equality?

Several studies have found that Spanish income inequality shrank very substantially between 1970 and 1990 (e.g. Alcaide, 2000; Ayala et al., 2006). This result is consistent with a positive impact of the political transition and the subsequent development of the welfare state in the country, and generated a strong consensus. By 1990, inequality in Spain would have fallen to levels that were similar to those in other developed European countries.[10]

However, I have argued elsewhere that this result arises from the use of sources without enough criticism (Torregrosa-Hetland, 2016). The main source in this case is household budget surveys; because these suffer from under-reporting of earnings, particularly those coming from self-employment and capital, they can potentially misrepresent the real levels of inequality. Several studies during the seventies were already devising ways to adjust for under-reporting, based on adjustment to the National Accounts and the ratios between income and expenditure (Alcaide, 2000; Instituto Nacional de Estadística, 1977; Pena & Callealta, 1996). My own procedure built on these ones, and also introduced a contrast between wage-earners and self-employed, to uncover under-reporting by the latter (Martínez-López, 2013; Pissarides & Weber, 1989).[11]

As it turns out, part of the reduction in inequality revealed by household surveys was due to under-reporting. Basically, under-reporting was more intense for capital income, and this represented a higher share of total income in 1990 than in 1970, which affects the comparison between the two years. After adjusting for under-reporting, inequality can be seen to have been quite persistent during the transition and the first decade and a half of democracy (see Table 7.2). Here, the concept of disposable income is used (i.e. after direct taxes and transfers, but before indirect taxes and the effect of spending in kind), which is the most commonly used in similar literature: this is the income that households receive and can directly decide upon. The first row shows inequality between households, while the second represents inequality between individuals. Technically, this means that for the indices in the

Table 7.2 Inequality in disposable income, 1973–1990 (Gini index)

	1973	1980	1990
Disposable total income (households)	36.8	33.5	34.8
Disposable equivalent income (individuals)	34.6	32.6	33.0

Source Torregrosa-Hetland (2016)

first rows households are used as the unit of analysis (i.e. the household weights given in the surveys), and income is not adjusted for household size, while for the second row individual weights and adjusted income are used (with the OECD equivalence scale).

Both the unadjusted data and the corrections in previous literature pointed to an abrupt improvement in the distribution over time. The present results, on the contrary, reveal a far smaller change during the first decade (around 2 Gini points), which actually came to a halt in the eighties. There are thus indications of considerable persistence in inequality, particularly in the second subperiod, when the Spanish welfare state was under construction. This result contrasts with most of the previous literature based on surveys, but is not at odds with studies that use tax or macroeconomic data (Alvaredo & Saez, 2009; Onrubia et al., 2007; Prados de la Escosura, 2008). Even if redistribution increased through the period, it did not completely offset the growth in inequality in market income, as shown in Chapter 5.[12]

Table 7.3 displays the levels of income: mean disposable per capita equivalent income by deciles, in constant 1990 pesetas. All groups experienced an increase in their purchasing power.[13] But the profiles of income growth were dissimilar in the two subperiods: while during the seventies it was higher at the lower-mid levels, in the eighties it was the extremes that benefited the most (pointing towards the expansion in welfare state transfers in the case of the low-income households). Looking at the top 1%, there is even stagnation in the first subperiod (the oil-crisis decade) and a very significant recovery in the second. The ratios in the last rows confirm the same impression of a slight reduction of economic distances.

It should be recalled that the Gini index and other related indicators measure *relative* inequality (i.e. the Gini index would remain constant if all income was multiplied by the same factor). If absolute differences

Table 7.3 Levels and growth of disposable equivalent income, 1973–1990

	Mean (constant 1990 ptas)			Increase		
	1973	1980	1990	1973–80	1980–90	1973–90
Decile 1	257,168	279,276	359,219	8.6%	28.6%	39.7%
Decile 2	385,927	440,857	540,182	14.2%	22.5%	40.0%
Decile 3	475,042	543,928	652,221	14.5%	19.9%	37.3%
Decile 4	558,261	633,925	754,046	13.6%	18.9%	35.1%
Decile 5	640,977	727,475	863,084	13.5%	18.6%	34.7%
Decile 6	737,294	826,796	974,459	12.1%	17.9%	32.2%
Decile 7	854,088	950,880	1,111,928	11.3%	16.9%	30.2%
Decile 8	1,015,400	1,119,565	1,302,864	10.3%	16.4%	28.3%
Decile 9	1,260,337	1,373,365	1,615,610	9.0%	17.6%	28.2%
Decile 10	2,369,292	2,399,594	3,004,124	1.3%	25.2%	26.8%
Top 1%	5,691,256	5,705,531	8,444,164	0.3%	48.0%	48.4%
Total	855,313	929,507	1,117,712	8.7%	20.2%	30.7%
Deciles 10/1	9.21	8.59	8.36	0.15	0.88	0.68
Deciles 10/5	3.70	3.30	3.48	0.09	1.35	0.77
Deciles 5/1	2.49	2.60	2.40	1.57	0.65	0.87

Source Torregrosa-Hetland (2016)

in income within a society are also thought to be important, we can calculate an absolute Gini: the same index without normalisation to the mean (as put forward by Ravallion, 2003). Doing this exercise for the three years, an increase of 24% is obtained in the absolute inequality index between 1973 and 1990. Relative economic distances did not change that much, but they did in absolute terms, in actual consumption capacity.

The composition of income shows quite a different picture in 1990 than twenty years earlier. While the capital share decreased in the last years of the dictatorship, as a consequence of the crisis, it increased again later in the context of liberalisation and resumption of growth (going from 4 to 7%). Capital income was concentrated at the top throughout the period: almost absent in the lower classes, it constituted over 10% of income for the upper decile and around 30% for the top 1%. Furthermore, most advanced industrial economies have experienced an increase in the dispersion of labour income in recent decades, which is intensified in the case of Spain by the strong and cyclical incidence of unemployment, as well as by a considerably fragmented labour market. These forces counteracted the equalising forces found in the system: the introduction of progressivity in taxes, and the expansion of public benefits (total transfers increased from 14 to 25% of disposable income).

Indeed, the redistributive role of the state did grow. Not only was progressive taxation introduced, even with all the aforementioned insufficiencies, but the public budget was significantly tilted towards social spending. Figure 7.2 shows the evolution of public social spending in its different forms: old age and survival, disability and temporary sickness, unemployment, family benefits, health, and education. The democratic state spent more on pensions and also on unemployment. In the case of pensions, this was a continuation of the trend initiated with the Social Security Law of 1967. Unemployment protection was more of a novelty (on its precedents, see Espuelas, 2013b). As discussed in Chapter 5, needs increased as well, particularly with regard to the latter. On the other hand, after the mid-seventies the Spanish state has spent relatively less on families, which during the Francoist period reflected traditional views, but which represents a clear insufficiency in the later decades (Espuelas, 2013a; León, 2011; Navarro, 2006).[14]

Spending on health and education were also reinforced by the democratic state. Importantly, not only does this mean redistribution today (since the value of the service represents a greater transfer, in relative terms, for poor families), but it also implies potential social mobility. Indeed, social mobility in terms of occupation increased for the cohorts born in the seventies, particularly women (Gil-Hernández et al., 2017). However, this is not necessarily associated with decreases in inequality. Whether the welfare state will fulfil its promises in this sense remains to be seen.

So, to go back to the initial question, did transition to democracy fail to reduce inequality? As in other countries, redistribution increased but it was unable to outcompete forces pulling in the opposite direction. A more unequal pre-distribution won the game. While there is no space here to dwell on the causes of inequality in market income, its recent increase in developed countries has been linked to factors such as globalisation, skill-biased technological change, and the role of inheritance, among others (Atkinson, 2000; Easterly, 2004; Krugman, 2000; Piketty,

a

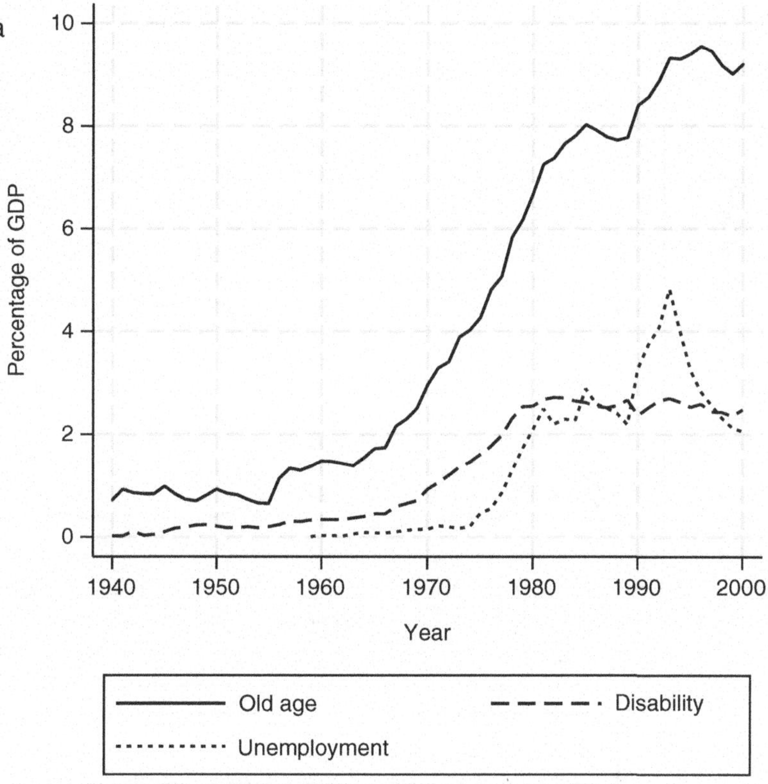

Fig. 7.2 Public social spending in Spain (1940–2000). (a) Old age, disability and unemployment, (b) Family, health and education (*Source* Espuelas, 2013a. *Notes* Functional classification, following the OECD classification. Disability therefore includes temporary payments in case of sickness or work accident. The categories do not coincide with the differentiation between spending in monetary transfers and in kind)

2011). Furthermore, Roine et al. (2009) have shown how reductions in the top marginal tax rates caused an expansion in the inequality *of pre-tax income*, via incentive effects. Following the general international trends, top marginal rates in Spanish income tax indeed decreased from a maximum of 68.47% in 1982 to 56% in 1988 (when the number of brackets was also reduced, to sixteen).

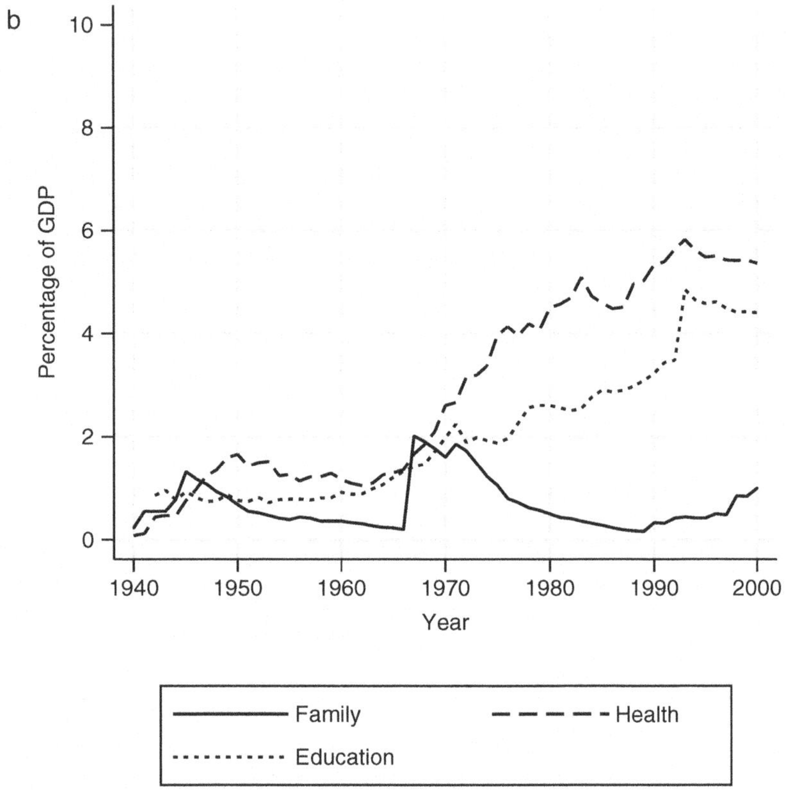

Fig. 7.2 (continued)

Economic growth and the decline in inequality in the years after 1950 were thought to have facilitated the transition in the seventies. Prados de la Escosura (2008) interpreted in this way the elimination of absolute poverty and the growth of the middle class, which would have permitted the stabilisation of democracy, unlike what happened in the interwar period. But that evolution does not seem to have gone much further. This is, of course, the result of a political choice, reflecting the equilibrium attained in the young parliamentary state.

Notes

1. Of course, given the exit of the United Kingdom from the European Union, the EU-14 will not be a good reference for future trends, as it has been for the past several decades. The UK's departure will automatically bring up the average tax revenue of the comparison group.
2. Inflation reduces the real value of public debt, as well as that of other stocks set in nominal terms. The government can also earn money directly by issuing currency, which is known as seigniorage (and might lead to inflation). Finally, financial repression is a set of instruments aimed at keeping interest payments low, such as by establishing a cap on interest rates or forcing institutions to hold public debt.
3. For an estimation of flexibility in the Spanish tax system, in terms of elasticity of tax revenues to GDP, see Edo Hernández (2002).
4. Procyclicality is expected in models of "opportunistic political budget cycles", so it would be highly likely in new democracies. In this sense, Spain defied expectations: "*political bargaining became* less *fragmented and opportunistic with the end of Spanish autocracy*" (Battilossi et al., 2013, p. 289).
5. Because the autonomous communities cannot impose taxes on tax bases already used at the central or local levels, they have largely only enacted some forms of environmental and gaming taxation.
6. At the time the autonomous communities were created, existing public debt was kept at the central level. Apportioning it would have undoubtedly been complicated, but this meant that debt servicing became a bigger part of central spending (with less revenue), while the capacity of the communities to borrow against their revenues remained intact (López Laborda & Monasterio, 2007).
7. The empirical question was to ask how much, in monetary terms, someone with income level X should pay in taxes. Strictly progressive answers are those that display progression across all income levels enquired about. The data comes from the "Role of Government III" wave of the International Social Survey Program, and was compared with the current OECD tax system as published in "Taxing Wages".
8. This phenomenon is known as "bracket creep". Because inflation causes reductions of tax thresholds in real terms, individuals without real increases in their earnings could have been pushed into the tax. This is a very widespread phenomenon in high inflation scenarios when thresholds are not adjusted, and has caused the expansion of income taxes in

several contexts, including the oil crises and, earlier, the two world wars (Torregrosa-Hetland & Sabaté, 2021).

9. This was also observed by José Fernández-Albertos in *El País* in October 2018: https://elpais.com/elpais/2018/10/03/opinion/1538588319_708794.html.
10. The same result was obtained by studies analysing inequality of consumption, such as Gradín et al. (2008); see further references in Torregrosa-Hetland (2016).
11. In short, the adjustment consists of an upwards correction of household income by revenue sources, to match the corresponding flows in the National Accounts. In this sense, it is similar in spirit to the recent "Distributional National Accounts" initiative (Piketty et al., 2018), which is nevertheless conceptually wider. See the details in Torregrosa-Hetland (2016).
12. On the other hand, it should be noted that the three observations here are to a certain extent also a result of short-term fluctuations: 1973 was the culmination of the pre-oil-shock growth in Spain, while 1980 was a period of economic distress, and in 1990 the country was back on the ascending side of the cycle. Unfortunately, this is the only data available for the period. The *Encuesta Continua de Presupuestos Familiares*, a yearly rotating panel starting in 1985, might have complemented the image, but it is known to have an even more serious income under-assessment problem (Eurostat, 1999; Pou & Alegre, 2002).
13. It should be borne in mind that disposable income is still subject to indirect taxes, so changes in consumption taxation also affected final material well-being.
14. The figures for social spending do not include tax expenditure, which is carried out under income tax in connection with the family of each taxpayer. But this expenditure is less transparent and progressive. In 2004, deductions for descendants amounted to 11,310 million euros (data from IEF Badespe), which represents 1.3% of Spanish GDP (from Prados de la Escosura, 2017).

References

Agrawal, D. R., Foremny, D., & Martínez-Toledano, C. (2020). Paraísos Fiscales, Wealth Taxation, and Mobility. *SSRN Electronic Journal*.

Albi, E. (2007). The business community, policy-makers, and tax reform (1977–2004). In J. Martínez-Vázquez & J. F. Sanz-Sanz (Eds.), *Fiscal reform in Spain: Accomplishments and challenges* (pp. 59–97). Edward Elgar.

Alcaide, J. (2000). La renta nacional de España y su distribución. Serie años 1898 a 1998. In J. V. Fuertes (Ed.), *1900–2000. Historia de un esfuerzo colectivo: cómo España superó el pesimismo y la pobreza* (pp. 741,810). Fundación BSCH.

Alvaredo, F., & Saez, E. (2009). Income and wealth concentration in Spain from a historical and fiscal perspective. *Journal of the European Economic Association, 7*, 1140–1167.

Alvira, F., García, J., & Delgado, M. L. (2000). *Sociedad, impuestos y gasto público. La perspectiva del contribuyente*. Centro de Investigaciones Sociológicas.

Aróstegui, J. (1999). La transición política y la construcción de la democracia (1975–1996). In J. Martínez (Ed.), *Historia de España. Siglo XX: 1939–1996* (pp. 245–364). Cátedra.

Atkinson, A. (2000). The changing distribution of income: Evidence and explanations. *German Economic Review, 1*, 3–18.

Atkinson, A. (2018). *Inequality: What can be done?* Harvard University Press.

Ayala, L., Jurado, A., & Pedraja, F. (2006). Desigualdad y bienestar en la distribución intraterritorial de la renta, 1973–2000. *Investigaciones Regionales, 8*, 5–30.

Battilossi, S., Escario, R., & Foreman-Peck, J. (2013). Fiscal policy response to cycles under two regimes: Spain 1950–1998. *Cliometrica, 7*(3), 267–294.

Boeri, T., Börsch-Supan, A., & Tabellini, G. (2001). Would you like to shrink the welfare state? A survey of European citizens. *Economic Policy, 16*(32), 7–50.

Bosch, N., Espasa, M., & Solé Ollé, A. (Eds.). (2010). *The political economy of inter-regional fiscal flows*. Edward Elgar.

Bozio, A., Garbinti, B., Goupille-Lebret, J., Guillot, M., & Piketty, T. (2020). *Predistribution vs. Redistribution: Evidence from France and the U.S* (2020/22; World Inequality Lab—Working Paper).

Castillo, J. M. (1994). *El fraude fiscal en España*. Comares.

Centro de Investigaciones sobre la Realidad Social. (1995). *Survey, Spain, April 1995: Social Inequalities* (Issues ICPSR06968-v1).

Centro de Investigaciones Sociológicas. (1991). *La política fiscal y la declaración de la renta correspondiente a 1990. Impuestos (VIII)* (No. 1971; Estudio).

Colomer, J. M. (1998). *La transición a la democracia: El modelo español*. Anagrama.

Comín, F. (2012). Default, rescheduling and inflation: Public debt crises in Spain during the 19th and 20th centuries. *Revista de Historia Economica—Journal of Iberian and Latin American Economic History, 30*(3), 353–390.

Conde-Ruiz, J. I., Díaz, M., Marín, C., & Ramírez, J. R. (2015). *Una Reforma Fiscal para España* (Policy Papers). FEDEA.

Cowell, F. A., Van de gaer, D., & He, C. (2018). Inheritance taxation: Redistribution and predistribution. In *Inequality, Taxation and Intergenerational Transmission (Research on Economic Inequality, Vol. 26)* (pp. 1–13). Emerald Group Publishing Ltd.

Cruces, G., Perez-Truglia, R., & Tetaz, M. (2013). Biased perceptions of income distribution and preferences for redistribution: Evidence from a survey experiment. *Journal of Public Economics, 98*(C), 100–112.

Cuevas, J., & Pons, M. A. (2021). Reformas y cambios en el sistema financiero durante la Transición, 1974–1985. In J. de la Torre & M. Rubio (Eds.), *Economía en Transición. Del tardofranquismo a la democracia* (Chapter 5). Marcial Pons.

de La Fuente, A., Barberán, R., Uriel, E., de La Fuente, A., Barberán, R., & Uriel, E. (2014). A system of regionalized public accounts for Spain. Methodology and Results for 2005. *Hacienda Pública Española* [Review of Public Economics], *209*(2), 99–150.

Del Pino, E. (2005). *¿Se han modificado las preferencias de los ciudadanos sobre las políticas de bienestar en España (1985–2005)?* (Issues 05–03).

Díaz García, C., & Delgado Lobo, M. L. (1994). *Formación de la opinión fiscal: ¿influyen los mensajes de los líderes de opinión?* (9/94; Papeles de Trabajo).

Easterly, W. R. (2004). Globalization, inequality, and development: The big picture. *Monetary and Economic Studies, 22*(S1), 57–87.

Edo Hernández, V. (2002). Importancia recaudatoria y flexibilidad del sistema impositivo español según las principales fuentes estadísticas. *IX Encuentro de Economía Pública, Hacienda y Medio Ambiente*.

Escario, R., Sabaté, M., & Gadea, M. D. (2011). La sombra monetaria del déficit en la España de la peseta. *Investigaciones De Historia Economica, 7*(1), 151–181.

Espuelas, S. (2013a). *La evolución del gasto social público en España, 1850–2005* (Vol. 63). Banco de España.
Espuelas, S. (2013b). Los obstáculos al desarrollo de los seguros sociales en España antes de 1936: El caso del seguro de desempleo. *Revista De Historia Industrial, 22*(52), 77–110.
Eurostat. (1999). *ECHP data quality* (Issue 108/99).
Fernández-Albertos, J. (2011). The making of egalitarian Spain: Growth, demographics, politics and the income distribution, 1960–1990. *Revista Española De Sociología, 16*, 47–72.
Fernández-Albertos, J., & Kuo, A. (2018). Income perception, information, and progressive taxation: Evidence from a survey experiment. *Political Science Research and Methods, 6*(1), 83–110.
Fernández Ordóñez, F. (1980). *La España necesaria.* Taurus.
Foremny, D. (2020). *What do we know about the taxes we pay?* https://observatoriosociallacaixa.org/en/-/que-sabemos-sobre-los-impuestos-que-pagamos-.
Gil-Hernández, C. J., Marqués-Perales, I., & Fachelli, S. (2017). Intergenerational social mobility in Spain between 1956 and 2011: The role of educational expansion and economic modernisation in a late industrialised country. *Research in Social Stratification and Mobility, 51*, 14–27.
Gradín, C., Cantó, O., & del Río, C. (2008). Inequality, poverty and mobility: Choosing income or consumption as welfare indicators. *Investigaciones Economicas, 32*(2), 169–200.
Guillén, A. M., & León, M. (2011). *The Spanish welfare state in European context*. Ashgate.
Hvidberg, K. B., Kreiner, C., & Stantcheva, S. (2020). *Social position and fairness views* (No. 28099; NBER Working Paper).
Instituto Nacional de Estadística. (1977). *La Renta nacional y su distribución 1976*. INE.
Krugman, P. R. (2000). Technology, trade and factor prices. *Journal of International Economics, 50*(1), 51–71.
Lagares, M. J. (1990). La aceptación social del sistema tributario: el Impuesto sobre la Renta de las Personas Físicas. In E. Albi (dir), *La Hacienda Pública en la Democracia. Estudios en homenaje al profesor Enrique Fuentes Quintana* (pp. 109–132). Ariel.
León, M. (2011). The quest for gender equality. In Ana M. Guillén & M. León (Eds.), *The Spanish welfare state in European context* (pp. 59–76). Ashgate.
López Laborda, J., & Monasterio, C. (2007). Regional governments: Vertical imbalances and revenue assignments. In J. Martínez-Vázquez & J. F. Sanz

Sanz (Eds.), *Fiscal reform in Spain: Accomplishments and challenges* (pp. 422–452). Edward Elgar.

Martínez-López, D. (2013). The underreporting of income by self-employed workers in Spain. *Series, 4*(4), 353–371.

Martínez-Vázquez, J. (2007). The Spanish tax reform: Overview and lessons. In J. Martínez-Vázquez & J. F. Sanz Sanz (Eds.), *Fiscal reform in Spain: Accomplishments and challenges* (pp. 532–553). Edward Elgar.

Martínez-Vazquez, J., & Torgler, B. (2009). The evolution of tax morale in modern Spain. *Journal of Economic Issues, 43*(1), 1–28.

Monasterio, C. (2002). El laberinto de la financiación autonómica. *Hacienda Pública Española* [Review of Public Economics], *163*, 157–187.

Navarro, V. (2006). *El subdesarrollo social de España. Causas y consecuencias.* Anagrama.

Oates, W. E. (1999). An essay on fiscal federalism. *Journal of Economic Literature, 37*(3), 1120–1149.

Onrubia, J. (2007). The reform of the tax administration in Spain. In J. Martínez-Vázquez & J. F. Sanz Sanz (Eds.), *Fiscal reform in Spain: Accomplishments and challenges* (pp. 484–531). Edward Elgar.

Onrubia, J., Rodado, M. C., Díaz, S., & Pérez, C. (2007). Progresividad y redistribución a través del IRPF español: Un análisis de bienestar social para el periodo 1982–1998. *Hacienda Pública Española, 183*, 81–124.

Pan-Montojo, J. L. (2007). *Los inspectores de Hacienda en España: Una mirada histórica.* Centro de Estudios Financieros.

Pena, J. B., & Callealta, F. J. (1996). *Distribución personal de la renta en España: corrección y modelización de la información básica: desigualdad y análisis.* Pirámide.

Piketty, T. (2011). On the long-run evolution of inheritance: France 1820–2050. *The Quarterly Journal of Economics, 126*(3), 1071–1131.

Piketty, T., Saez, E., & Zucman, G. (2018). Distributional national accounts: Methods and estimates for the United States. *The Quarterly Journal of Economics, 133*(2), 553–609.

Pissarides, C. A., & Weber, G. (1989). An expenditure-based estimate of Britain's black economy. *Journal of Public Economics, 39*(1), 17–32.

Pou, L., & Alegre, J. (2002). *La Encuesta Continua de Presupuestos Familiares: Descripción, Representatividad y Propuestas de Metodología para la Explotación de la Información de los Ingresos y el Gasto* (Issue 172/2002).

Prados de la Escosura, L. (2008). Inequality, poverty and the Kuznets curve in Spain, 1850–2000. *European Review of Economic History, 12*, 287–324.

Prados de la Escosura, L. (2017). *Spanish economic growth, 1850–2015*. Springer International Publishing.
Ravallion, M. (2003). The debate on globalization, poverty and inequality: Why measurement matters. *International Affairs, 79*(4), 739–754.
Repullo, R. (1992). Financing budget deficits by seigniorage and implicit taxation: The cases of Spain and Portugal. In D.-E. Fair & D. de Boissieu (Eds.), *Fiscal policy, taxation and the financial system in an increasingly integrated Europe* (pp. 235–253). Kluwer Publishers.
Rodríguez Cabrero, G. (2011). The consolidation of the Spanish Welfare State (1975–2010). In A. M. Guillén & M. León (Eds.), *The Spanish welfare state in European context* (pp. 33–54). Ashgate.
Roine, J., Vlachos, J., & Waldenström, D. (2009). The long-run determinants of inequality: What can we learn from top income data? *Journal of Public Economics, 93*(7–8), 974–988.
Singhal, M. (2013). *Quantifying Preferences for Redistribution* (NBER Working Paper).
Stiglitz, J. (2012). *The price of inequality: How today's divided society endangers our future*. W. W. Norton.
Torregrosa-Hetland, S. (2015). *Tax system and redistribution: The Spanish fiscal transition (1960–1990)*. University of Barcelona.
Torregrosa-Hetland, S. (2016). Sticky income inequality in the Spanish transition (1973–1990). *Revista de Historia Economica—Journal of Iberian and Latin American Economic History, 34*(1), 39–80.
Torregrosa-Hetland, S., & Sabaté, O. (2021). Income tax progressivity and inflation during the World Wars. *European Review of Economic History* (forthcoming).
Uriel, E. (2003). *Una aproximación a las balanzas fiscales de las Comunidades Autónomas*. Fundación BBVA.

8

Conclusions: The Spanish Fiscal Transition and Beyond

We used to think that the transition to democracy in Spain had been exemplary, and that the *fiscal* transition had managed to reduce inequality in the country. We now know better. Inequality was not reduced by the new democracy. On the contrary, in terms of disposable income it remained largely static from the mid-seventies, moving cyclically. Market income grew more unequal at the same time. The tax system was profoundly modernised, falling into line with that of other Western European countries, and becoming capable of raising more revenue. But this did not equate to progressivity. Labour income still shouldered much of the burden, in terms of both personal income tax and social contributions, while tax evasion was concentrated among capital and high income. Therefore, even if taxes funded redistributive spending, it was not the rich who paid for it. Total redistribution did not prove all that high by comparative standards.

Why was this? The lack of overall tax progressivity contradicts the predominant political discourse about the objectives and effects of the tax reform. For example, Francisco Fernández Ordóñez, the minister of public finance between 1977 and 1979, stated in the press that the

© The Author(s), under exclusive license to Springer Nature Switzerland AG 2021

S. Torregrosa Hetland, *The Spanish Fiscal Transition*, Palgrave Studies in Economic History,
https://doi.org/10.1007/978-3-030-79541-2_8

reform had the goal of "*paying better; that is, in a fair way, following the old principle and desire that those who have more pay more*".[1] In hindsight, this objective was not completely fulfilled.

The previous chapters have discussed the factors that led to and constrained the reform. Although limited, the survey data about the public's attitudes towards taxation and inequality reflects a strong demand for equalisation, but this might have decreased over time. The press gave voice to some opinions that were very much in favour of progressive reform, to which there was no clear alternative at the beginning. From the right to the left, almost all parties (at least, all major parties) shared an understanding that tax reform was necessary. The Spanish state needed higher revenues, and these had to tap into economic capacity, as was being done elsewhere in Europe. This basis of the consensus between the parties, and more broadly in Spanish society, has been highlighted by previous writings (Fuentes Quintana, 2004; Lagares, 1999). The research presented here affirms this assertion but qualifies it to some extent. It is true that during the first years of democracy no alternative tax plans were put on the table: the pages of the conservative newspapers showed that immobility was not popular in the exceptional years of the transition. But much of the agreement seems to have been superficial and based on a very broad understanding of some of the concepts. As soon as the parties had to sit down in Parliament and discuss concrete measures, differences came to the surface, anticipating the "reform of the reform" programme of the eighties (Pan-Montojo, 1996).

The book's interpretation is that political institutions and the economic context both strongly influenced how citizens' demands were translated into policies. Several constraints limited the effective culmination of the reform. Malapportionment in Parliament is one: the electoral law was designed during the transition period under significant conservative influence, giving birth to a system that benefited rural, conservative districts. The importance of this element should not be underestimated, since it largely shaped the party system that emerged after the first democratic elections of 1977. Successful parties gained access to power during the constitutional talks, as well as media attention and public funds for their activities. Other political aspects that might have affected the process deserve further consideration, such as the relationship between political participation and income levels, and the actions of pressure groups, which are mentioned in narrative evidence.

Economic distress and changes in public finance theory are very much interrelated. Rising unemployment and sluggish growth certainly made it difficult to increase taxation sharply. The reform of social security was delayed by resistance to increasing labour costs, and the introduction of VAT was also deferred due to fears about foreseeable inflationary effects. In 1977, the model aspired to was the product of postwar Keynesian economics, developed under a period of unprecedented growth and social peace in Western democracies. The era of oil shocks brought about a different context, in which emphasis would be placed on the promotion of private savings and investment. Finally, international openness came to reinforce this process, by providing capital owners with a credible exit strategy—since openness came without enough harmonisation or cooperation.

To be sure, there is still more to be learned about the Spanish fiscal transition, and about other similar processes. This book is part of an ongoing effort in the international academic community to delve into the role of taxation in shaping societies and bringing their inner structures to light, from various disciplinary perspectives such as economic history, sociology, and political science. Further analyses are needed to be able to tell a fully comparative story.

An idea that this book illustrates is that not all countries go through the same stages in their fiscal development. History is not linear, and this is also true of the taxation arena. Even if Spain had tried to introduce the postwar fiscal model in the late seventies, it did so "too late" and soon started the gradual reform of the system. Spain never had a functioning income tax with heavy effective taxation of top incomes, as other countries did in the fifties and sixties—even if effective taxation was lower than might be assumed (Torregrosa-Hetland & Sabaté, 2021). The lasting impact that progressive taxation left in other societies therefore cannot be found in the Spanish case. In a way, because of the dictatorship, the country bypassed the classic tax system of the golden age period.

This last chapter tries to look beyond the Spanish fiscal transition, to situate it in a wider context in both chronological and geographical terms. The first subsection looks forward, describing further changes to the tax system in relation to international trends. The second looks at recent experiences of tax reform in Latin America, reflecting on common ground as well as differences.

8.1 Looking Forward

As noted earlier, the system established between 1977 and 1986 is basically the one that we have today. This holds true in terms of the balance between different types of taxes, as well as the total tax revenue they provide. Of course, it has undergone multiple piecemeal reforms, tweaks to the tax rates, and so on. But there have been no wholesale redesigns—even though there have been initiatives and proposals to this end, as we shall see.

Dominant thinking about tax policy has changed over the last few decades. General, progressive, and redistributive taxation was at its peak in the sixties and seventies, with the "Carter Report" of 1966 favouring as integrated and comprehensive a model of personal taxation as possible. Proliferation of deductions and exemptions, however, made the real systems differ from the model, and plagued them with horizontal and vertical equity problems.[2] The proposed solutions rested on new theoretical approaches, related to the development of optimal tax theory during the seventies. These focused on the behavioural effects of taxation (i.e. the disincentive to work or save, and thus the negative impact of tax rates on the tax base). Tax policy proposals tended to reduce progressivity, especially at the top, and prioritise the objective of neutrality over equity considerations (Buggeln et al., 2017; Slemrod, 1995; Steinmo, 2003).[3] They were part of a supply-side, business-friendly economic programme that emphasised efficiency.

In practice, there was a reduction in the tax burden on capital and high incomes, through reductions in the corporate tax rates and in the top marginal income tax rates. The reforms were usually combined with a broadening of the base by limiting tax deductions, as well as a reduction in the number of tax brackets, in the wake of Reagan in the United States. These reforms have been cited as a factor in the recent increase in inequality, mainly in Anglo-Saxon economies (Atkinson & Piketty, 2007). Of course, even if the arguments used are economic, tax reforms are always political (Peters, 1991), and in this sense they cannot be disentangled from wider changes such as the rise of neoliberalism and the crisis of social democracy in post-industrial societies (Levy & Temin, 2007).

In Spain, the reform of the reform was first put forward by the People's Alliance (*Alianza Popular*, AP) in its 1982 electoral platform. But the influence of the new ideas also reached the centre and left of the political spectrum. The tide had turned. The best expression of this attitude change came by way of Enrique Fuentes Quintana, the main champion of tax reform from the sixties. But by the end of the eighties, Fuentes was criticising the tax that he himself had helped to establish, and was praising the benefits of "linear tax" (Fuentes Quintana, 1987). Linear tax is a tax on income with a single rate, which has some progressive effects due to the exemption of a portion of income (threshold). According to its advocates, it would help to prevent the disincentive effect of high marginal rates, and to simplify—albeit at the price of less effective escalation.

The first significant reform of personal income tax came in 1991. It responded to prolonged mobilisation against the obligation of married couples to file joint returns, which made them subject to higher tax rates than would have been the case if they had filed separately.[4] This was a middle-class mobilisation—at that point, there were still relatively few married Spanish women working outside the home.[5] As a result of it, compulsory joint taxation was ruled unconstitutional in February 1989, and since then married couples have been allowed to file separately. The reform also tackled the definition of payments in kind (another means of avoidance), and introduced special treatment for irregular income and long-term capital gains (Romero Jordán & Sanz-Sanz, 2007). Also in 1991, a new tax amnesty was declared, and net wealth tax was finally introduced, now without the adjective "extraordinary".[6]

New income tax reforms took place in 1998 and 2006. The former was passed by a government led by the Popular Party (*Partido Popular*), a descendant of AP, while the latter again corresponded to the social-democratic Spanish Socialist Worker's Party (*Partido Socialista Obrero Español*). In 1998, tax credits for dependants (deducted from the tax payment) were transformed into tax allowances (deducted from the tax base). This effectively meant that taxpayers on higher income would benefit most from family adjustments.[7] Other changes were the reduction in the number of brackets and tax rates (continuing the trend of the previous years), as well as a significant increase in the threshold for the filing obligation. The 2006 reform introduced partial dualisation of the tax, which meant that income from long-term capital gains became subject to a proportional tax, while the progressive schedule applied to other forms of income. (Later, a progressive scale was established for capital gains, but with lower rates than for other income forms.) All in all, the tax has undergone a process of "simplification" similar to that in other Western countries: in 2020, it had five brackets (the maximum in 1982 had been 34), and the top marginal tax rate was 45% (compared with 68.47% in 1981).[8] The result was that income tax progressivity increased until 1988, stagnated for the next fifteen years, and then decreased between 2003 and 2007 (Onrubia & Picos, 2013; Onrubia et al., 2007). Over the last three decades, Spain has raised by income tax around two percentage points of GDP less than the EU-14 average (8 versus 10%) (Torregrosa-Hetland, 2021).

Other changes to the main taxes in the system have also followed international trends and led to further convergence with European Union countries, despite the aforementioned limitations of institutionalised harmonisation. The corporation tax rate was increased in 1985 (from 33 to 35%), but then reduced after 2006; today, it stands at 25% (average effective rates are considerably lower, given the application of deductions). This is in line with the international trend towards lighter capital taxation. The 1995 reform responded to some issues raised by firms, for example, with respect to international openness and competitiveness, and the reduction of compliance costs. Social contributions have also seen their rates reduced progressively, from 31.1% in 1982 to 28.3% in 2010 (del Blanco García et al., 2011); at the same time, the separation of the funding of contributory and non-contributory pensions has progressed—but the conversation about how to make the pension system fairer and more sustainable is still ongoing. When it came to value added tax, the higher rate for luxuries was dropped in 1992, while a new reduced rate of 3% was introduced—but since then the trend has been one of successive increases, sometimes related to financing needs (today, the general rate is 21%, while the lower ones are 10 and 4%). Most changes to this tax were actually related to the adaptation of European rules and tendencies, but Spain still has a particularly inefficient VAT (Durán-Cabré, 2014) that rises yearly by between 6 and 7% of GDP, one point below the EU-14 average (Torregrosa-Hetland, 2021).[9]

Earlier on, this book mentioned some recent studies about the distribution of the tax burden among Spanish households, covering the period 2013–2017. A comparison between the results shown here for 1990 and those of López Laborda et al. (2016) for 2013 is certainly a big jump, particularly since the latter includes a smaller selection of household taxes. But the 1990 data can be adjusted for the main methodological differences.[10] Doing this shows that redistribution appears to have increased over this period of more than twenty years. The 2013 tax redistribution index in the same study is 1.17 (which corresponds to 2.82% of pre-tax income inequality between households), while in 1990 it is 0.34 (0.91%).[11] The effective tax rate calculated for the top percentile in 2013 is 33%, significantly more than the 24% of 1990, but the tax system still had a regressive profile at the bottom. However, this increase in redistribution took place, as in other countries, in connection with more unequal pre-tax income: the Gini moved in the same period from 37.3 to 41.4—leading to more unequal post-tax income as well. In addition, as the authors of the study noted, the reduction of inequality via taxes pales in comparison with redistribution via spending, which forms the lion's share: in 2013, it reduced inequality by 30%.

But despite what these recent studies have found, the public might still know little about the distribution of the tax burden, and whether it corresponds to their ideals of fairness. Tax policy is often perceived as a highly technical issue, and this information is not often presented in an accessible manner. This is at least partly in contrast to the cases of the United Kingdom and the United States, mentioned in Chapter 5, where yearly estimations are carried out by public bodies. In the early days of the reform, Enrique Fuentes Quintana defended the idea that the reform had to be "institutionalised". By this, he meant that a specific institution was needed to "keep an eye" on the process. In 1981, a bill was made for the creation of the *Consejo de Equidad Fiscal* (Council for Tax Equity): an independent body dedicated to studying and advising on the efficacy and fairness of the tax system (including the regional distribution of tax effort and spending), inspired by the French *Conseil des impôts* created in 1971.[12] The proposal, however, never made it to Parliament. One might suppose that had it existed, it might have published a stream of studies about the effects of the tax system and improved public awareness.

Despite the apparent stability and merely piecemeal reforms, in truth calls for comprehensive tax reform have emerged and re-emerged periodically over the last twenty years. These calls advocate for consideration of the tax system as a whole: assessment of its effects on revenue, incentives, administration, equity, and other matters, along with proposals for modification of nearly all taxes.[13] A tax reform of the sort would be a new "constitutional" tax reform, to use the terminology of Levi (1988): a renegotiation of the fiscal contract. However, this is difficult to achieve in the absence of impetus by way of a deeper crisis—in the seventies, this was democratisation, along with the economic downturn and its associated high deficits (Martínez-Vázquez, 2007).

8.2 Fiscal Transitions in the Late twentieth Century

The book will end by looking abroad. Countries that entered the seventies with low and regressive taxation may have faced similar constraints as Spain, or could do so in the near future. Parallels are easily found in Latin America, to where we turn now.

Even if there are many significant differences within this large region, there are also some common lines. When it came to average tax revenues as a share of GDP, the trajectory was of considerable increase during the sixties, starting from very low levels (data from 18 countries in Morán & Pecho, 2017), followed by a long period of stagnation, combined with intense volatility, in the seventies and eighties. A deep trough was entered around 1989, of below 14% of GDP (Cornia et al., 2014).[14] Then a significant expansion began in the nineties, with previous levels recovered by the end of the decade, and acceleration continued after 2002. As a result, by 2009, average tax as a share of GDP was situated at 18.5%, and in some cases considerably higher (particularly in Brazil and Argentina, in which taxes amounted to more than 30% of GDP).

Two distinct waves of Latin American tax reforms have shaped this evolution—and, one might say, they took place in the opposite order than in Spain. In the eighties and nineties, neoliberal tax reforms intended to increase efficiency and reduce progressivity, in connection to broader economic liberalisation inspired by the Washington Consensus. This materialised as the reduction of tariffs, partly replaced by value added taxes, as well as the reduction in the rates and number of brackets of income taxes (Cornia et al., 2014). Top marginal rates on personal income were set at around 25–30%, very low in comparison with European standards. These changes coincided with an unfavourable economic context (the effects of the oil shocks and the debt crisis of 1982), and may even have exacerbated it, as low revenue led to spending cuts. They also contributed to an increase in income inequality.

Since around 2000, sometimes earlier, new shifts have taken place. Tax revenue has not only increased: it has also become more progressive, with more emphasis on direct taxation—even though the systems generally remain tilted towards consumption taxes.[15] This led to increased redistribution and reductions in inequality, which have caught the attention of many (for example, Bértola & Williamson, 2017; Cornia, 2014).[16] The new wave of reforms was facilitated by the culmination of democratisation processes—and was sometimes made in conjunction with them, as in the case of Chile (Boylan, 1996). But the reforms also drew from a reaction against former policies, a voting shift towards the left, and a context of economic expansion related to the higher prices of exported commodities. The latter meant that the public budgets of several countries became more dependent on natural resources revenue, which carries risks in terms of volatility and lack of incentives for fiscal capacity building. Taxes on natural resources made particularly strong contributions to public revenue in Venezuela, Ecuador, Bolivia, and Mexico

(Cornia et al., 2014). This is, of course, an issue that did not affect Spain. But parallels abound in other respects.

Against this backdrop, Martínez-Vázquez (2007) offered some "lessons" from the Spanish tax reform to other countries, albeit with the necessary caution. Three of them are taken up here: analysis, administration, and comprehensiveness. With regard to the first, Martínez-Vázquez argued that analysis and preparation by the *Instituto de Estudios Fiscales* facilitated reform in Spain by improving the quality of political debate. All parties referred to the same studies, which left less leeway for populism. Of course, decisions are made politically, but it can well be an advantage that they are made with some common understanding of the existing situation and the probable consequences of proposed changes. Similar roles in analysing actual and alternative tax reforms may be played by the United Nations Economic Commission for Latin America and the Caribbean (ECLAC) or the Inter-American Development Bank (IADB).

In Spain, the reform of taxes was conducted before the reform (i.e. strengthening) of the tax administration. Martínez-Vázquez (2007) argued that this was the correct order, since the enforcement of a system perceived to be unfair could reduce legitimacy. However, this has not been without controversy, with some having argued—at the time of reform as well as later—that insufficient administrative development hindered the new system's success. In Latin America, the eighties left a legacy of improved administration and revenue-raising capacity, even if this was based on regressive taxes, which could have turned out to be positive for later reforms (Atria et al., 2018; Bird & Zolt, 2014).

The third point that Martínez-Vázquez (2007) made about the Spanish reform was that it was comprehensive, covering all taxes. It also came in the context of broader *fiscal* reform, of increased spending on welfare state functions. And also, beyond the fiscal arena, it was related to general economic reforms, such as financial and labour market liberalisation (De la Torre & Rubio-Varas, 2021). This comprehensive character allowed the reform to be seen as the other side of the coin to wage restraint, in the frame of the Moncloa Pacts, and the later increase in consumption taxes as a payment for further welfare state expansion. Indeed, some have seen in the recent Latin American developments the emergence of a new fiscal contract, which expanded revenue to fund more and better public transfers and services (Bird & Zolt, 2014; Cornia et al., 2014). The former authors argued that the reinforcement of progressive taxation should be accompanied by the incorporation of elites as users of (improved) public services—their account is based on Hirschman's famous framework of "voice" or "exit", with Latin American elites often having taken the "exit" option. Yet an area of particular success in recent Latin American social policy is that of conditional cash transfers such as the *Oportunidades* programme in Mexico and *Bolsa Familia* in Brazil, which support poor families in exchange for school attendance by their children and healthy behaviour. Indeed, the increases in redistribution in recent decades have been mostly accomplished via spending, and not so much via tax progressivity. This is also in parallel with Spain—and with other countries in the period after 1970.

The achievement of tax progressivity, of course, is tantamount to the achievement of a solid, progressive income tax. This book has argued that this very objective encountered some serious constraints in the Spanish case. Similar, or even more severe, limitations may be at play in Latin America. Indeed, these countries deal with the same international order but do so from a peripheral region, with levels of inequality among the highest in the world and pervasive informality. Latin American income taxes, even after the last wave of reforms, are generally very narrow. They provide little revenue, and provide it by taxing very few people—mostly within the top decile of the income distribution—at low rates (Barreix et al., 2017). These are still "class taxes", like the original income taxes were in other Western countries.

Furthermore, they are not really comprehensive taxes: they often do not employ a broad, coherent definition of income as the tax base. In recent years, several countries have introduced presumptive taxation schemes for small firms, in an attempt to facilitate their coming into the tax net (Cornia et al., 2014). What the Spanish experience can tell us about this is that such schemes might be necessary, or positive, to a point, but risk to become entrenched. Spanish presumptive taxation schemes have been difficult to reform and still today constitute a hole whereby income escapes taxation, with effects similar to fraud. Even if experts agree on this, a political consensus to change it has yet to emerge.

Previous studies have found income tax evasion to be very high, often around or over 40% of tax due (Gómez Sabaini et al., 2012). Furthermore, in many countries (for example, Brazil), broad exemptions or privileged treatments are enjoyed by capital income (interests, dividends, capital gains). This is made more explicit in countries that employ a dual income tax, such as Uruguay (since 2007) or Peru (since 2009).[17] Dualisation might not be complete everywhere, as in Spain, but the trend has clear implications. It breaks with the model of comprehensive, general taxation of income, establishing instead a privilege for capital income. In a way, this recalls the earlier schedular taxation—with the fundamental difference that, a hundred years ago, it was labour that was meant to be treated with a lighter tax burden (Mehrotra & Ott, 2016; Slemrod, 1995).

So, have these countries also bypassed the classic income tax? This would be consistent with some interpretations of the current political economy of taxation. According to Ganghof (2001), governments in the second globalisation operate in a "cuatrilemma" where they have to give up on at least one of the following: "competitiveness" (low taxation on capital), "allocative efficiency" (equal taxation on corporations and sole proprietorships), "comprehensiveness" (equal taxation on capital and labour income of individuals) or "progressivity" (increasing rates on labour income, as defined there). Different countries occupy different places in the quadrant of possible responses, but it is fair to say that progressivity has been compromised by many.

In the world of welfare state and regressive taxation, this might not matter. As was advanced in Chapter 1, many have argued that the more redistributive welfare states are funded mainly by regressive taxes, since it is politically or economically difficult to maintain extensive *and* progressive taxation (Kato, 2003; Lindert, 2004; Steinmo, 1989, 1993; Wilensky, 2002). This appreciation was initially based on the comparison between the United States and Sweden, but has since been extended to further cases, although not many (Prasad & Deng, 2009). What initially seemed like a paradox has now been quite broadly accepted—and fits with the public finance claim that it is optimal to redistribute through expenditure, and forget about progressive taxation.

One might think that the Spanish trajectory fits with this idea. The country expanded its welfare state at the same time as it introduced value added tax and continued to rely on heavy social contributions. As much as the expansion of public revenues in the late seventies could only be achieved by increasing the burden at the top, it would seem that further, sustained expansion during the economic crisis was only politically feasible if it also limited the progressivity of taxes. Was this the kind of compromise on which modern welfare states rest?

This book has shown that the insufficiencies in terms of revenue, and progressivity of revenue, limited overall redistribution. Indeed, redistribution in late twentieth-century Spain lagged behind that of the European core, and even of "liberal" welfare states such as the United States and the United Kingdom (in the categorisation of Esping-Andersen, 1990). These are also the countries on which the welfare state–regressive taxation nexus was first discussed and developed—but latecomers might not have been able to go down the same road. In Spain, convergence was ultimately left incomplete: welfare state development, delayed by the dictatorship, was hindered by a new international political economy, where the combination of sluggish growth, economic openness, and neoliberal theory made progressive taxes harder to defend and implement. This, in turn, limited the state's redistributive capacity. Were the late transitioners too late?

The answer to this question might hinge upon the future of international coordination: the downward pressure on top tax rates, and the facilities to evade them, both depend on a lack thereof. Of course, this is no easy problem to solve. But recent developments (international tax evasion scandals and the fiscal crisis stemming from the current Covid-19 pandemic) might have put further strain on the status quo. The scandals have sparked calls for coordinated efforts against tax evasion and avoidance, with a leading role to be taken by the OECD, while the pandemic has lent strength to arguments of "shared sacrifice" of the kind used to resolve previous fiscal problems during unprecedented crisis—the world wars (Scheve & Stasavage, 2016). The end of the story is nowhere in sight.

Notes

1. Francisco Fernández Ordóñez: “La reforma fiscal, ¿un ademán solitario?”, *El País*, 18 June 1980; author’s translation.
2. Vertical equity refers to the treatment of people at different income levels, and horizontal equity to the treatment of those at the same level. The idea is that people with different economic capacity should be taxed differently (i.e. more tax at higher income), while those at the same level should be treated in the same way (i.e. pay the same tax).
3. Steinmo (2003) suggested that changes were also important with regard to demand for redistribution, which was affected by the evolution of dominant ideas about fairness in income distribution, as well as about the capacity of the tax system to approach the ideal.
4. Because the tax was progressive, an income of, say, 3 million pesetas paid more than two separate incomes of 1.5 million pesetas each. This usually meant that, in the case of a married couple, the wife’s income as secondary earner was subject to a higher marginal tax rate than the income of the husband. The conflict has been approached through several mechanisms in different countries; for example, Sweden introduced compulsory separate taxation in 1971, while France uses a system of income splitting (*quotient familial*).
5. The labour force participation rate of women in Spain in 1978 was 27.8%, which by 1989 had grown to 33.9%, but this would be lower for married women in particular (Nicolau, 2005, Table 2.26).
6. The net wealth tax was suspended between 2008 and 2010, then re-introduced in the context of the economic crisis. Today, Spain is one of very few OECD countries that still has such a tax, while many have abolished it since the early nineties.
7. Because they were taxed at higher rates, and the reduction of the tax base affects the tax rate. This effect, however, was neutralised in 2006.
8. This is the top marginal tax rate that would apply in the absence of changes by autonomous communities. Several of these have indeed enacted different tax schedules for their part of revenues, as discussed in Chapter 7.
9. For example, only five countries in the EU used super-reduced rates in 2020 (France, Ireland, Italy, and Luxembourg are the others). In terms of the standard rate, Spain is very close to the EU-average of 21.5%. See https://ec.europa.eu/taxation_customs/sites/taxation/files/resources/documents/taxation/vat/how_vat_works/rates/vat_rates_en.pdf.

10. For this, the same definition of pre-tax income (including social benefits as well as private transfers) is used, the same taxes (not the corporation tax, the social contributions of employers, the inheritance tax, or local taxes) are included, and the same units of analysis (households, or alternatively households with the OECD modified equivalence scale) are applied.
11. This corresponds to inequality between households. Redistribution is somewhat smaller when calculated using equivalence scales, particularly in 1990, when the system is shown to be regressive, as in the main results of the book.
12. Ref: Archivo General de la Administración – Ministerio de Hacienda – Dirección General del Tesoro y Política Financiera – índice IDD(1)031.000 – E. 1995 – 55/15249.
13. Some examples are Ruiz-Castillo et al. (2002), Díaz and Sebastián (2004), Comisión de Expertos para la Reforma del Sistema Tributario (2014), Esteller and Durán (2014), Conde-Ruiz et al. (2015).
14. The data in Morán and Pecho (2017) starts in 1960, but excludes social contributions, while that of Cornia et al. (2014) includes them but starts in 1973. Both series refer to central governments, but include sub-national governments in some countries, particularly the latter. In any case, the two accounts of the general trends in the period are very similar.
15. Between 1990 and 2009, taxes on income and property grew from 3.4 to 5.6% of GDP, on average. While this increase is remarkable, in the last year they represented 30% of total tax revenue, compared to 51% from VAT, excises, and taxes on international trade (the rest are social security and others). There have also been some initiatives to reduce the regressivity of consumption taxes (for example, Ecuador introduced excises on luxury items in 2008).
16. In a study that analysed fiscal redistribution in six Latin American countries since the nineteenth century (including taxes and spending), Chile and Argentina were found to have become more progressive since the mid-nineties (Arroyo & Lindert, 2017). Progressivity is, however, relatively low, and the systems redistribute "to the rich and the poor" (for example, in Peru the system is not progressive overall). The authors also noted that social spending has generally risen since the eighties, but invests relatively less on the young (education) than on the old (pensions—to urban, formal, often privileged groups).

17. The dual income tax model comes from the Nordic countries—it was introduced in Sweden in 1991, Norway in 1992, and Finland in 1993 (Denmark also had it between 1987 and 1994). The pure dual income tax uses a single rate for capital incomes, while preserving the progressive structure for labour income.

References

Arroyo, L., & Lindert, P. (2017). Fiscal redistribution in latin America since the nineteenth century. In L. Bértola & J. Williamson (Eds.), *Has latin American inequality changed direction? Looking over the long run* (pp. 243–282). Springer.

Atkinson, A., & Piketty, T. (2007). *Top incomes over the 20th century: A contrast between continental European and English-speaking countries*. Oxford University Press.

Atria, J., Groll, C., & Valdés, M. F. (Eds.). (2018). *Rethinking taxation in Latin America*. Springer International Publishing.

Barreix, A., Benítez, J. C., & Pecho, M. (2017). *Revisiting personal income tax in Latin America*. OECD Publishing.

Bértola, L., & Williamson, J. (Eds.). (2017). *Has Latin American inequality changed direction? Looking over the long run*. Springer International Publishing.

Bird, R. M., & Zolt, E. M. (2014). Taxation and inequality in the Americas: Changing the fiscal contract?. In *Taxation and development: The weakest link?* (pp. 193–237). Edward Elgar Publishing.

Boylan, D. M. (1996). Taxation and transition: The politics of the 1990 Chilean Tax Reform. *Latin American Research Review, 31*, 7–31.

Buggeln, M., Daunton, M., & Nützenadel, A. (2017). The political economy of public finance since the 1970s: Questioning the leviathan. In *The Political economy of public finance: Taxation, state spending and debt since the 1970s* (pp. 1–31). Cambridge University Press.

Comisión de Expertos para la Reforma del Sistema Tributario. (2014). *Informe*.

Conde-Ruiz, J. I., Díaz, M., Marín, C., & Ramírez, J. R. (2015). Una Reforma Fiscal para España. In *Policy Papers*. FEDEA.

Cornia, G. A. (Ed.). (2014). *Falling inequality in Latin America.* Oxford University Press.

Cornia, G. A., Gómez-Sabaini, J. C., & Martorano, B. (2014). Tax policy and income distribution during the last decade. In *Falling inequality in Latin America* (pp. 295–317). Oxford University Press.

De la Torre, J., & Rubio-Varas, M. (Eds.). (2021). *Economía en transición. Del tardofranquismo a la democracia.* Marcial Pons.

del Blanco García, Á., Gutiérrez Lousa, M., Alonso San Alberto, D., Fernández de Beaumont Torres, I., Martín Román, J., & Rodríguez García, Á. (2011). *Evolución del sistema fiscal español: 1978–2010* (13/2011; Documentos).

Díaz, M., & Sebastián, M. (2004). Ideas para una reforma fiscal en España. In J. Pérez, C. Sebastián, & P. T. De Lorca (Eds.), *Políticas, Mercados e Instituciones Económicas. Estudios en Homenaje a Luis Ángel Rojo.* Editorial Complutense.

Durán-Cabré, J. M. (2014). Los impuestos sobre el consumo en el sistema fiscal español: revisión y propuestas de reforma. In A. Esteller Moré & J. M. Durán Cabré (Eds.), *Por una verdadera reforma fiscal*. Ariel Economía.

Esping-Andersen, G. (1990). *The three worlds of welfare capitalism.* Cambridge University Press.

Esteller, A., & Durán, J. M. (2014). *Por una verdadera reforma fiscal*. Ariel.

Fuentes Quintana, E. (1987). El impuesto lineal: Una opción fiscal diferente. *Papeles De Economía Española, 30*(31), 175–192.

Fuentes Quintana, E. (2004). Los Pactos de la Moncloa y la Constitución de 1978. In E. Fuentes Quintana (Ed.), *Economía y economistas españoles* (Vol. 8, pp. 163–238). Galaxia Gutenberg: Círculo de Lectores.

Ganghof, S. (2001). *Global markets, national tax systems, and domestic politics: Rebalancing efficiency and equity in open states' income taxation* (01/9; MPIfG Discussion Paper).

Gómez Sabaini, J. C., Jiménez, J. P., & Rossignolo, D. (2012). *Imposición a la renta personal y equidad en América Latina: nuevos desafíos* (No. 119; Serie Macroeconomía Del Desarrollo). ECLAC.

Kato, J. (2003). *Regressive taxation and the welfare state: Path dependence and policy diffusion.* Cambridge University Press.

Lagares, M. J. (1999). La Hacienda Pública en las Facultades de Ciencias Económicas y en la sociedad española durante la segunda mitad del siglo XX. In E. Fuentes Quintana (Ed.), *Economía y economistas españoles* (Vol. 7, pp. 571–617). Galaxia Gutenberg.

Levi, M. (1988). *Of rule and revenue.* University of California Press.

Levy, F., & Temin, P. (2007). *Inequality and institutions in 20th century America.* NBER Working Paper No. 13106.

Lindert, P. H. (2004). *Growing public.* Cambridge University Press.

López Laborda, J., Marín, C., & Onrubia, J. (2016). *Observatorio sobre el reparto de los impuestos entre los hogares españoles. Primer informe* (2016/21; Estudios Sobre La Economía Española).

Martínez-Vázquez, J. (2007). The Spanish tax reform: Overview and lessons. In J. Martínez-Vázquez & J. F. Sanz Sanz (Eds.), *Fiscal reform in Spain: Accomplishments and challenges* (pp. 532–553). Edward Elgar.

Mehrotra, A. K., & Ott, J. C. (2016). The curious beginnings of the capital gains tax preference. *Fordham Law Review, 84*(6), 2517–2536.

Morán, D., & Pecho, M. (2017). La tributación en los últimos cincuenta años. In *CIAT: Cincuenta años en el quehacer tributario de América Latina* (pp. 1–37).

Nicolau, R. (2005). Población, salud y actividad. In A. Carreras & X. Tafunell (Eds.), *Estadísticas Históricas de España: Siglo XIX-XX* (pp. 77–154). Fundación BBVA.

Onrubia, J., & Picos, F. (2013). Progresividad, redistribución y bienestar a través del IRPF español en el periodo 1999–2007. *Revista De Economía Aplicada, 21*(63), 75–115.

Onrubia, J., Rodado, M. C., Díaz, S., & Pérez, C. (2007). Progresividad y redistribución a través del IRPF español: Un análisis de bienestar social para el periodo 1982–1998. *Hacienda Pública Española, 183*, 81–124.

Pan-Montojo, J. L. (1996). Una larga e inconclusa transición: la reforma tributaria, 1977–1986. In J. Tusell & A. Soto (Eds.), *Historia de la transición. 1975–1986* (pp. 264–304). Alianza.

Peters, G. B. (1991). *The politics of taxation: A comparative perspective.* Wiley–Blackwell.

Prasad, M., & Deng, Y. (2009). Taxation and the worlds of welfare. *Socio-Economic Review, 7*, 431–457.

Romero Jordán, D., & Sanz-Sanz, J. F. (2007). Personal income taxation: The cornerstone of the tax system in a democracy. In J. Martínez-Vázquez & J. F. Sanz-Sanz (Eds.), *Fiscal reform in Spain: Accomplishments and challenges* (pp. 151–207). Edward Elgar.

Ruiz-Castillo, J., Castells, A., Cruz Amorós, M., Díaz de Sarralde, S., Gago, A., Garde, J. A., Gimeno, J. A., Herce, J. A., Iturriaga, R., Jiménez-Ridruejo, Z., López, J., Loscos, J., Medel, B., Romero, J., Ruiz-Huerta, J., Segura, J., & Zornoza Pérez, J. (2002). *Una alternativa fiscal para España.* Fundación Alternativas, Exlibris.

Scheve, K., & Stasavage, D. (2016). *Taxing the rich: A history of fiscal fairness in the United States and Europe*. Princeton University Press.

Slemrod, J. (1995). Professional opinions about tax policy: 1994 and 1934. *National Tax Journal, 48*, 121–147.

Steinmo, S. (1989). Political institutions and tax policy in the United States, Sweden, and Britain. *World Politics, 41*(4), 500–535.

Steinmo, S. (1993). *Taxation and democracy. Swedish, British, and American approaches to financing the modern state*. Yale University Press.

Steinmo, S. (2003). The evolution of policy ideas: Tax policy in the 20th century. *The British Journal of Politics & International Relations, 5*(2), 206–236.

Torregrosa-Hetland, S. (2021). La reforma fiscal y sus restricciones económicas. In J. De la Torre & M. Rubio-Varas (Eds.), *Economía en Transición. Del tardofranquismo a la democracia* (Chapter 4). Marcial Pons.

Torregrosa-Hetland, S., & Sabaté, O. (2021). *Income taxes and redistribution in the early 20th century*. Lund Papers in Economic History: General Issues; no. 224.

Wilensky, H. L. (2002). *Rich democracies: Political economy, public policy, and performance*. University of California Press.

Index

A

Ability to pay 10, 14, 153, 190
Alianza Popular (AP) 66, 70, 78, 87, 135, 219
Average effective tax rate 124, 127
Avoidance 157, 166, 170, 174

B

Banking secrecy 84, 97, 109, 158

C

Compliance 157, 159, 162–167, 169–177
Comprehensive tax reform 29, 46, 222
Consent 155, 157
Convergència Democràtica de Catalunya (CDC) 87
corporation tax 8

D

debt 188
Decentralisation 8, 50, 59, 76, 84, 185, 191, 194, 195
deficit 188
Democratisation 1, 9–13, 15, 18
Deterrence 156, 157
Disposable income 10, 16, 123, 127, 128, 137, 201, 202, 204, 215
Distribution of the tax burden 118, 120, 127
Dual income tax 226

E

Economic growth 2, 15, 42, 44, 49, 63, 91, 174, 206

© The Editor(s) (if applicable) and The Author(s), under exclusive license to Springer Nature Switzerland AG 2021
S. Torregrosa Hetland, *The Spanish Fiscal Transition*, Palgrave Studies in Economic History, https://doi.org/10.1007/978-3-030-79541-2

education 6
Electoral system 5, 84–90
European Economic Community 28
Evasion 154, 155, 158, 159, 161–163, 165–167, 169, 171, 172, 174
excises 7

F

Fair tax system 71
Fernández Ordóñez, Francisco 6, 7, 9, 57, 68, 87, 96, 98, 107, 117, 190, 200, 215
Financial repression 188, 189
Fiscal competition 194
Fiscal contract 13–15, 17
Fiscal federalism 191
Flexibility 45, 189
fraud 3
Fuentes Quintana, Enrique 29, 36, 45–47

G

Generality 153, 159–161, 174
Gini index 125, 135, 136, 140

I

Income inequality 11, 18, 27, 136, 142, 186, 199, 201, 223
Inequality 1, 3, 4, 7, 9–12, 16, 18, 64, 123–126, 134, 136, 137, 140, 142, 145, 154, 171, 172, 194, 196, 199–204, 206, 208, 215, 216, 219, 221, 223, 225, 229
Inflation 51, 91–93, 95, 99, 101, 102, 104, 109, 111
Inheritance tax 96, 101, 102
Instituto de Estudios Fiscales 46

L

Larraz, José 31, 32, 50
Latin America 2, 13, 88, 218, 222, 224, 225
Law for Urgent Fiscal Reform Measures 96
Legitimacy 35, 58, 86, 93, 154, 170, 185, 195, 197, 224
Liberal tax system 29, 34
Linear tax 219

M

Malapportionment 87–89

N

Navarro Rubio, Mariano 32, 37, 38
Net wealth tax 46, 95, 97, 101, 219

O

Openness 93–95, 108

P

Partido Comunista de España (PCE) 85–87, 103
Partido Nacionalista Vasco (PNV) 87
Partido Socialista Obrero Español (PSOE) 86, 90, 98, 103
Personal income tax 93, 94, 98–100, 102
Presumptive assessment 158, 162, 170

Progressivity 2, 6, 9–11, 16, 117–119, 121, 125, 126, 131, 133–136, 140, 142
Public debt 170, 188, 193, 207
Public deficit 37, 92, 188
Public opinion 58, 70, 78, 90, 195, 197

R
Redistribution 2, 118, 119, 121, 123, 125, 126, 133–138, 140–143, 145

S
Schedular tax 31–33, 38, 39, 60, 99, 154, 156, 161, 162, 226
Second globalisation 2, 13, 226
seigniorage 189
Social contributions 103, 104, 108
Social security 8, 15, 35, 36, 40, 41, 43, 47, 48, 51, 65, 66, 77, 78, 84, 92, 103, 105, 118, 124, 134, 138, 189, 192, 217
Social spending 12, 13, 66, 86, 138, 188, 204, 205, 208
Sufficiency 188, 189

T
tariffs 7
Tax administration 189, 190, 197
Tax incidence 118, 119, 121–123, 136, 137
Tax inspection 156, 157, 161
tax rates 2
tax reform 3
Third-party reporting 158, 168, 174
Third wave democracies 13

U
Under-assessment 165, 166, 170
Under-reporting 159, 162, 165, 166, 168, 174
unemployment 188
Unión de Centro Democrático (UCD) 86, 87, 89, 90, 97, 98, 100, 101, 103, 107

V
Value added tax 6–8, 15, 27, 40, 45, 46, 84, 102, 130, 135, 140, 142, 186, 187, 193, 221, 223, 227
voluntary compliance 6

W
Welfare state 6, 59, 192, 196–199, 201, 202, 204

The manufacturer's authorised representative in the EU is Springer Nature Customer Service Centre GmbH, Europaplatz 3, 69115 Heidelberg, Germany. If you have any concerns regarding our products, please contact ProductSafety@springernature.com

Printed and bound by CPI Group (UK) Ltd, Croydon, CR0 4YY
30/09/2026
02225698-0007